THE BIBLE
and
RECONCILIATION

Confession, Repentance, and Restoration

JAMES B. PROTHRO

Baker Academic
a division of Baker Publishing Group
Grand Rapids, Michigan

© 2023 by James B. Prothro

Published by Baker Academic
a division of Baker Publishing Group
Grand Rapids, Michigan
www.bakeracademic.com

Printed in the United States of America

Library of Congress Cataloging-in-Publication Data
Names: Prothro, James B., 1986– author.
Title: The Bible and reconciliation : confession, repentance, and restoration / James B. Prothro.
Description: Grand Rapids, Michigan : Baker Academic, a division of Baker Publishing Group, 2023. | Series: Catholic biblical theology of the sacraments | Includes bibliographical references and index.
Identifiers: LCCN 2023015034 | ISBN 9781540964786 (paperback) | ISBN 9781540967343 (casebound) | ISBN 9781493444588 (ebook) | ISBN 9781493444595 (pdf)
Subjects: LCSH: Penance. | Reconciliation—Biblical teaching. | Reconciliation—Religious aspects—Catholic Church. | Confession—Catholic Church. | Bible. Old Testament—Theology.
Classification: LCC BX2260 .P76 2023 | DDC 234/.166—dc23/eng/20230621
LC record available at https://lccn.loc.gov/2023015034

Nihil Obstat:
Scott Powell, Ph.D.
Censor Librorum

Imprimatur:
+Most Reverend Samuel J. Aquila, S.T.L.
Archbishop of Denver
Denver, Colorado, USA
August 17, 2023

Baker Publishing Group publications use paper produced from sustainable forestry practices and post-consumer waste whenever possible.

23 24 25 26 27 28 29   7 6 5 4 3 2 1

"An outstanding contribution to the Catholic Biblical Theology of the Sacraments series. Prothro offers a detailed and engaging survey of confession, repentance, and restoration in the Bible and effectively demonstrates that the sacrament of reconciliation is rooted in the witness of Scripture. Readers looking for an overview of biblical narratives and practices that shows how God acts with mercy toward sinners and offers forgiveness and grace to the penitent will find this book to be a trustworthy guide."

—David J. Downs, University of Oxford and Keble College

"This work is a great resource on the deep biblical roots of the sacrament and the more general Christian life of penance, reconciliation, and conformity to Christ. Exploring the teaching of the Old and New Testaments on sin, contrition, penance, and reconciliation and situating the sacrament in this wider context, Prothro invites the reader to a life of repentance and love and of hope in the merciful God who will bring to completion the work of salvation that he has begun in us."

—Lawrence Feingold, Kenrick Glennon Seminary

"Moving sequentially through the Bible, Prothro unfolds the grand narrative of God, in his holiness, reconciling the sinful world to himself. Irrespective of their ecclesial traditions, readers will find a beautiful, biblical exposition of God acting mercifully in his justice to draw sinful people to repentance, to forgive and restore them, and to teach and form them in the process. There's holy ground here that's common to us all."

—Jonathan Mumme, Hillsdale College

Praise for the Catholic Biblical Theology of the Sacraments Series

"This series gives to students of the Bible a deeply enriched view of the mesh of relationships within and between biblical texts that are brought to light by the liturgy of the sacraments."

—Jennifer Grillo, University of Notre Dame

"Theologically trained, exegetically astute biblical scholars here explore the foundations of Catholic sacramental theology, along paths that will change the theological conversation. This series points the way to the theological and exegetical future."

—Matthew Levering, Mundelein Seminary

"The sacraments come to us clothed in images that carry their mystery and propose it to our hearts. These images come from Scripture and are inspired by the Holy Spirit, who wills to transfigure us each into the full measure of Christ. The books in this series will over time surely prove themselves to be agents in this work of the Spirit."

—John C. Cavadini, McGrath Institute for Church Life, University of Notre Dame

A CATHOLIC BIBLICAL THEOLOGY
OF THE SACRAMENTS

SERIES EDITORS

Timothy C. Gray

John Sehorn

ALSO IN THE SERIES

The Bible and Baptism: The Fountain of Salvation
  Isaac Augustine Morales, OP

*The Bible and the Priesthood: Priestly Participation
in the One Sacrifice for Sins*
  Anthony Giambrone, OP

For Elizabeth Hope

For whatever was written in former days
was written for our instruction,
so that by steadfastness and by the encouragement
of the scriptures we might have hope.

—Romans 15:4

Contents

Sidebars

the teaching and practice of the postbiblical Church, showing the sometimes surprising ways in which Tradition embodies the Church's ongoing reception of the biblical Word.

In the case of the sacraments, attention to the analogy of faith means, among other things, keeping always in mind their origin and end in the eternal life of the Blessed Trinity, their relationship to the missions of the Son and the Spirit, their ecclesial context, their doxological character, their soteriological purpose, their vocational entailments, and their eschatological horizon.

The series' intended readership is broad. While the primary audience is Catholics of the Roman Rite, it is hoped that Catholics of the non-Roman rites as well as Eastern Christians who are not in full communion with the Bishop of Rome, whose sacramental theory and practice are very close, will find much to appreciate. Protestant Christians, of course, vary widely in their views of sacramental worship, and their reception of the series is likely to vary similarly. It is our hope that, at the very least, the series helps Protestant believers better understand how Catholic sacramental teaching is born of Scripture and animated by it.

We pray that all those who read these volumes will together delight in the rich food of God's Word (cf. Isa. 55:2), seeking the unity in faith and charity to which we are called by our common baptism into the life of the Blessed Trinity. To him be the glory.

Timothy C. Gray
John Sehorn

Acknowledgments

I am thankful to Jim Kinney of Baker Academic and to series editors Tim Gray and John Sehorn for inviting me to write this volume. My academic considerations of sin and its being dealt with in justification and reconciliation started years ago with my doctoral work, but it did not stretch to the sacrament or encompass the full breadth of the biblical canon. The process of researching and writing this book has been a formative experience for me and has affected my own piety for the better.

I am especially thankful to John Sehorn, who has read carefully every word of this book chapter by chapter. Amid his busy schedule, he consistently offered helpful insights, criticism, and encouragement that have improved the final product. I am thankful to my colleagues Michael Barber, Mark Giszczak, Israel McGrew, and Brant Pitre for discussions about Job, Matthew, and biblical theology. Conversation with my colleagues in patristics Elizabeth Klein, Christopher Mooney, and Carl Vennerstrom inspired (and sometimes corrected) my reading of postbiblical material. Thanks go also to Matthew Levering and the Academy of Catholic Theology for inviting me to prepare and present my thoughts on what a sacramental "biblical theology" might look like.

The team at Baker Academic has been a dream to work with in bringing this book to completion. Jim Kinney has been nothing but patient, encouraging, and professional. The same can be said of Baker's team of copyeditors, designers, and typesetters. Special appreciation goes to Tim West and Shannon Lee, who worked through and suggested improvements throughout the manuscript, and to Paula Gibson, who designed the beautiful cover.

The spiritual and emotional support I have received in writing this book has made it a joy to write despite other pressures. I want in particular to thank my pastor, Fr. Daniel Cardó, and our chaplain, Fr. James Claver. They give good medicine in the confessional. I always encounter the mercy of God in them. I am ever grateful to my wife, Ashley, who is always by my side, for her love, patience, and support of my work and well-being.

This book is for my sweet daughter, Elizabeth. May God's word always fill you with hope in his manifold mercy.

Abbreviations

AB	Anchor Bible	JSOTSup	Journal for the Study of the Old Testament Supplement Series
ABD	*Anchor Bible Dictionary*. Edited by David Noel Freedman. 6 vols. New York: Doubleday, 1992.	LHBOTS	The Library of Hebrew Bible/Old Testament Studies
ANF	*Ante-Nicene Fathers*	LNTS	The Library of New Testament Studies
BMSEC	Baylor-Mohr Siebeck Studies in Early Christianity	NABRE	New American Bible, revised edition
BZNW	Beihefte zur Zeitschrift für die neutestamentliche Wissenschaft	NET	New English Translation
CBQ	*Catholic Biblical Quarterly*	*NIB*	*The New Interpreter's Bible*. Edited by Leander E. Keck. 12 vols. Nashville: Abingdon, 1994–2004.
CBTS	A Catholic Biblical Theology of the Sacraments		
CCC	*Catechism of the Catholic Church*	NICNT	New International Commentary on the New Testament
ConBNT	Coniectanea Neotestamentica	NICOT	New International Commentary on the Old Testament
ConcC	Concordia Commentary		
DRV	Douay-Rheims Version	NIGTC	New International Greek Testament Commentary
ECC	Eerdmans Critical Commentary		
ESV	English Standard Version	NJB	New Jerusalem Bible
ESVCE	English Standard Version-Catholic Edition	NJPS	*Tanakh: The Holy Scripture: The New JPS Translation according to the Traditional Hebrew Text*
FC	Fathers of the Church		
ICC	International Critical Commentary		
JBL	*Journal of Biblical Literature*	NovTSup	Supplements to Novum Testamentum
JSOT	*Journal for the Study of the Old Testament*	*NPNF¹*	*Nicene and Post-Nicene Fathers*, Series 1

NPNF²	*Nicene and Post-Nicene Fathers*, Series 2	RSV	Revised Standard Version
NRSV	New Revised Standard Version	SP	Sacra Pagina
NSBT	New Studies in Biblical Theology	SVSPPS	St. Vladimir's Seminary Press Popular Patristics Series
NTL	New Testament Library	*TBei*	*Theologische Beiträge*
NTM	New Testament Monographs	TDNT	*Theological Dictionary of the New Testament.* Edited by Gerhard Kittel and Gerhard Friedrich. Translated by Geoffrey W. Bromiley. 10 vols. Grand Rapids: Eerdmans, 1964–76.
NTS	*New Testament Studies*		
OTL	Old Testament Library		
OTP	*Old Testament Pseudepigrapha.* Edited by James H. Charlesworth. 2 vols. New York: Doubleday, 1983, 1985.		
OtSt	Oudtestamentische Studiën	WBC	Word Biblical Commentary
PHSC	Perspectives on Hebrew Scriptures and Its Contexts	WSA	Works of Saint Augustine
		WUNT	Wissenschaftliche Untersuchungen zum Neuen Testament
RBS	Resources for Biblical Study		

1

Confession and Reconciliation

An Encounter with Divine Mercy

For the LORD your God is gracious and merciful, and will not turn away his face from you, if you return to him.

—2 Chronicles 30:9

In Luke 15:11–32, Jesus tells a parable of a lost son restored. The son has for years, we are to understand, enjoyed the benefits of living in his father's home, in the company of the rest of the household. His father is a landowner, and the son has the privilege of being an heir to the estate, the duty of managing property and servants, fellowship with the others in the household, and the continual experience of his father's love and care. But one day, he chooses to leave. He asks for his share of what he, with his brother, would inherit from their father's estate. He wants to enjoy the goods that he gets from being his father's son without living as his father's son—without being under his father's authority, without discharging his duty in the household, and so without the communion of his father and the rest of the family.

We are not told the father's reaction, only that he grants the request, not forcing the son to remain against his will. So the son goes off to a faraway land and spends his inheritance on debauched, profligate living. But, having spent it all, he is left destitute, undignified, and debased. He realizes that even his father's servants are better off. So he packs up and heads home, surely a long and difficult journey, hoping to rejoin the household simply as a servant. But when he finally nears the house, his father runs to him and embraces him. The son confesses, "Father, I have sinned against heaven and before you; I am no longer worthy to be called your son" (Luke 15:21). But the father calls for a fine robe, a ring, and sandals to replace his destitute son's rags. And he summons the rest of the household together to rejoice and celebrate not the hiring of a servant but the return of his son. When the son's older brother is indignant at this celebration, the father insists, "We had to celebrate and rejoice, because this brother of yours was dead and has come to life; he was lost and has been found" (Luke 15:32).

For nearly two millennia, this parable has been used as an image of re-pentance and forgiveness between God and God's people. God's children sin in various ways, failing to live out their identity under the Father, and some choose to leave the household altogether. But God wants his children home, and he embraces them with mercy and grace when they turn back in repen-tance. The road is not always easy, and it can be more arduous the farther away we have strayed. But God envelops the repentant with love and restores them to their dignity as daughters and sons and to their place within the family.

This encounter with God's mercy receives special expression in the sacra-ment of reconciliation, through which God's wayward children are forgiven and restored by God's grace to life in "the household of God, which is the church" (1 Tim. 3:15). It is a sacrament that has gone by many names accord-ing to its different parts, "each revealing a different facet" of the complex and beautiful reality of repentance and restoration.[1] It can be called the sacrament of conversion, confession, or penance, pointing to the acts by which one turns from sin to God and seeks restoration. It can be called the sacrament of forgive-ness, pointing to God's forgiveness of the guilt of one's sin. Most comprehen-sively, it can be called the sacrament of reconciliation, the restoration of the sinner through forgiveness and repentance to live again in love and friendship with the Father and the rest of the household.[2] It is a sacrament that has seen various formal expressions throughout the history of the Church and across different rites today. But in all of its names, and in all of its expressions, the sacrament offers the same fundamental gift: an "encounter with the Lord's mercy," the embrace of the Father welcoming wayward children home through

---

1. David W. Fagerberg, "The Sacramental Life," in *The Oxford Handbook of Catholic Theology*, ed. Lewis Ayres and Medi Ann Volpe (New York: Oxford University Press, 2019), 253.
    2. See CCC 1423–24.

the Church.[3] The pages that follow are an invitation to study this encounter with God's mercy, the call to repentance, and God's grace to restore sinners from death to life—God's "love which is more powerful than sin."[4]

Sin and Reconciliation in the Story of Scripture

This is a book about the sacrament of reconciliation. More specifically, it is a book about the *Bible* and the sacrament of reconciliation and how Scripture shows forth and proclaims the realities involved in the sacrament—sin and forgiveness, confession and repentance, and the work of Christ through his body, the Church. To get our bearings, then, we need to have some understanding of the problem of sin and God's plan of salvation overall, and then to consider the sacrament in particular.

Sin and Its Consequences

God created human beings to make them "share in the divine life."[5] Humans are made in God's "image" and "likeness" in their being, their character, and their role in the world (Gen. 1:26, 28). God made humans with a rational soul and free will, capable of knowing themselves, knowing God, and of responding freely to God in love.[6] We are created, one might say, hardwired for love and goodness, able to receive God's gifts with thanks and to give of ourselves in love. Reflecting the communion among Father, Son, and Holy Spirit, "the human person" was made "a social being" by nature, created for fellowship with God and others.[7] Humans were also created to exist in harmony with the rest of creation, caring for it as little lords reflecting God's lordship over the world. In the first creation account in Genesis, God commands humans to procreate and "fill" the earth and exercise "dominion" over other creatures (Gen. 1:26, 28). This dominion was not to be one of capricious force, but one that mirrors God's own rule over the world, a creative and loving care.[8] Men and women take

3. Francis, *Evangelii gaudium*, §44.
4. John Paul II, *Dives in misericordia*, §13.
5. Vatican Council II, *Lumen gentium*, §2. Unless otherwise noted, texts and translations of conciliar documents are taken from Norman P. Tanner, ed., *Decrees of the Ecumenical Councils*, 2 vols. (London: Sheed & Ward, 1990).
6. See *CCC* 357.
7. Vatican Council II, *Gaudium et spes*, §12.
8. See Stephen G. Dempster, *Dominion and Dynasty: A Theology of the Hebrew Bible*, NSBT 15 (Downers Grove, IL: InterVarsity, 2003), 56–62.

part in God's continued creative work by being fruitful and tending creation to nourish it for life. In the second creation account, Adam's dominion is described as "serving" (Hebrew *'avad*) and "guarding" (*shamar*) the garden (Gen. 2:5, 15).

Humans were created in holiness and justice. Their ability to love and serve God, their friendship with God, and their harmony with one another and with creation were unimpeded by any rupture or dysfunction.[9] But that harmony was soon broken by human sin. Part of being able to love and act in ways that are truly just and good—the hardwiring required—is a will that can receive and give love in our relationships with God and others. But the free will made for love can also be misused. The first humans, heeding the voice of temptation, used their God-given reason to question whether God's plan was truly for their good, and they chose to seek blessing and life apart from God. Genesis narrates the sin of Adam and Eve as one of trying to become like gods themselves and to use the good things they enjoyed as God's children apart from the will and plan of the creator (Gen. 3:5–6). Genesis depicts this through the image of a particular tree: the tree was a good creation of God with its own place in the world, but it was not meant to be food for Adam and Eve, and God warned them not to eat its fruit. Fixing their eyes on this created thing and their own advantage, however, they rejected God's command and ate. Rather than glorifying God as God and receiving his gifts with praise, and instead of taking part in the life and glory for which God made them, humans sought their own glory out of sync with God's plan (Rom. 1:21).

This sin affects all the heirs of Adam and Eve, now born in *Adam's* likeness and image (Gen. 5:3). Sin did not destroy what God made humanity for or take away their rational soul. But it introduced disorder into humanity's relationships with God and creation and within themselves, distorting the divine image in which we were made and our ability to reflect God's holiness in the world. Between God and humans, sin brings guilt and ruptures communion. Between one human and another, the possibility of broken promises and the fear of betrayal sets each against the other in defensiveness and competition. Their harmonious relationship with each other and, indeed, with creation becomes marked by a prideful desire to "dominate" and "to use rather than to love."[10] And this tendency toward pride and self-preservation enters also into the human person. Human reason is still made to know God,

---

9. See *CCC* 356–57.

10. Michael Dauphinais and Matthew Levering, *Holy People, Holy Land: A Theological Introduction to the Bible* (Grand Rapids: Brazos, 2005), 35. See *CCC* 400.

God's "Image" and "Likeness" and Original Sin

The divine "image" and "likeness" have been discussed piously in more than one way. God made human beings with a rational soul, with intellect and will, designed to receive and embody divine goodness, truth, and incorruptibility. Our rational soul is not undone by sin, though sin darkens natural reason and "weakens" and even "saps" the will's capabilities.[a] Many distinguish the rational soul as the divine *image* and God's *likeness* as our actual state of embodying divine attributes. If so, the image is "disfigured" but not lost,[b] while the likeness is lost with original sin.[c] However, the two concepts are not separate but form a unity in God's intent for humanity, and both are restored to perfection through grace, so the terms can overlap. Biblical authors can say both that people born after the fall have dignity as being in God's "image" (Gen. 9:6) and God's "likeness" (James 3:9) and yet that in Christ the human self is renewed in God's "image" (Col. 3:10; cf. Rom. 8:8–9; 1 Cor. 15:49; 2 Cor. 3:18).

a. Council of Trent, *Decree on Justification*, Session VI.1.
b. *CCC* 1701.
c. E.g., *CCC* 518, 705, 708, 2566.

but it becomes "darkened" by preoccupation with the self and by desires to use created things against the will of their creator (see Rom. 1:21–23; Eph. 4:18–19). The human will, designed to choose love and service, is marked by "a leaning towards evil"—concupiscence—which is further encouraged and reinforced from outside influences and the "multitude of evils" in which we are "submerged" in the fallen world.[11] Finally, as a consequence of sin, death entered the world. Humanity sought life and blessing apart from the only One who can truly give it. And the people God "created . . . for incorruption," made to receive the gift of immortality (Wis. 2:23; cf. the "tree of life" in Gen. 2:9; 3:22), along with the cosmos God created to sustain life, became subject to decay (see Rom. 5:12–14; 8:19–21). This, too, reinforces our sinful inclinations, as the fear of death and the needs and desires of our corruptible bodies influence us to act against God's call for holiness and self-giving for the good of others (cf. Rom. 6:12; 7:5, 23; Gal. 5:17; Heb. 2:15). The apostle

11. Vatican Council II, *Gaudium et spes*, §13.

Paul summarizes this aspect of human existence since Adam as a kind of "slavery" under the dominion of sin and death (see Rom. 6:20; 7:14; cf. 2 Pet. 2:19), one from which fallen humanity cannot free itself.[12]

Christ the Redeemer

Mankind after the fall existed in a distorted relationship with God, with the rest of God's creation, and was subject to the dominion of sin and death. Made to be God's loving children, we opposed God's good will and stood as his "enemies" (Rom. 5:10; James 4:4). Made for love and justice, we became "inventors of evil" (Rom. 1:30). Made to receive God's gift of immortality, we became heirs of death.

But God did not choose to destroy humanity or do away with the world and begin again from scratch. God planned a means of *restoring* his world and human persons to their fullest dignity in glory and immortality, in justice and love. He set it in motion through his people Israel, preparing in them the plan of salvation. And he manifested his love and mercy in the death and resurrection of Jesus Christ.

> For while we were still weak, at the right time Christ died for the ungodly. . . . God proves his love for us in that while we still were sinners Christ died for us. (Rom. 5:6, 8)

> But God, who is rich in mercy, because of the great love he had for us, even when we were dead in our transgressions, brought us to life with Christ. . . . For by grace you have been saved through faith, and this is not from you; it is the gift of God; it is not from works, so no one may boast. For we are his handiwork, created in Christ Jesus for the good works that God has prepared in advance, that we should live in them. (Eph. 2:4–5, 8–10 NABRE)

The Son of God entered the world to restore the human race to the dignity for which it was created, to restore Adam's heirs to their divine inheritance of blessing and life as God's sons and daughters. He took on human nature and joined it to his divine life. In his crucifixion he suffered the consequences of sin, even death itself, as an atoning sacrifice that paid the price to ransom humans from sin and death and reconcile them to God (see Mark 10:45; Rom. 3:25; 5:10; Col. 1:20; 1 Pet. 1:18–19; 2:24; 1 John 2:2; 4:10). More than that,

---

12. See Council of Trent, *Decree on Original Sin*, Session V.

when he gave himself unto death even though he deserved no condemnation, he condemned sin and defeated death itself; he, as a human, broke through death to incorruptible life (Rom. 8:3; 1 Cor. 15:54–57). Now, through the work of his Spirit, human beings who are joined to his death can share again in the life and blessing for which God made them—restored to the image of God through the God-man, Jesus Christ (see Rom. 6:3–11; 1 Cor. 15:45–49; Col. 3:1–11).

Risen and ascended to the right hand of the Father, the Son sent forth his Spirit to pour out the love and grace of God into human hearts (Rom. 5:5). Hearts that were prideful and inclined to avoid God are moved by the Spirit to faith (1 Cor. 12:3), that "filial existence" of dependent trust and confidence in God and God's love.[13] Through faith, the Spirit of Christ dwells within us, bringing us again to friendship with God as God's children and strengthening us in knowledge and holiness (Gal. 3:14; 4:4–7; Eph. 3:14–19; 1 John 5:1) so that our faith, the "root" and continual "foundation" of our salvation, is supplemented with virtue (2 Pet. 1:5) and active in love despite our selfish inclinations (Gal. 5:6, 16–18).[14] And, on the last day, the same Spirit will complete our restoration when the dead are raised and all the world is purified from evil (Rom. 8:11, 19–23; 2 Pet. 3:7, 10). This is the work of the triune God to make "all things new" (Rev. 21:5). He forgives our guilt, liberates our minds from darkness, heals our broken will, and reconciles us to his friendship now, and he will restore to us the gift of immortality through Jesus Christ.

The Spirit and the Ministry of Reconciliation

God's mercy is enacted for the world through the death and resurrection of Christ, a singular event at a particular place and time in the world's history, but one whose saving power is limitless, paying the ransom for every soul past, present, and future. Yet to individual souls this gift must be *mediated* and received through other humans. The message of the gospel is God's power to save, through which the Holy Spirit prompts and calls human hearts to faith (Acts 16:14; 1 Cor. 12:3). God's Spirit comes to dwell in us, join us to Christ, and pour out God's grace in our hearts for salvation. Salvation is effected by God's power and grace. But God's power and grace work through the mediation of humans. The gospel must be preached by human mouths if it is to be heard

13. Francis, *Lumen fidei*, §19.
14. Council of Trent, *Decree on Justification*, Session VI.8.

and believed (Rom. 1:16; 10:14–17; Gal. 3:1–5). And the gift of the indwelling Spirit is received in baptism, conferred by human hands (Acts 2:38–39).

Jesus entrusted this ministry to the Church. Ascended and enthroned on high, Christ sent his Spirit to the apostles to give them authority to evangelize, baptize, and build up the faithful in his name (cf. Matt. 28:18–20; John 20:21–22; Eph. 4:11–16; 2 Tim. 4:1–5). The authority of the Father, shared by the Son, is given through the Spirit to the Church (John 16:12–15), so that "repentance for the forgiveness of sins should be proclaimed in his name to all nations" (Luke 24:47 ESV). This is "the ministry of reconciliation" (2 Cor. 5:18). Through baptism sinners are spiritually "washed" and receive forgiveness of their guilt (Acts 22:16; 1 Cor. 6:11; 1 Pet. 3:21). Through baptism they are joined by the Spirit to Christ and to the fellowship of his body, the Church (Rom. 6:3–11; 1 Cor. 12:12–13). And through the grace of the Spirit dwelling within, their minds and wills are reformed and renewed in faith, love, and the hope of sharing in Christ's resurrection (2 Cor. 3:18; Gal. 5:16–18; Phil. 2:13; Col. 2:11–15). They are restored to God and God's household and are empowered to live in it as God's heirs.

Yet the work of God through the Church to save sinners cannot stop at conversion and baptism. For, while baptism remits the guilt and punishment of former sins, our salvation is a matter not merely of guilt but of the restoration of our whole selves, being conformed to Christ in mind and will and action and ultimately in our bodies. We still need grace to sanctify and heal what is imperfect in us and to counteract influences that tempt us to sin. And we still need forgiveness. As the apostolic letters in the New Testament show, believers still sin—they can even fall away (e.g., 1 Cor. 5:1–13; Gal. 5:2–4; 1 Thess. 3:5; 1 Tim. 1:19–20; 5:15)—and they need to be forgiven and restored. "If we say that we have no sin, we deceive ourselves, and the truth is not in us" (1 John 1:8). The ministry of reconciliation does not end with the conversion and baptism of an unbeliever, but is an ongoing and "uninterrupted task"[15] of guiding believers into ever deeper communion with God and reconciling the fallen, so that all God's children might return and remain home, reconciled to their loving Father and living under him in his household.

Therefore, the Church calls not only outsiders but also insiders to repent and "be reconciled to God" (2 Cor. 5:20). This invitation bears the power of God's grace and promise, not merely through the Spirit's work to move

15. CCC 1428.

hearts to repentance through preaching, but specifically through the sacramental ministry of forgiveness. As the Gospel of John narrates, the risen Jesus breathed the Spirit upon the apostles and tasked them, through the power of his Spirit, with administering his forgiveness on earth.

> Receive the Holy Spirit. If you forgive the sins of any, they are forgiven them; if you retain the sins of any, they are retained. (John 20:22–23)

This is part of the office of the "keys" granted to Peter and the authority of "binding" and "loosing" sins within the Church promised to the apostles with Peter (see Matt. 16:18–19; 18:18).[16] It is a ministry of forgiveness and spiritual "healing" for believers who falter in love and faithfulness (see James 5:16). Jesus makes "the apostles and all their successors . . . instruments of the mercy of God."[17] In them, he carries on his work of opposing sin and forgiving the penitent, restoring them to communion with himself through the Church, and strengthening them anew on the path to salvation.

The Sacrament of Reconciliation

Having considered God's work to save fallen humanity and, within it, the authority given to apostolic ministers to forgive and retain sins, we can now consider its expression in the sacrament of reconciliation itself. Reconciliation "is an institution of a very complex character."[18] It involves not a simple material element like water (baptism) or bread and wine (Eucharist) but the actions of two people—the penitent and the priest. Further, although the "affirmation of the authority of the Church to remit sin" was "constantly renewed" even in the earliest centuries, the Church's understanding of the sacrament's best use has developed over time.[19] Nonetheless, its fundamental elements have remained essentially consistent. The sacrament can be summarized simply in the three main movements involved: *confession*, *absolution*, and *penance*. But before looking at these, we should first ask *who* is called to the sacrament.

16. See *Lumen gentium*, §§11, 22.
17. Francis, *The Name of God Is Mercy: A Conversation with Andrea Tornielli*, trans. Oonagh Stransky (New York: Random House, 2016), 21.
18. Bernhard Poschmann, *Penance and the Anointing of the Sick*, trans. Francis Courtney, Herder History of Dogma (New York: Herder & Herder, 1964), 2.
19. Allan D. Fitzgerald, "Penance," in *The Oxford Handbook of Early Christian Studies*, ed. Susan Ashbrook Harvey and David G. Hunter (New York: Oxford University Press, 2008), 802.

Whom Is This Sacrament For?

From the earliest period, it has been acknowledged that the sacrament of reconciliation is instituted for *baptized Christians* who sin. This seems implied when comparing the gifts of this sacrament with the gifts of baptism. Baptism washes away all prior sins and the guilt of original sin inherited from Adam. Baptism is also a sacrament of initiation, one that forges one's union with Christ and his body, the Church (1 Cor. 12:13). Reconciliation, however, occurs when one who is already *in* the Church sins after baptism, when a child who has been living in God's house has disobeyed or left home. Jesus's words about the apostolic authority to "bind" and "loose" refer specifically to the case of one's *fellow disciple* (a "brother") sinning and being called to repentance by the Church or, if necessary, excommunicated from fellowship (Matt. 18:15). The calls to confession and promises of God's forgiveness in James 5:16 and 1 John 5:16 likewise speak of confessing to *one another* and of intercession for one's "brother" or sister in Christ.[20] An unbaptized person who seeks God's grace needs baptism; the gift of authority to hear specific sins and forgive is given to deal with sin among the baptized.

Early on we find affirmations of the Church's—particularly the bishop's—role to forgive and discipline Christian sin, even with references to Jesus's gift of the power of the "keys" and of binding and loosing. There was no question of the Church's authority to carry out this ministry, to excommunicate, to assign penance, and to absolve (often by the bishop's laying on of hands) and readmit the penitent to communion.[21] There were differences and debates, however, about which sins—and how many—could or needed to be brought before the Church. Generally, since Scripture speaks of various acts like fasting, almsgiving, forgiveness, and prayer obtaining rewards or being acceptable offerings to remit sins (e.g., Ps. 51:17; Sir. 3:30; Matt. 6:14; Luke 11:41), only grave sins—particularly murder, apostasy, and adultery—were brought to the Church as requiring *sacramental* penance and reconciliation. Venial sins did not exclude one from communion with God or the Church and so did not require the sacrament, but could be addressed by confessing in prayer to God

---

20. Compare also, from a book that may date to the first century, *Didache* 4.6; 14.1.

21. E.g., Tertullian, *Antidote for the Scorpion's Sting* 10; *On Modesty* 21; Origen, *Commentary on Matthew* 13.30–31; Cyprian, *Epistles* 9; 13 (Oxford ed. 16 and 19). The first Council of Nicaea stipulated periods of penance and instructions for readmission in certain cases (e.g., canons 11–14). Notably, the council also urged regular synods of bishops to keep their colleagues in check, lest any excommunicate a believer merely out of "pettiness or quarrelsomeness" rather than in pious discharge of their duty (canon 5).

and by ordinary practices of penance and charity, which "covers a multitude of sins" (1 Pet. 4:8; cf. Prov. 10:12).[22] But regarding grave sins, there were concerns that offering sacramental reconciliation to someone more than once would encourage laxity or create scandal. Some held that, while it was not beyond God's ability to grant salvation to a repeat offender, it was beyond the Church's authority to readmit them to full communion. Especially in times of persecution, when some rigorist sects insisted that no one could be readmitted to the Eucharist after grave sin, granting sacramental reconciliation even once to an apostate or adulterer or murderer was seen as generous. Bishops tended toward assigning long, public penances and sometimes offered absolution and the Eucharist again only at the deathbed.[23] The image of sacramental penance as a second "plank" after the "ship" of baptismal grace is wrecked is often used today to emphasize the need for sacramental penance and that second repentance is possible after grave sin, after the manner of Jerome and the Council of Trent. But the image originates not with Jerome but with the rigorist Tertullian, who denied more than one penance after baptism—and that only for lighter sins.[24] One can see the rigorism of the image: baptism puts us on a great ship transporting us across the water to salvation, but after one sin and reconciliation, we are left hanging on to only that single board to swim the rest of the way.[25]

However, even as fear of encouraging laxity made many cautious about being indulgent in canonical discipline, faith and hope in God's unlimited mercy remained intact, and the seeds of repeated reconciliations for grave and even venial sin began to bear fruit. As John Chrysostom counsels, "In the case of souls . . . there is no incurable malady," because the God to whom we turn in repentance is the creator who makes all things new.[26] Biblically, though the Letter to the Hebrews seems to deny salvation to those who sin gravely after baptism (Heb. 6:4–6; 10:26), God accepted and forgave (or at least promised

22. See Origen's enumeration of seven ways (including baptism, martyrdom, and sacramental reconciliation) in which sins are remitted in his *Homilies on Leviticus* 2.4.

23. On this period see the surveys in Poschmann, *Penance*, 19–121; Karl Rahner, *Penance in the Early Church*, Theological Investigations 15 (New York: Crossroad, 1982).

24. It is instructive to compare here the *Shepherd of Hermas* 6; 31 (Visions II.2; Mandates IV.3), which admitted only one sacramental reconciliation after baptism, after which salvation would be difficult and extraordinary. Tertullian agreed on only one reconciliation after baptism, but in his later work he rejected even *Hermas* as too lax, since *Hermas* allowed this reconciliation even after adultery, whereas Tertullian saw no possibility of penance for such grave sin (see Tertullian, *On Modesty* 1.6; 18.18; 20.2).

25. For the "plank" image, see Tertullian, *On Penitence* 4.2; Jerome, *Epistle* 80.9.

26. John Chrysostom, *Exhortation to Theodore* 1.15 (NPNF[1] 9:105).

to forgive) the penitence of great sinners like Ahab, Nebuchadnezzar, Simon Magus, and Peter after he denied Christ. And Paul granted reconciliation to a grave sinner in Corinth.[27] Theologically, one expects that the practice of reconciling and giving the Eucharist at a penitent's deathbed—even when the assigned length of penance had not been fulfilled—betrayed the knowledge that long penances were not strictly necessary.[28] Moreover, while confession and penance were in part seen in light of the penalty for sinning, the *medicinal* value of the sacrament's grace to restore one to spiritual health was also constantly present.[29] As penances began, in many places, to become less arduous, and as the medicinal value of the sacrament became recognized to heal and strengthen Christians in the fight against sin, the broader value of sacramental reconciliation became recognized not only as the bishop's task to address grave sin but also as part of the priest's ministry to treat venial sins.[30] Today, while only grave sins require sacramental reconciliation, the faithful are called to seek the sacrament at least once per year and are encouraged to make use of "the pious practice of frequent confession" to be strengthened in their life of grace.[31]

We will be able to revisit some of these matters in the following pages. However, as to the preliminary question of *whom* the sacrament is *for*, the answer is baptized Christians who sin.

Contrition and Confession

The sacrament begins with the interior repentance of the Christian who has sinned. By the grace and prompting of God, the person is moved to feel sorrow or *contrition* for sin and to seek reconciliation with God.[32] This in-

---

27. These (and other) biblical texts are used to counsel hope instead of despair in Chrysostom, *Exhortation to Theodore*, and to refute the rigorists in Pseudo-Ambrose, *Concerning Repentance*.

28. So Poschmann, *Penance*, 56–57.

29. See, e.g., Heb. 12:13; James 5:16; Tertullian, *On Penitence* 10; Origen, *Homilies on Leviticus* 2.4; Sayings of the Desert Fathers, *Syncletica* 3; John Chrysostom, *On Repentance and Almsgiving* 7.1.1–2; Pseudo-Ambrose, *Concerning Repentance* 2.8.66.

30. The shape and use of the sacrament in today's Roman Rite is traceable especially to Celtic practices in the sixth century (see Poschmann, *Penance*, 124–38).

31. Pius XII, *Mystici corporis Christi*, §88. Cf. CCC 1458.

32. As faith is a grace, moved in the mind and will by the Holy Spirit (e.g., Acts 16:14; 1 Cor. 12:3), so too are contrition and penitence. For one who has sinned venially and not lost the life of grace infused by the indwelling Spirit, contrition and penitence are fruits of that infused grace working within. For one who has sinned mortally, imperfect contrition is also a "gift of God and an impulse of the holy Spirit, not yet actually dwelling in the penitent, but only moving him" (Council of Trent, *Teaching Concerning the Most Holy Sacraments of Penance and Last Anointing*, Session XIV.4; cf. *Decree on Justification*, Session VI.14; CCC 1432, 1453). One may compare the actual

ternal penitence, recognizing one's sin with regret and desiring to be restored to communion with God, is the proper response and posture of *faith*, *hope*, and *love* for a believer who has sinned.[33] Faith believes God's word, both the truth of God's will for humans and God's promise of mercy. Love feels sorrow over our infidelities toward God and wants to repent and be faithful. And hope clings to God's promise and power to restore us through this sacrament.

This interior penitence and contrition are expressed outwardly in various ways as the person sorrows over sin or perhaps makes amends to a neighbor. In the sacrament, it is expressed in seeking a priest, being willing to do penance, and confessing particular sins. The naming of sins in confession—at least in number and kind—is important. One is encouraged to confess one's sinfulness generally, even daily. But when sins are brought specifically to the minister for forgiveness, the absolution envisioned is not a general or blanket one. Jesus shares his authority to forgive *and* retain sins, to loose *and* bind (see Matt. 16:19; 18:18; John 20:23). When specific sins, and especially grave sins, are being dealt with, the priest needs to know that the person is contrite rather than presumptuous (in which case the sin may need to be retained). Further, confession of specific sins is important for the minister to be able to diagnose not only that the person has sinned but how, so that he can assign a fitting penance and give helpful counsel, to determine a prognosis by which to apply Christ's healing mercy. "If a sick man is ashamed to disclose his wound, the doctor does not heal with medicine what he is unaware of."[34] "Therefore confess your sins to one another, and pray for one another, so that you may be healed" (James 5:16).[35]

---

graces and movements of the Spirit by which God prompts unbelievers to seek baptism before the Spirit's indwelling and the infusion of grace within (e.g., through preaching, God's commandments considered in examination of conscience, feelings of shame or of God's love that awaken one's desire for reconciliation). A lack of attention to such actual graces and preparation leaves one in a theological conundrum, trying to account for how one who does not have (infused) grace can rightly repent and confess when faith and repentance are themselves graces—e.g., in Aquinas's argument that grace infused in the absolution after confession works retroactively to prompt the confession (see Poschmann, *Penance*, 171–72). On actual and infused grace, see CCC 2000–2001.

33. Compare John B. Sheerin, *The Sacrament of Freedom: A Book on Confession* (Milwaukee: Bruce Publishing, 1961), 89. Similarly, though it speaks of the repentance that leads adults to baptism, see the connection between contrition and the theological virtues in Council of Trent, *Decree on Justification*, Session VI.6.

34. Council of Trent, *Teaching Concerning the Most Holy Sacraments of Penance and Last Anointing*, Session XIV.5.

35. This is one reason the Church has discouraged reconciliation services in which the priest offers absolution to many people at once with only a general confession, except in cases of necessity. See, e.g., John Paul II, *Reconciliatio et paenitentia*, §33.

Recognition and confession of specific sins is beneficial on the penitent's side as well. In our relationship toward God, confessing is an act of humble faith, and naming the sin specifically is a response of love and hope toward the God we have wronged. When we act against our loved ones, we express our love and contrition better by confessing our actual wrong, and we show greater hope in the strength of their kindness to forgive even this specific sin, however great. Psychologically, our confidence in God's mercy is strengthened when we hear, with our ears, God's word of forgiveness through the priest not just for "being imperfect" or for "sinning" in general but for *this* sin. Further, the process of self-examination and self-diagnosis that we undertake before confession is helpful in our own walk of faith, as we put a name to what we have done and grow in awareness of how we are tempted. This, in addition to any counsel received in the confessional, can aid in our attempt to avoid sin and pursue holiness after we leave the confessional.[36]

Forgiveness and Reconciliation

The penitent's initial actions in this sacrament are contrition and confession. The priest's actions, in response, are to welcome the penitent in God's name and hear the confession, standing in for the Father who embraces the prodigal who wants to come home. Unless the priest discerns something that requires the sins to be "retained"—such as clear evidence of unrepentance—his response will be to pronounce absolution.[37] The formula of the absolution has differed historically. At times it has been expressed only as a prayer of intercession, the Church asking God in the name of Jesus to forgive the penitent.[38] The importance of such intercession is biblical and has its origins in Jesus's own prayer that God would forgive those who sinned against him (Luke

---

36. See Jana M. Bennett and David Cloutier, *Naming Our Sins: How Recognizing the Seven Deadly Vices Can Renew the Sacrament of Reconciliation* (Washington, DC: Catholic University of America Press, 2019).

37. Forgiveness is not conditioned on the performance of the penance or how earnestly one does it, though this can affect the degree to which the penance's healing work takes effect. The rigorist position of the Jansenists, denying the validity of absolution before satisfaction, was condemned (see Robert L. Fastiggi, *The Sacrament of Reconciliation: An Anthropological and Scriptural Understanding* [Chicago: Hillenbrand, 2017], 67–68). The blood of Christ, not our acts of "satisfaction," pays for the guilt of sin (John Paul II, *Reconciliatio et paenitentia*, §31). However, the absolution does require prior *acceptance* of the assigned penance and the *intention* to perform it. This willingness is part of our contrition and desire to be reconciled and live again as God's children (see further below).

38. This remains true in some Eastern rites, where supplicative prayer is used in order to emphasize "that Christ, not the priest, is the true minister of the sacrament" (Fastiggi, *Reconciliation*, 51).

23:34; cf. Acts 7:60; James 5:16). But Jesus also pronounced forgiveness of sins directly (Mark 2:5; Luke 7:48). And his institution of the sacrament, granting the apostles his own Spirit so that whoever's sins "*you* forgive" are forgiven (John 20:23), suggests that in absolution the priest speaks not merely with the intercessory voice of Christ's bride but directly in the stead or "in the person of Christ."[39] Indeed, this is what gives the sacrament a special character as a sacrament, since interceding for others' forgiveness is something all believers can do in any setting (cf. 2 Tim. 1:16, 18; 1 John 5:16). Accordingly, the Councils of Florence and Trent identified the "form" of reconciliation—the words that determine the sacrament—as the personal, declarative absolution that the priest speaks as Christ's representative: *ego te absolvo*, "I absolve you."[40]

Through the absolution spoken by the priest, Jesus pronounces and confers his forgiveness for the sins confessed. The sacramental grace given works to counteract the effects of sin for the salvation of the penitent. Above all, through forgiveness, the person is restored to *friendship with God*. The sins that ruptured the relationship are brought to God and, by the merits of Christ, are forgiven. The breach in fellowship is healed, and they are reconciled. For those who sinned mortally and fell from friendship with God, they are forgiven anew and infused with grace as at baptism, joined again to the One in whom there is "no condemnation" (Rom. 8:1) and whose Spirit transforms sinners to "become the righteousness of God" (2 Cor. 5:21).[41] They are thus also reconciled with their brethren in the Church and restored to full participation in the life of Christ's body. For those absolved only of lighter faults, they receive forgiveness and a strengthening of the grace already at work within them. Confession of venial sins is, so to speak, not done because one needs to be readmitted to God's family, "but to become a better member of the family and grow in grace."[42] In both cases, however, the sin is forgiven and eternal punishment remitted, and God's grace works to restore his wayward children and to continue to renew his image in them.

---

39. See Lawrence Feingold, *Touched by Christ: The Sacramental Economy* (Steubenville, OH: Emmaus Academic, 2021), 25, 196–97.

40. Council of Florence, *Bull of Union with the Armenians* (see Tanner, *Decrees*, 1:548); Council of Trent, *Teaching Concerning the Most Holy Sacraments of Penance and Last Anointing*, Session XIV.3. On matter and form in sacramental theology, see Feingold, *Touched by Christ*, 134–38, 151–52; Roger W. Nutt, *General Principles of Sacramental Theology* (Washington, DC: Catholic University of America Press, 2017), 66–73.

41. The Council of Trent thus describes this restoration, for one who has fallen into mortal sin, as a kind of re-justification (*Decree on Justification*, Session VI.14).

42. Sheerin, *Sacrament of Freedom*, 20.

Penance and Satisfaction

A final but no less important component of the sacrament of reconciliation is penance done in satisfaction for the sins forgiven. The whole life of a Christian is to be one of repentance, of inwardly turning from sin to follow the Lord and expressing this repentance outwardly in one's behavior. It is part of a life of faith, hope, and love, a response to the divine "kindness" that is "meant to lead you to repentance" (Rom. 2:4). Expressions of the virtue of penance are especially found in *prayer*, *fasting*, and forms of *almsgiving*. But other forms of penance in the Christian life—such as making amends for wrongs we have done to others, meditating on a passage from Scripture, or attending counseling or spiritual direction regarding a habitual fault—can be "suitable for the realization . . . of the precise goal of penitence."[43] That goal is one's "love and surrender to God"[44] and ultimately one's conformation to God's image and glory in Christ.

All expressions of humble faith and love are penitential in that sense, part of our conformation to Christ in self-denial and self-giving love toward God and neighbor. The penance assigned by the priest in the sacrament is part of this life of repentance, here assigned with regard to one's restoration after the particular sins that have just been absolved. To live again in his father's household, to be truly *reconciled* and live in renewed relationship with him, the prodigal must not only receive his father's forgiving embrace on the street but come into the house and act as a son. If we want to be forgiven rather than punished, yet we refuse to be renewed in our obedience to God, we are still acting like prodigals wanting the benefit of our Father's gifts without living as his children. The assignment of a penance calls us, in a particular way, to be reconciled to God.

What is more, fulfilling our penance plays a role in counteracting the consequences of sin in us. For, while the eternal penalty of sin is remitted in Christ's absolution through the priest, sin also brings about "temporal" or noneternal consequences in our relationships and in our will and character. David is forgiven his adultery and murder and will not be put to death, but the child born of his adulterous union does not live, and David's selfishness and lust will influence his son to rebel against him and take his wives (2 Sam. 12:7–15). God pardons Israel's rebellion and will not destroy the nation;

43. Paul VI, *Paenitemini*, §2.
44. Paul VI, *Paenitemini*, §1.

nevertheless, the generation that rebelled will have to wander and relearn to cling to God in the desert for forty years as a fitting penance for the forty days they spied out the gift of the land that they rejected (Num. 14:20–35; cf. Ps. 99:8). One can consider these consequences from the perspective of divine justice as penalties that need satisfaction. One can also consider them within the structure of our person and relationships: committing sin knowingly, whether grave or light, wounds our own resolve in love and reinforces dysfunction in our relationships to God or others. Both ways of describing it are true; therefore, since this sacrament is given to address the problem of Christian sin, penance has both a *judicial* and a *"medicinal* character."[45]

From the perspective of divine *judgment*, penance addresses the temporal penalties for the sin, so that those penalties do not have to be applied in other ways or after this life (i.e., in purgatory).[46] One sees this belief anticipated in the atoning and sacrificial value ascribed to prayer, fasting, and almsgiving in the Old Testament (see Tob. 4:10–11; 12:8–9; Ps. 51:17; Sir. 3:30; 35:4; Dan. 4:27) and continued in Jesus's preaching about laying up treasure not on earth but in heaven (see Matt. 6:4, 6, 17–21; Luke 11:41; 12:33). Paul, likewise, warns the Corinthians that participating in the Eucharist without self-examination and penitence is a reason some are experiencing physical illness as judgments from God, and he calls them to obviate this with self-judgment (see 1 Cor. 11:27–32). If, as Paul says, the shoddy works of the saved will be burned away at the judgment so that only what is pure and precious will endure and be rewarded (1 Cor. 3:13–15), penance now can be thought of as an anticipation of that purification, removing what is shoddy in us and turning to produce works that will pass the test.

From the *medicinal* side, acts of penance play a role in healing our will and training us in works of love and friendship with God. Penances of prayer and Scripture reading call us to commune and converse again with God, to reengage our relationship with the Father. Fasting trains us in self-control

---

45. John Paul II, *Reconciliatio et paenitentia*, §31 (italics original).

46. See CCC 1470. Though the term "purgatory" comes later, the notion of a final purification in the process of the soul's entrance to beatitude—being finally healed of all impurities and completing any remaining penalty for our sins—received early affirmation especially in discussions of penance (sacramental or otherwise). Cf. Clement of Alexandria, *Miscellanies* 7.10.56; Tertullian, *Treatise on the Soul* 58.1; Origen, *Homilies on Jeremiah* 20.9; Lactantius, *The Divine Institutes* 7.21. Augustine, *Expositions of the Psalms* 37.3, speaking explicitly of the "chastening fire" that will finally purify the redeemed (as opposed to the damned, who are not made pure) after this life, prays, "Purify me in this life, and make me such that I will not need that chastening fire" (trans. Boulding, 147).

and is an act of submitting our bodily desires to God. Almsgiving is an act of love toward God and neighbor and trains us in habits of self-giving. In all of these, self-denial counteracts the habit of selfishness that our sins reinforce. "Penance is that counterforce which keeps the forces of concupiscence in check and repels them."[47] It is a "medicine" that "aims at the 'liberation' of man" from bondage to carnal desires that we so often gratify despite the harm they do.[48] If every act of sin shapes our will in the habit of sinning, penance offers salutary healing to strengthen us in self-control and shape us in habits of virtue and piety. This aspect of the sacrament, following the absolution from guilt, is also a gift of God's mercy through the Church to renew us in his likeness and train sinners in holiness and love. "While we still have time to be healed, let us place ourselves in the hands of God the physician, and pay him what is due. What is that? Sincere, heartfelt repentance."[49]

The Bible and Reconciliation

The preceding pages in this introductory chapter have given a brief overview of the place of this sacrament within God's manifold work to restore his fallen people, and they have also outlined the elements of the sacrament specifically. This prepares us now to turn to the Bible and look for those realities as they are disclosed in its pages: how God responds to sin in his world, God's call to repentance, and God's work to restore his people in Christ through the ministry of the Church.

A book investigating this sacrament by turning to Scripture could be organized in many ways and could have many purposes—perhaps using Scripture to defend, critique, or further develop the Church's thinking and practice on a particular issue. Other books might begin with Scripture to ground the Church's practice and then address social, psychological, or theological reasons that keep some Catholics away from the sacrament. My goals in writing this book are informed especially by the following paragraph from the dogmatic constitution *Dei Verbum* from the Second Vatican Council:

> Sacred theology takes its stand on the written word of God, together with tradition, as its permanent foundation. By this word it is made firm and strong

47. John XXIII, *Paenitentiam agere*, §12.
48. Paul VI, *Paenitemini*, §2.
49. *2 Clement* 9.7–8 (trans. Holmes, 149).

and constantly renews its youth (*iuvenescit*), as it investigates, by the light of faith, all the truth that is stored up in the mystery of Christ. The holy scriptures contain the word of God and, since they are inspired, really *are* the word of God; therefore the study of the "sacred page" ought to be the very soul of theology (*anima sacrae theologiae*).[50]

Theology rests on God's word, written in Scripture and received through the living tradition of the Church, which is guided into all truth by the same Spirit that inspired the texts (John 16:13; 1 Pet. 1:21). The written word is the foundation of the Church's faith and life, a permanent and perpetual base that cannot be forgotten or taken for granted. Turning to the Bible in light of the Church's faith, then, reveals again the "foundations" of what we believe in divine revelation. It shows why we believe what we believe and informs our understanding of what we do, why, and how we might do it better. More than that, however, the words of the Bible—read in the light of faith—bear in themselves an invigorating power. For they are not merely words for study that *inform* us, but words through which God's Spirit *forms* us in faith, hope, and love. The writings of Scripture are divinely inspired and, by the power of the Spirit, are life-giving and have a rejuvenating effect. The study of Scripture is the very "soul" or life-breath (*anima*) of theology, not only informing us about what to believe but also shaping us in how we believe and live it as God's Spirit energizes our own souls.

This study hopes, first, to show the "foundations" or basic convictions on which the sacrament stands. This will mean, in part, emphasizing passages that have traditionally been used as supports or "proofs" of its institution in the New Testament, such as Christ's commission of the apostles. But the sacrament's foundations are much broader than a few prooftexts. The sacrament itself is about sin, divine mercy, and the ways that God has established for dealing with sin among his people both communally and individually. Christ's commissioning the apostles with authority to forgive sins and the Church's use of this authority in the sacrament make sense only within the greater story of sin and redemption as it unfolds throughout salvation history. The meaning of a sentence is not understood unless we understand the words within it, yet the significance of those words together is not fully understood until we reach the sentence's end. So too with Scripture, from a canonical perspective: "Through all the words of Sacred Scripture, God speaks only

---

50. Vatican Council II, *Dei Verbum*, §24 (italics Tanner's).

one single Word"—the single truth of God's being and saving will—and that one Word is disclosed through the many words of Scripture's stories, songs, and instructions and received in the living tradition of the Church.[51] All of Scripture's diverse texts, written in different circumstances to make different points to their original audiences, when read in their contexts and within their place in God's unfolding "pedagogy" in Israel and the Church, ultimately testify to the same truth and the same saving plan.[52]

The approach I take in this book is to follow the biblical canon, from Genesis to Revelation, noting the realities of the problem of sin and God's unfolding response in salvation history.[53] The overall organization follows a kind of broad narrative frame (creation and fall, the patriarchs, Israel's monarchy, exile, return, and the advent of Christ) into which nonnarrative parts of the canon are set (Psalms, Wisdom literature, Pauline and Catholic Epistles).[54] My approach is both descriptive and synthetic, seeking to hear and describe the testimony of different books or sets of books while also drawing them together to the see the truth expressed through these many witnesses and at different periods. In both the New and the Old Testaments, we find retellings of the biblical story focused and filtered through the lens of a particular theme or mystery of faith. In Nehemiah, as the people prepare to renew their covenant with God, Israel's story is retold from Abraham through the exile with a focus on God's mercy amid the people's sinfulness (Neh. 9:1–10:1). In Acts, beginning from the mystery of Christ's crucifixion, Stephen retells the same story with emphasis on figures such as Moses and Joseph, who like Christ were rejected by the very people they were appointed to deliver (Acts 7:2–53).[55]

---

51. CCC 102; cf. *Dei Verbum*, §12. See the emphasis on this "one single Word" in Denis Farkasfalvy, *A Theology of the Christian Bible: Revelation, Inspiration, Canon* (Washington, DC: Catholic University of America Press, 2018). For an emphasis on the individual historical words that communicate that Word, see James B. Prothro, "Theories of Inspiration and Catholic Exegesis: Scripture and Criticism in Dialogue with Denis Farkasfalvy," *CBQ* 83 (2021): 294–314.

52. Vatican Council II, *Dei Verbum*, §§15–16.

53. My approach is similar, though not always identical, to the proposals for "biblical theology" in Geerhardus Vos, *Biblical Theology: Old and New Testaments* (Grand Rapids: Eerdmans, 1948); Augustin Cardinal Bea, "Progress in the Interpretation of Sacred Scripture," *Theology Digest* 1 (1953): 67–71; Brevard S. Childs, *Biblical Theology in Crisis* (Philadelphia: Westminster, 1970), 131–32; Benedict XVI, *Jesus of Nazareth: From the Baptism in the Jordan to the Transfiguration* (New York: Doubleday, 2007), xvii–xxi.

54. The overall frame is paralleled, though not precisely, by Augustine's organization of "six ages" from creation to the present (see his *Instructing Beginners in Faith* 18.29–24.45).

55. See Chris Bruno, Jared Compton, and Kevin McFadden, *Biblical Theology according to the Apostles: How the Earliest Christians Told the Story of Israel*, NSBT 52 (Downers Grove, IL: IVP Academic, 2020).

They look back as beneficiaries of their tradition and from the vantage point of their current faith. Here, too, and with a good deal more space than those short retellings are given in our Bibles, I aim to rehearse the biblical material through the lens this sacrament provides on divine mercy and God's work of restoring sinners through the grace of repentance.

Like inner-biblical retellings of Scripture's story, this book will be necessarily selective. I have highlighted material that provides insight on individual parts of the sacrament—sin and the need to confess it, the call to repentance and acts particularly involved with it (e.g., prayer, fasting, almsgiving), individual and communal restoration, Christ's commissioning of the apostles with authority to forgive, and the use of that authority in the New Testament. Somewhat like the examples from Nehemiah and Acts, I have also focused especially on recurring *patterns* of divine and human responses to sin as they are illustrated, described, or commanded in the various books of Scripture. The sacrament of reconciliation, as highlighted above, is aimed at restoring relationships between the sinner and God in the Church, and it consists of a pattern of actions on the part of the penitent, the priest, and the God who is at work through it all. The foundations of the sacrament, in my view, are not merely to be shown by in-depth arguments about individual topics (the value of almsgiving, distinctions between lighter and graver sins, etc.) or institutions that might correspond to the sacrament typologically (detailed discussions of Levitical institutions). They are best shown by highlighting how sin is dealt with in the relational context in which such realities make sense together—how prodigals leave and, through confession and repentance, are restored to life in the Father's household.[56]

It is hoped that readers will benefit from this presentation of the sacrament's biblical foundations, whether they avail themselves of sacramental reconciliation or not. And I hope in particular that Catholic readers who make use of this sacrament, and especially those who teach others about it, will be strengthened and *rejuvenated* by the biblical words and examples highlighted here. One of the contributions a "biblical," as opposed to "dogmatic," way of doing theology can make—even when they agree in substance—is to re-articulate truths in the Bible's own mode, using its images and metaphors and stories.[57] Indeed, due to its divine inspiration, the Bible is uniquely privileged

56. For a more detailed discussion, see James B. Prothro, "Patterns of Penance and the Sin of Cain: Approaching a Sacramental Biblical Theology," *Nova et Vetera* 21 (2023): 1371–89.
57. See Xavier Léon-Dufour, *Dictionary of Biblical Theology* (New York: Seabury, 1973), xxi–xxii. According to Angelo Tosato, receiving the Bible in its own mode is *the* touchstone

in the way it speaks and the power with which it addresses the Church. Long before Vatican II, Pope Leo XIII criticized preachers for speaking only in distilled philosophical formulas: their words may be true, "but they must be feeble and they must be cold, for they are without the fire of the utterance of God and they must fall far short of that mighty power which the speech of God possesses."[58] The Bible does not provide mere fodder to be synthesized into theological formulas. It addresses us and invites us to see our present life under God in light of the past and to hear ourselves addressed, corrected, and edified by the words of Scripture (see 2 Tim. 3:16–17). We are invited not merely to know *about* forgiveness but to beg for it with the psalmist; not only to know *that* Peter denied Christ but to weep with him in his sorrow and rejoice at his restoration; not merely to know *that* the redeemed must repent but to see ourselves wandering in the wilderness with Israel; not merely to know *that* God is merciful but to feel the Father's embrace of the returning prodigal. My hope, ultimately, is that priests, deacons, and catechists—whether they are already steeped in Scripture or not—will benefit from the pages that follow as they turn to Scripture to be edified and, in turn, to prepare to instruct and edify others. For the sake of accessible reference for those who want to read for themselves the passages briefly addressed here, chapter and verse numberings from Scripture are taken from the New Revised Standard Version (NRSV) and correspond to those of most other English translations.[59] I have also used longer (and more searchable) titles for ancient Jewish and Christian works rather than their academic abbreviations.[60] If this book is successful, it will prove not only informative but formative, pointing in its own small way to God's wonderful gift of forgiveness and his call, through Scripture and the ministry of Christ's Church, to be reconciled to God.

---

of Catholic biblical interpretation (*The Catholic Statute of Biblical Interpretation* [Rome: Gregorian & Biblical Press, 2021], 14).

58. Leo XIII, *Providentissimus Deus*, §4.

59. Versifications in the NRSV are standard to most English Bibles (e.g., RSV, ESV). Readers who use the "Catholic editions" of the RSV, NRSV, or ESV will find some differences only in the additions to Esther and Daniel, which I will note when significant. Those who use the NJB or NABRE, which usually follow versifications from critical editions of the Hebrew Old Testament despite English conventions, will find differences in verse numberings of some psalms and occasionally in chapter numberings of other books.

60. Translations of the Apostolic Fathers are taken from Michael W. Holmes, *The Apostolic Fathers: Greek Texts and English Translations*, 3rd ed. (Grand Rapids: Baker Academic, 2007).

2

Sin, Mercy, and Promise

Foundations in Genesis 1–11

Let them thank the LORD for his mercy,
such wondrous deeds for the children of Adam.

—Psalm 107:8 (NABRE)

The sacrament of reconciliation is an encounter with God's mercy. God acts with mercy toward those who know God and yet have fallen into sin, offering forgiveness to the penitent and grace that strengthens and heals the fallen as part of God's work to restore them fully to the divine image. This is a grace that is given particularly in the New Covenant by the death and resurrection of Christ and through the ministry of the Holy Spirit in the Church. But its foundations and patterns are visible even in the first pages of the Bible. The first eleven chapters of Genesis show us examples of sin by those who know God and God's desire to restore them.

The stories of Genesis 1–11 present human beginnings that have set the "roots" and trajectory "of human life."[1] As one author puts it, they present "beginnings that wrote history."[2] We have already outlined the foundational

---

1. Leon R. Kass, *The Beginning of Wisdom: Reading Genesis* (Chicago: University of Chicago Press, 2006), 10.

2. Hieronymus Horn, *Anfänge, die Geschichte Schrieben: Das Buch Genesis (1–11) neu kommentiert* (Stuttgart: Katholisches Bibelwerk, 2013).

sin of Adam and Eve and its effects. And the flood narrative is, of course, important for understanding the depth of fallenness within the human person—that "the inclination of the human heart is evil from youth" (Gen. 8:21)—and God's saving solution in the sacrament of baptism, which 1 Peter 3:21 says was "prefigured" in the flood. But these stories do not merely show *that* humanity fell. They also depict conversations between God and those who know God and yet fall into sin, such as Adam and Cain. These stories showcase human characters—representative of all humans, in different ways—in their relationship with God after sin, as God mercifully comes to encounter them and invites them to repentance. Likewise, even where sin and punishment are depicted on a more global than individual scale, as with the flood and Babel, these narratives show us God's character as one who deals with sin in ways that can be beneficial to the sinner and, in God's providence, prepare for the salvation of all in Christ.

"Where Are You?" Penalty and Promise for Adam and Eve

Some might not think of the fall of Adam and Eve as a story from which to learn God's mercy. Sin, guilt, and punishment? Yes. The Puritan *New England Primer*, a children's schoolbook first published by Benjamin Harris in the late 1600s, started its alphabet with *A*, at which letter children were to memorize: "In Adam's fall, we sinned all." More foundational for the Catholic faith, it is to Adam's sin that Paul points in describing humanity's fallenness and need for salvation in Christ. Sin "entered" the world through Adam, bringing "death" and "condemnation" with it (see Rom. 5:12–21; cf. Wis. 2:24).

This *is*, very definitely, a story about sin and its consequences. Adam and Eve sin. Created to be God's viceroys over creatures, they instead "obey" a creature, ultimately "siding with the serpent" and believing the serpent's word against God's.[3] Created to eat from the tree of life and become like God in holiness and immortality, they eat from the tree of knowledge of good and evil, whose fruit God warned would bring death (Gen. 2:17). They heed their own passions over God's warning and promise—the delight of their *eyes* at the tree's appearance, their desire to *taste* its fruit, and their prideful *ambition* to become wise (Gen. 3:6). And they, with all humanity after them, reap the

---

3. T. Desmond Alexander, *From Paradise to the Promised Land: An Introduction to the Pentateuch*, 4th ed. (Grand Rapids: Baker Academic, 2022), 17–18.

Sin, Desire, and Pride

Interpreters have long discerned a parallel between Eve's temptations in Genesis 3:6—the tree's outward splendor, her desire to taste it, and her prideful ambition—and those which summarize the "desire" or "lust" of the fallen world in 1 John: "For all that is in the world—the desires of the flesh and the desires of the eyes and pride of life—is not from the Father but is from the world" (1 John 2:16 ESV). Indeed, alongside other enumerations such as the seven "deadly" vices, these three can be used to categorize the root problem of sin for the heirs of Adam and Eve. According to Augustine, "There are these three, and apart from either the desire of the flesh or the desire of the eyes or the ambition of the world you find nothing to tempt human cupidity."[a]

a. Augustine, *Homilies on the First Epistle of John* 2.14 (trans. Ramsey, 50).

fruits of the disorder now introduced into God's once harmonious creation. The woman and man compete, their own roles to procreate and tend creation are marred by dysfunction (Gen. 3:16–19), and they receive the judgment of death—"To dust you shall return" (Gen. 3:19; cf. Ps. 90:3).

However, if our memory of this foundational narrative is only geared to see the "bad news" of sin and punishment, we will miss the good news of God's love as God responds to sin with mercy and promise. Something that sometimes goes unnoticed is God's response, before any penalty is pronounced. After Adam and Eve attain experiential "knowledge" of good and evil by transgressing God's command, they cover themselves and hide (Gen. 3:7–8).[4] If the narrative were meant only to show that sin entered the world and incurred divine punishment, we might expect the next line to give us a God's-eye view of things. It might read something like Genesis 6:3 or 6:7,

4. The "knowledge" of good and evil associated with sin here is sometimes taken to suggest that innocence and knowledge are incompatible. But the phenomenon of God's command implies (or creates) already a mental distinction between good and evil objectively. Given the experiential sense of "knowing" (Hebrew *yada'*, as in "Adam *knew* his wife") and the fact that their "knowledge" results directly in an experience of shame, it is better to understand the tree's name as indicating an *experiential*, not objective, knowledge of sin by committing sin, a name the snake twists into a promise of godlike autonomy or omniscience. Compare Gerhard von Rad, *Genesis*, OTL (Philadelphia: Westminster, 1973), 81, 89.

where a report of increased sin on earth is followed by a pronouncement of punishment from on high. But this account of the primordial sin in Genesis 3 instead depicts a God who seeks the sinner out. When Adam and Eve sin and hide, the first thing God does is come to them and ask a question. "But the LORD God called to the man, and said to him, 'Where are you?'" (Gen. 3:9). We are presented with a God who came "walking" around nearby (Gen. 3:8), not coming directly to where they were to drive them from Eden, but apparently surreptitiously coming near to where (God apparently knew) they were and inviting them with a question, *Where are you?*

God's approach and this question are important. Legal conflicts in the Bible frequently show us accusations that come in the form of questions. We see accusatory questions later in this scene, when God asks Adam directly if he has eaten from the forbidden tree and asks Eve what she has done (Gen. 3:11, 13). But this first question is different. God comes first not with accusation but with *invitation*. Why, when God seems to know where they are enough to stroll about nearby, would God ask where they are? "The answer is as immediate as it was obvious to nearly every early Jewish and Christian interpreter: *in order to give Adam and Eve an opportunity to repent.*"[5] God's question intimates that something is new and wrong in their relationship, hinting to Adam that God knows he is hiding.[6] But it is not yet accusatory. God's question is open, inviting Adam's free response and calling him to acknowledge why he is hiding. God asks no such questions of the snake, for whom God has only curses. God responds to sin by approaching the sinner with an invitation to confess. It is the response of "the good shepherd who seeks the lost sheep," and with an air of "tenderness" before "toughness."[7]

But Adam does not confess. He admits to hiding and some shame, but dissembles, at which point God responds with accusatory questions. These offer further opportunities for Adam, and then Eve, to express contrition. But instead they cast blame. Adam blames Eve, and by extension God ("The woman whom *you* gave to be with me," Gen. 3:12; italics added), and Eve

---

5. Gary A. Anderson, *The Genesis of Perfection: Adam and Eve in Jewish and Christian Imagination* (Louisville: Westminster John Knox, 2001), 138 (italics original).

6. Christoph Klein describes God's approach as that of an "intentional" father (*Wenn Rache der Vergebung Weicht: Theologische Grundlagen einer Kultur der Versöhnung*, Forschungen zur systematischen und ökumenischen Theologie 93 [Göttingen: Vandenhoeck & Ruprecht, 1999], 33).

7. Victor P. Hamilton, *The Book of Genesis: Chapters 1–17*, NICOT (Grand Rapids: Eerdmans, 1990), 193.

blames the deceptive snake. We see the deepened rupture of relationships, and we glimpse a problem that is not merely their single act of eating but their prideful disposition to defend themselves to the denigration of others. Then come the pronouncements of penalty and the consequences of sin. Competition between the man and woman will increase, their disharmony with creation will frustrate their natural vocations to procreate and to tend the earth, and the disunity introduced between their soul and body as they sought the delight of the eyes and stomach over blessedness will result in the soul's separation from the body in death (Gen. 3:16–19).[8]

Although this passage does not show us an example of explicit confession or a pronouncement of forgiveness, we can see in it the foundations of the sacrament of reconciliation. God's response to sin is to *seek out* the fallen, to come to them and invite them to reengage their relationship with God after it has been ruptured. Further, God's open question invites their *free response of confession* and contrition before he corners them with accusations and threats of wrath. This is the invitation extended in the sacrament, to acknowledge our sin and humbly bend the knee before the creator who loves us, not merely because we "fear his just punishments" but, ideally, in a response of love toward the God we have offended. We can also see some foundations for the forms penance has taken in Jewish and Christian life, as the faithful sought to counteract Eve's temptation by disciplining their desires with fasting and their temptation to pride with confession, as well as the use of "dust"—here an image of death—along with ashes as an outward symbol of the inward penitence Adam lacked (e.g., Neh. 9:1; Job 42:6).

This passage also shows us the consequences of sin and God's character in dealing with sin. Notice the order and character of the curses and penalties. God curses the *snake* first. God asks the snake no questions to invite piety or confession. God does not accuse the snake to call it to repentance. Though Adam and Eve have erred and are culpable, an outsider—one apparently not invited to repentance here—is responsible for beguiling them. And, while Adam and Eve (and their descendants) will bear the consequences of their sin, it is against this deceiver, identified in theological tradition as a demonic figure, that God's anger and opposition are first directed.[9] God is against sin

8. See Michael Dauphinais and Matthew Levering, *Holy People, Holy Land: A Theological Introduction to the Bible* (Grand Rapids: Brazos, 2005), 23–39.

9. There are varied terms and depictions of angelic influences toward evil in the Bible and in Jewish and Christian tradition, and there is a similar complexity regarding the demonic leader

and sin's effects in his people, and God's first act of wrath is against the "opponent" or "adversary" who introduced God's creatures to evil (1 Pet. 5:8).

God's wrath is directed first against sin. That means he will punish human sinners, yes, but God's opposition against sin means also that he opposes sin's effects in humans and desires to redeem and restore them. This is clear in God's curse of the snake, when God promises not only that there will be enmity and opposition between this snake figure and "the woman"—here Eve—but also that a descendant of Eve will strike the snake with his heel and crush him (Gen. 3:15). Christian tradition has long seen here a promise of redemption, the coming of Christ, in whose death and resurrection sin is condemned and the curse of death overturned—the New Adam whose obedience reconciles the world to God (see Rom. 5:12–21; 8:3). Christ will defeat the power of sin and Satan, and Paul even states that God will "crush Satan under your feet" (Rom. 16:20)—referring to Christ's body, the Church. God's first punishment of sin is to promise the defeat of Satan and the condemnation of sin itself in the coming Redeemer, through whom the faithful will be raised to victory over the evil that once conquered humanity.[10]

In fact, as we see God's condemnation of sin itself foretold here, we can also see how the penalties experienced by sinners become the very vehicles of their redemption. Christ's own death opens the gates of life, and through dying and being crucified "with" Christ, sinners are joined again to the blessing of eternal divine life (cf. Mark 8:24–35; Rom. 6:3–11; Phil. 3:10–11). And the consequences of sin's dysfunction experienced in the family and childbearing, likewise, become the means through which redemption will come. For God does not remove the blessing of fertility from Adam and Eve, the "mother of all living" (Gen. 3:20). Rather, God blesses it even more. The now difficult interrelations of marriage, the wife's painful act of childbearing,

---

often called "Satan." Archie T. Wright's cautious and detailed study views Justin Martyr as "likely" the first to identify this "Satan" directly as the snake in Genesis (*Satan and the Problem of Evil: From the Bible to the Early Church Fathers* [Minneapolis: Fortress, 2022], 226). Others see earlier identifications in the serpent who fights against God and deceives the world in Rev. 12:9, in the "devil" who introduced death into the world in Wis. 2:24, and perhaps in the crushing of Satan under the Church's feet in Rom. 16:20 (cf. Gen. 3:15).

10. This promise that God will crush Satan under the feet of the Church is encapsulated in depictions of Mary standing on the head of a serpent. She is the "symbol and most perfect realization" of the Church (*CCC* 507), a "woman" who by grace opposed the devil and was hated by him for bringing the Messiah to the world (see Rev. 12:1–18). Mary's role in salvation history as a "new Eve" appears in Christian theology as early as the second century (e.g., Justin Martyr, *Dialogue with Trypho* 100; Irenaeus, *Against Heresies* 3.22).

and the husband's toil to provide become the means by which, generation by generation, the long-awaited descendant of Eve will be born. Indeed, from this point in Scripture onward, every genealogy is gospel, a sign of hope that God is continuing the human race toward the advent of Christ, God's promise of redemption in response to human sin.

"Where Is Your Brother?" The Sin of Cain

The fall of Adam and Eve shows the beginnings of sin in the world and sets a backdrop for all of salvation history. Cain's murder of his brother, Abel, presents something similar. Here we see the problem of sin continue in humanity, the murderous beginnings of civilization in Cain and in Cain's posterity (Gen. 4:17–24), and the first instance of God's frequent pattern of esteeming the younger brother, here Abel, over the elder (as with Jacob and Esau; Gen. 25:23). Yet, as with Adam and Eve, the text also invites us into a conversation—two conversations, in fact—between God and one who has sinned that illumines for us the reality of sin, God's invitation to confess, and God's merciful application of penalty.

The brothers' first action in the story is to bring an offering of homage to the Lord—Abel (a shepherd) with a firstling from his flock and Cain (a gardener) with produce from his harvest. God accepts Abel's offering, but not Cain's. Many look to the types of offerings they bring to determine *why* God favored Abel, but the Hebrew text leaves it ambiguous.[11] The focus, for the reader, is instead on God's words to Cain and Cain's murderous response. Cain is angry and feels dejected (his face "fell") at God's disapproval (Gen. 4:5). But God responds with a word that is both a rebuke and an encouragement. "Why are you angry, and why has your countenance fallen? If you do well, will you not be accepted? And if you do not do well, sin is lurking at the door; its desire is for you, but you must master it" (Gen. 4:6–7). The syntax is dense here, and translation is difficult.[12] Yet on any translation the text

---

11. The Septuagint's translation locates the problem in how the offerings were prepared. God says that Cain has sinned if his offering is not *divided* rightly (*orthōs de mē dielēs*)—not cut up and apportioned correctly—even if it is *offered* rightly (*orthōs prosenenkēs*, Gen. 4:7). The Letter to the Hebrews summarizes the difference in their offerings as a matter of "faith" (Heb. 11:4).

12. See, among others, Kass, *Beginning of Wisdom*, 139–40n21. The NJPS translation, set in stanza form and intentionally wooden, gives a sense in English of some of the difficulties: "Surely, if you do right, / There is uplift. / But if you do not do right / Sin couches at the door; / Its urge is toward you, / Yet you can be its master."

assumes that Cain knows a moral code and has transgressed it. God's question intimates that Cain, who clearly knows enough of piety to be bringing an offering in the first place, should know how he has erred. God's words are meant to check Cain's pouty jealousy, warn him that sin and temptation are near at hand, and direct him to turn again toward God and make an acceptable sacrifice next time.

We see here a God who seeks those who have done wrong and calls them to repentance. God even warns Cain that in his current state he is in danger of greater sin, calling Cain to self-control and changed behavior. God rebukes with love here, for Cain's good. But God's good word becomes an occasion for Cain's internal sinfulness to bring him to graver wrongdoing—an image of sinful inclinations within humans turning God's good commandments into an occasion for transgression, as Paul describes in Romans 7:7–12.[13] The next verse narrates Cain's response to God's exhortation: "Cain said to his brother Abel, 'Let us go out to the field.' And when they were in the field, Cain rose up against his brother Abel, and killed him" (Gen. 4:8).

The gravity of this sin should strike us. The narrative frames Cain's murder against his intimate relationship with the victim, twice reiterating that Abel was Cain's "brother." That this murder comes directly on the heels of God's warning and exhortation to do good, likewise, throws Cain's actions into sharp relief. Further, the verbs in Genesis 4:8 betray Cain's continued, stubborn intentionality in the progression of his actions. He first *invites* Abel away from other family and, once they have arrived, he *rises* to attack Abel and, in doing so, *kills* him. Interpreters sometimes reason that, this being the first murder, Cain must have intended only to hit Abel, and that we should imagine Cain being surprised that Abel never got back up.[14] But this is difficult to sustain. God's words in 4:7 already imply that Cain knows right from wrong, and in 4:8 we are not presented with a Cain who merely hit his brother in a rage but one who lured him away to do premeditated harm, who retained that intention all the while that he walked with his brother to the field, and who then chose to stand and attack him by surprise.

Cain's sin is, as we would classify it, both grave and mortal. It is neither light nor unintended. This is important to note as we read this episode in the

13. That Cain is echoed in Rom. 7, in fact, is suggested by N. T. Wright, *The Climax of the Covenant: Christ and the Law in Pauline Theology* (London: T&T Clark, 1991), 226–30.

14. E.g., Nahum M. Sarna, *Understanding Genesis*, Heritage of Biblical Israel 1 (New York: Jewish Theological Seminary of America, 1966), 31.

context of confession and penance. For with Cain, as with Adam, God's first response is an open question that aims, as John Chrysostom puts it, "to drag the murderer toward repentance."[15] God asks, "Where is your brother Abel?" (Gen. 4:9). Even in the case of such a sin—surely graver than whatever had made his earlier offering unacceptable—God's first response is to invite a free confession by the sinner. But, as with Adam, Cain dissembles, and God turns from invitation to accusation. God tells Cain directly that he knows his sin and can hear Abel's innocent blood crying out from the earth for vengeance. And God imposes a penalty: the earth that Cain has defiled with murder will no longer be hospitable to him, and Cain will become a wanderer, now even farther away from Eden (Gen. 4:10–12).

Cain had been unwilling to lament his brother's death or admit his responsibility for it. Now that he is accused and hears his punishment, he begins to express sorrow. The terms in 4:13 bear ambiguity, since the Hebrew *'awon* can indicate guilt or punishment, and the verb *nasa'* ("bear") can be used of bearing a burden (like guilt) or perhaps "bearing away" or forgiving sin. Cain's words might be translated "My punishment is too much for me to bear" (as in most English versions) or "My guilt is too great to be forgiven" (compare the Septuagint and Vulgate), and some even interpret Cain on the latter reading as the first penitent.[16] But on either translation, any contrition on Cain's part is imperfect. He does not lament his crime as such, but bemoans his banishment from home and from God's presence and complains that he—a murderer—will himself be murdered by others in his wanderings.

Cain has sinned gravely, and his contrition is imperfect, motivated more by a fear of punishment than love of God and others. But God does not spurn imperfect contrition even after such a sin. Rather, God promises to *protect* Cain's life by placing a "mark" or "sign" (Hebrew *'ot*) of some kind on him "so that no one who came upon him would kill him" (Gen. 4:15).[17] And this despite the death penalty elsewhere stipulated for murder (e.g., Gen. 9:6; Num.

15. John Chrysostom, *On Repentance and Almsgiving* 2.1.3 (trans. Christo, 17).

16. Such interpretations are not in the majority but are registered by the early rabbis in *Genesis Rabbah* 22.13. Some patristic Christian authors, reading the Septuagint, use the passage similarly. The Septuagint has God tell Cain that he has sinned and must "be silent" (Gen. 4:7); this was applied to commands that some penitents should abstain from singing in worship. Compare Pseudo-Ambrose, *Concerning Repentance* 2.104.

17. The text makes explicit that its function is to ward off attackers, though what the mark or sign was is ambiguous. *Genesis Rabbah* 22.12 records several opinions, including that God caused the sun to shine for Cain (as a "sign" giving assurance of God's promise), gave Cain leprosy, gave Cain a dog, and made a conspicuous horn grow out of Cain's body.

35:33). *God wants Cain to bear his punishment, but not to die from it.* Gerhard von Rad calls this perhaps "the most enigmatic part of the narrative."[18] Considered in the light of what is revealed elsewhere in the biblical canon, however, we can see here a manifestation of God's character as one who takes "no pleasure in the death of the wicked, but that the wicked turn from their ways and live" (Ezek. 33:11). The penalties God imposes on Cain are *fitting*, exiling him from the ground he polluted and from the family he violated by fratricide. Yet the consequences are not necessarily *final*. God still lets Cain live, and God still allows him the "blessing" of fertility, so that Cain—while suffering penalty—can come to have a share in fulfilling God's command to multiply and fill the earth with his wife in a new land (cf. Gen. 1:28; 4:16–17).

We are meant to see the gravity of Cain's sin in this narrative, and the horror of it should deter us from following in his footsteps. But we need that deterrence precisely because of our tendency to be like Cain, not only in our potential for outright murder but in all manner of crimes against our sisters and brothers. Jesus commands his followers not only not to murder but not to harbor anger against their brethren (Matt. 5:21–22), and 1 John 3:11–12 calls us to see every sin against a brother or sister as akin to fratricide, calling us instead to the love of neighbor that Cain refused. But this narrative invites us also to see ourselves in Cain's place when we have sinned and to respond rightly where Cain did not. We can be assured of God's mercy for us in his responses to Cain. Even after grave sin, even when contrition is imperfect, God desires and provides for the sinner's repentance and blessing.

Sin, Penalty, and Preparation: From the Flood to Babel

The primordial history of Genesis 1–11 continues after Cain to depict God's mercy, justice, and plan of redemption. However, we do not see the same kinds of personal conversation and interaction between sinners and God as in Genesis 3–4. Instead, these stories depict God working from on high to punish sin and yet provide for life and redemption in the world.

Eve's descendants continue to populate the world, through Cain's line and also through that of her third son, Seth (Gen. 5:3). Seth's descendants have some bright lights among them, particularly Enoch and Noah, both of whom are said to have "walked" in close fellowship with God (Gen. 5:24; 6:9).

18. Von Rad, *Genesis*, 109.

But they appear to be unique. By the time of Noah, God sees not only that humanity in general is wicked but that "every inclination of the thoughts of their hearts was only evil continually" (Gen. 6:5). Impiety toward God and injustice among humans wreak havoc in creation, and God visits judgment upon the world through a flood. Yet God preserves Noah and his family and so preserves the human race through which God promised to send the Redeemer. The flood waters deal death and purify the world for life. According to 2 Peter, God's action in the flood signals both threat and promise, showing that "the Lord knows how to rescue the godly from trial, and to keep the unrighteous under punishment" (2 Pet. 2:9). The flood is for the world a kind of purification, a type for the divine fire that will purify the world at the final judgment, refining and preserving what is good and destroying finally what is evil (2 Pet. 3:5–7; cf. 1 Cor. 3:13–15).

God's punishment and provision are presented on a global and not individual scale here. How God dealt with the souls of individuals or how God appealed or prompted any to repent before sending the flood is not addressed. But the text shows starkly the problem of sin from which Christians are delivered in baptism (as 1 Pet. 3:21 indicates) and, if they lapse again into mortal sin, through the sacrament of reconciliation. It also shows God's desire for reconciliation and continued relationship with human beings. For God stipulates to Noah that more clean animals, fit for sacrifice, be brought than other animals—seven pairs instead of only one (Gen. 7:2–3).[19] This is so that, when Noah's family finally leaves the ark, they can resume their worship of God by sacrifice (Gen. 8:20). God punishes the world's sin. Yet God arranges things so that through this punishment the world may be purified, life and the hope of redemption preserved, and humans restored to an active relationship of worship and love toward God.

Nonetheless, though this cleansing did forestall increased wickedness by those notorious sinners destroyed in the flood, the problem of sin continued in Noah's line. Even when God is pleased with Noah's sacrifice (Gen. 8:20), God still acknowledges that human desire remains inwardly bent toward evil (Gen. 8:21). Noah's own drunkenness and the familial conflicts that ensue parallel the temptation toward physical *desire* and the familial dysfunction

---

19. This is consistent enough in the story's present canonical form: Noah is commanded to bring more clean animals suitable for sacrifice, some of which he sacrifices immediately after leaving the ark. But otherwise only one pair of each kind is mentioned. Such threads, repeated but apparently ignored in the flood narrative, make this one of the most notorious texts suggesting a need for source- or tradition-critical theories for the Pentateuch's composition.

we saw already in Eve and Adam (Gen. 9:20–23). The last of the episodes in Genesis 1–11 shows a sin of communal human *pride*. The story of the tower of Babel begins in a setting in which all mankind speaks the same language and settles in the land that will become Babylon, "Babel" in Hebrew (Gen. 11:1–2). There, they concoct a plan to build a city and a great tower that reaches to the heavens. They do this to secure a reputation for themselves and also a settled location: "Let us make a name for ourselves; otherwise we shall be scattered abroad upon the face of the whole earth" (Gen. 11:4). In what is likely a counter to Babylonian celebration of its city as the center of the world and of its ziggurat as the point where the high gods made contact with earth, Genesis presents such a tower not as a divine gift but as a manifestation of human "ambition" and "impiety," an Adam-like "human effort to become like God" (cf. Jer. 51:53).[20]

This sin, like the prideful desire of Adam and Eve to be like God and seek blessing in their own way rather than the way God intended, will be punished. But here too the mode of God's punishment is not final but is fit into God's plan of redemption for the human race. Indeed, the text presents God's response less as a punishment than as a prophylactic action meant to forestall human pride. If things go on this way, God says, "nothing they presume to do will be out of their reach" (Gen. 11:6 NABRE). God reverses their work by confusing their languages, so that the people cannot understand or cooperate with one another. God also reverses their desire for security in a settled location. God confuses their tongues and so causes them to scatter and spread out over "all" the earth (Gen. 11:8, 9). This is not just a punishment forcing them to do what they did not want. The command to multiply and fill the earth has been God's command and blessing for humans since Adam (Gen. 1:28; 9:1, 7). Further, just as the command to multiply now plays a role in the future birth of the Savior, the command to fill the earth in a way prepares for that as well. In the book of Acts, Paul explains God's work among non-Israelite nations to Athenian philosophers thus: "From one ancestor he made all nations to inhabit the whole earth, and he allotted the times of their existence and the boundaries of the places where they would live, so that they would search for God and perhaps grope for him and find him—though indeed he is not far from each one of us" (Acts 17:26–27). Looking back on

20. Gordon J. Wenham, *Genesis 1–15*, WBC 1 (Nashville: Nelson, 1987), 239–40. See further John H. Walton, *Ancient Near Eastern Thought and the Old Testament*, 2nd ed. (Grand Rapids: Baker Academic, 2018), 80–81.

Genesis through the lens of this speech, we can see again that God's chosen mode of penalty for sin is applied in a way that points toward salvation. He confuses their tongues and causes different groups to split off, disunited in different lands. But in God's providence, each people's system of culture and language becomes a unique and fertile environment for the nations to develop traditions—imperfect though they are apart from the fullness of divine revelation—by which to conceive of the invisible creator, speak of him, and honor him through what is knowable of God through creation (cf. Wis. 13:5–9; Acts 14:15–17; Rom. 1:19–20). Here, too, in this punishment, God provides for humanity's ultimate redemption with an interest in his relationship with each individual sinner.

These chapters set the stage for the rest of Scripture. They show us sin at its roots in the snake's temptation and in the internal desires and pride of human beings. They show us sin's consequences as sin breeds more sinning and as the rupture in human relationships with God, one another, and creation deepens. And they show us God's merciful heart for fallen humanity. He comes to individuals to invite them to contrition and repentance, as we saw in God's encounters and conversations with Adam, Eve, and Cain. In imposing a fitting penalty for sin, God provides a mode of redemption for humanity. God continues to bless humankind, amid their brokenness and penalty, and seeks to restore them to himself. Most importantly this is seen in God's promise of a descendant of Eve, Christ himself, who will conquer sin through the mess of family and the blessing of childbirth. We will see God's work of redemption and his mercy amid human sin continue as God shapes the family, the people, through whom Christ will come in Abraham.

3

Mercy, Penalty, and Mediation

The Patriarchs and the Exodus

You were a forgiving God to them,
but an avenger of their wrongdoings.

—Psalm 99:8

God's mercy and invitation to repentance continue in the next phase of the biblical narrative, the beginnings of the nation of Israel in God's calling of Abraham and the journey of the Hebrews from Egypt toward the land of Canaan. As in Genesis 1–11, the plotline highlights God's unfolding promise, now focused in a single nation. It is Abraham's line through which all the nations will find blessing in Christ (Gen. 12:3; Gal. 3:16), and the story of this family, beginning with that promise in Genesis 12, now "moves forward with the hope that people may yet be reconciled to God."[1]

Both the New and the Old Testaments point back to this part of Scripture as especially instructive for the life of God's people. Of course, it is important for the story of salvation in the election of Israel and the promise to Abraham,

---

1. T. Desmond Alexander, *From Paradise to the Promised Land: An Introduction to the Pentateuch*, 4th ed. (Grand Rapids: Baker Academic, 2022), 6.

which Paul interprets as a proclamation of the Christian gospel ahead of time (Gal. 3:8, 16). On an individual level, too, these stories are instructive as we consider our lives in relationship with God, our struggles with sin, and God's call to repent and cling to him. Abraham is looked to as a kind of paradigm of the life of faith in the New Testament (see John 8:39–40; Rom. 4:1–25; Heb. 6:11–15; 11:8–19; James 2:20–24). In his journey of faith—and in Jacob's as well—we see God's patient and providential way of blessing Abraham while also calling him to greater faithfulness. The journey of the children of Israel toward the promised land is especially instructive as we see them sin after being delivered. The New Testament—following the Old—exhorts readers to attend to the events of Israel's wandering in the wilderness as reminders of God's kindness and as warnings of the seriousness of sin for Israel and the Church (cf. Pss. 95; 106; 1 Cor. 10:1–12; Heb. 3:7–19; Jude 5). In these passages, we see penance and reconciliation displayed in God's forgiveness, his imposition of corrective penalties, and his work through priestly mediators.

Abraham's Journey of Faith

Turning the page from Genesis 1–11 to Genesis 12 draws us from foundational stories depicting humanity's primordial beginnings to a recognizable place and time in ancient Mesopotamia around 2000 BC. This matches the salvation-historical narrative, as the promise that the snake-crusher, the New Adam, will be a descendant of Eve now narrows to a single family. God calls Abram and his wife, Sarai, who are currently old and childless, to move to the land of the Canaanites, promising to give them countless descendants and make them a "great nation," with kings and princes, a nation through which all the peoples of the world will find "blessing" (Gen. 12:2, 3; 15:5; 17:6, 16).[2] The royal dignity promised to this pair is encapsulated by the elevated names God gives them: Abraham, "exalted father," and Sarah, "princess" (Gen. 17:5, 15).[3]

Abraham and the nation that comes from him will, thus, mediate God's blessing and salvation to the fallen world. God will bless their family, and in them the rest of the world will be blessed. One can see this mediatory role

2. The *hithpael* verb in Gen. 12:3 (and parallel verses) can be read reflexively, that nations will "bless *themselves* by" Abram (e.g., RSV), or passively, that they will "*be* blessed" in Abram (e.g., ESV). The passive reading is taken by the Septuagint and in the New Testament, where it is read as a prophecy of Christ (Gal. 3:8).

3. See Victor P. Hamilton, *The Book of Genesis: Chapters 1–17*, NICOT (Grand Rapids: Eerdmans, 1990), 463–64, 476.

in Abraham's story already, long before we come to the examples of Moses and Israel's priesthood, as God blesses others for the sake of Abraham or Abraham's obedience and intercession (cf. Gen. 22:16–18; 26:5, 24). God is ready to spare the sinful cities of Sodom and Gomorrah because of Abraham's prayers. God spares Lot and his family, Abraham's kin, and spares the city of Zoar on account of Lot (Gen. 19:21–22, 29). God also commands the king Abimelech to have Abraham pray for him so that he might be spared (Gen. 20:7, 17). Yet God does not compromise his justice in heeding his mediators (Gen. 18:25), as though a word from Abraham could arbitrarily alter God's action, as we see in the ultimate destruction of Sodom or the punishment of Lot's wife for disobeying the angels (Gen. 19:23–26).[4] Indeed, by divine providence, Abimelech is "innocent" and has not violated Sarah, though Abraham and Sarah deceptively let him believe that she was unmarried and available (Gen. 20:4–6). Nonetheless, as God works justice and mercy from on high, he chooses also to work *through* the mediation of Abraham and Abraham's family, welcoming and accepting their prayers on behalf of others.

Even so, as with other chosen mediators of God, Abraham's walk of faith shows his own struggles. Abraham believes God and offers devout worship to God (Gen. 12:7–8; 13:4, 18; 15:6; 21:33). Yet the trust to which God calls him is robust and challenging. Abraham and Sarah are old, and Sarah is beyond her childbearing years (Gen. 17:17; 18:11). And, following the ages ascribed to him in the text, twenty-five more years pass from the time God promised to make him a great nation to the time that Sarah's promised son, Isaac, is born (cf. Gen. 12:4; 21:5). That is a long time to wait for God to fulfill his promise. Moreover, it is a promise whose fulfillment would be nothing short of miraculous—not only hard to wait for, but easy to second-guess and doubt. Abraham, admirably, does not seem in the text to have abandoned hope in this promise, but he clearly did struggle with *how* and *when* it would be fulfilled.

Abraham and Sarah first appear to assume that God will grant them a natural child. God's preservation of Sarah, when she and Abraham tell Pharaoh that she is only Abraham's sister out of fear that they may kill Abraham and

4. Lot's righteousness is not portrayed starkly in Gen. 19 other than perhaps in a desire to protect his guests from the Sodomites. His willingness to give them his daughters instead, and his daughters' later seduction of him, along with his fearful bargaining with the angels, may suggest he is spared more because he is Abraham's kin than for virtue (cf. the interpretation in *Jubilees* 16.7–9). Other writings, including the New Testament, read Lot more sympathetically as a type of the righteous who are hounded by an evil generation and will be delivered (Luke 17:28–34; 2 Pet. 3:6–8; cf. Wis. 10:6–9; 19:17; Pseudo-Philo, *Biblical Antiquities* 45.2).

take her (Gen. 12:10–20), seems also to betray God's desire to protect Sarah as the mother of the line of promise. But in the canonical text, Sarah's role as natural mother in God's promise to Abraham is not explicit at first. So, after a long period of waiting, Sarah suggests that God perhaps intended Abraham to have descendants by another, with the child belonging to Sarah only by a kind of surrogacy: Sarah's slave Hagar will become a subsidiary wife to Abraham under Sarah's authority and produce a child (Gen. 16:1–2). One can understand why Sarah would suggest recourse to this practice, just as one can understand their desire to lie to Pharaoh to protect Abraham, but the consequences of this deviation from the creator's intention become quickly visible. Hagar bears a son, Ishmael, and jealousy and competition between the wives set in quickly (Gen. 16:4–5). On Abraham's side, his lack of patience in God's word of promise breeds attachment, bringing him to cling to the hope of God's blessing through Ishmael. God tells Abraham that he will fulfill his promise through *Sarah* explicitly in Genesis 17:15–16. But Abraham, laughing at the statement that Sarah will give birth, pleads that God would redirect the blessing through Hagar: "If only Ishmael could live in your favor!" (Gen. 17:18 NABRE).

God's work in this situation demonstrates his providential mercy to humans amid the mess of sin. God maintains his promise to bring the great nation of blessing and salvation through Sarah, despite natural expectation, as a sign that nothing is "too wonderful" for God (Gen. 18:14; cf. 17:19; 21:12). Yet God has mercy on Hagar and Ishmael when they are treated cruelly by Sarah and promises to make Ishmael a great nation too (cf. Gen. 16:11; 17:20; 21:13).[5] God is merciful toward Pharaoh and Abimelech in keeping them from interfering with God's promise by violating Sarah. And, despite his failings, God preserves Abraham and grants him blessings from these kings and through Ishmael (cf. Gen. 12:16; 17:20; 20:14–16).

Nonetheless, as we see God's mercy and providence *amid* the fallenness of his chosen vessels, we also see God gradually calling them *out* of it toward greater faithfulness. John of the Cross describes God's way of strengthening the faith of believers as like that of a mother raising and training her child: at first, she coddles and carries them, lavishing sweet care and feeding them,

---

5. This sets a pattern repeated also with Jacob and Esau, Rachel and Leah, Israel and Judah, and others. "Ishmael inherits the Abrahamic promise but not the Abrahamic covenant. Isaac inherits both" (Jon D. Levenson, *Inheriting Abraham: The Legacy of the Patriarch in Judaism, Christianity and Islam*, Library of Jewish Ideas [Princeton: Princeton University Press, 2012], 51).

but then she weans the child from her breast and stops carrying the child. This can be distressing to the child, but it is for the child's good and growth. God, too, strengthens the soul by a similar, gradual pedagogy. And we can see this with Abraham. When Abraham doubts when and how God will give him an heir, God makes a formal covenant and swears a solemn oath to reassure him (Gen. 15:7–21). But after Abraham and Sarah try to get the promise through Hagar, God commands that Abraham be "blameless" before him (Gen. 17:1), ties the promise explicitly to Sarah, and commands that Abraham and the males of his household be circumcised (Gen. 17:9–14). This demands a strong demonstration of faith and self-sacrifice, calling Abraham to "seal" and enact his trust in God by sacrificing—surely painfully—a part of the very organ on which God's promise depends (cf. Rom. 4:11).[6] Once Sarah's son, Isaac, is finally born, God allows Hagar and Ishmael to be sent away, leaving Abraham to trust that God's promise will come through *Isaac* alone (Gen. 21:9–13). Then, in the greatest "test" of Abraham's belief in God's promise, God asks Abraham to sacrifice Isaac, his only and beloved son (Gen. 22:1–2). God does not, as Genesis 22 makes clear, want Abraham to kill him in fact, and an angel is sent to bar Abraham from harming Isaac. But the test is a final call for Abraham to demonstrate his faith in God's word over his own attachments and security—security he valued in telling kings that Sarah was his sister, security he valued in Ishmael (whom he could see and hold) over the promise of a future miraculous child, and now the security he has in Isaac and trying to keep him safe until Isaac has his own children to continue Abraham's line.[7] This final test calls Abraham to put his utter faith in God's word and God's ways, and Abraham passes the test, his faith being "completed" or "perfected" by his works of obedience (James 2:22).

We can see in Abraham's journey of faith a God who keeps his promises, who is merciful and just, and who wants his people—mediators through whom

---

6. On the pain of circumcision, which Abraham undergoes at the age of ninety-nine according to Gen. 17:24, compare the adult circumcision of the Shechemites, whom the pain rendered invalid for two days (Gen. 34:25). The ancient Jewish philosopher Philo read circumcision as purposed to physical and spiritual purity in restraining carnal lusts (Philo, *Special Laws* 1.5, 8–10); the rite of course took on other significances among Abraham's descendants.

7. The more theological question of how God could *command* such a thing, regardless of intent or function, is of course vast. Some early Jewish receivers of this text even posited a demonic figure issuing the command (*Jubilees* 17.15–18.13). For a theoretical discussion of how to approach such passages, see Matthew J. Ramage, *Dark Passages of the Bible: Engaging Scripture with Benedict XVI and Thomas Aquinas* (Washington, DC: Catholic University of America Press, 2013).

John of the Cross: Weaning Baby Souls

If new believers are like "newborn infants" (1 Pet. 2:2), John of the Cross imagines the next stage as that of spiritual toddlerhood, in which God, like a mother, strengthens believers by withholding some of the consolations of infancy.

> God nurtures and caresses the soul, after it has been resolutely converted to his service, like a loving mother who warms her child with the heat of her bosom, nurses it with good milk and tender food, and carries and caresses it in her arms. But as the child grows older, the mother withholds her caresses and hides her tender love; she rubs bitter aloes on her sweet breast and sets the child down from her arms, letting it walk on its own feet so that it may put aside the habits of childhood and grow accustomed to greater and more important things. The grace of God acts just as a loving mother by re-engendering in the soul new enthusiasm and fervor in the service of God.[a]

a. John of the Cross, *Dark Night* 1.1.2 (trans. Kavanaugh and Rodriguez, 361).

God will bless others—to turn to him again and again in faithfulness through repentance. We do not see much explicit contrition here, nor does the narrator explicitly blame Abraham for sins even if he does show us their consequences. But we do see God's patient pedagogy to call Abraham to greater and greater faithfulness after failure. Circumcision and the command to offer Isaac to God, in particular, show us a God who imposes a difficult and painful (physically or emotionally) task that is fit to Abraham's failure and prods him on to greater faith precisely where he had faltered. Abraham's faith is exemplary because, in all his questions and failings, he not only continues to seek and trust God but is ready to hear and heed God's call. He grows in fidelity through such challenges to become stronger where he was weak. Repentance and obedience are part of Abraham's proving himself a "friend of God" (see 2 Chron. 20:7; Isa. 41:8; James 2:23), part of his life of faith and growth in his personal relationship with God. Our penances, too, as we will continue to see, are part of our growth and training as God's children, part of walking in the "footsteps of the faith that our father Abraham had" (Rom. 4:12 ESV).

Sin and Blessing in Jacob's Broken Family

God continues to keep his promise after Abraham. He reiterates the promise of a nation, blessing, and blessing for the world explicitly to Isaac (Gen. 26:2–5, 24) and gives him twin sons through his wife, Rebekah. He continues this promise as well in the life of the younger twin, Jacob, whom God grants the name "Israel" (Gen. 32:28; 35:10) and through whom God elects to continue the line of blessing. Jacob's twelve sons will become the eponymous heads of the twelve tribes whom God delivers from Egypt and builds into the royal nation through which the Christ will be born. In Jacob's story, we see God continue this merciful promise despite sin in Jacob's family. And, not unlike Abraham, we see God call him personally to greater and greater faithfulness, as "Jacob repeatedly struggles to acquire a proper relationship both with men and with God."[8]

Sin and its consequences are evident in Jacob's interrelationships. He and his older twin, Esau, are prophesied to become separate nations, of which only Jacob's progeny will carry the line of salvation (Gen. 25:23). This prophecy is fulfilled, but not by the noblest means. Rebekah and Isaac each favor different sons (Gen. 25:27–28), setting them up for the competition we have seen since Adam and Eve's sin. Jacob is conniving toward his brother, who admittedly treats his birthright with little care (Gen. 25:34), and at Rebekah's urging Jacob deceives Isaac into giving him the family blessing that Isaac intended for Esau (Gen. 27). Esau becomes murderously angry, and Jacob has to flee— again with Rebekah's help. Jacob finds love in a new land, becomes enamored with a beautiful woman named Rachel, and makes a contract with her father, Laban, for seven years' labor as Rachel's bride price, which "seemed to him but a few days because of the love he had for her" (Gen. 29:20). But this time Jacob is the victim of his father-in-law's conniving. Laban apparently holds no hope of another match for his older daughter, Leah, and so switches the brides at the wedding feast, marrying Jacob to Leah. Laban allows Jacob to marry Rachel also, but at the price of seven more years' servitude. Jacob honors both brides with husbandly provision, but he continues to love Rachel over Leah (Gen. 29:30), and this breeds sorrow and competition between the sisters. God grants Leah children, whose names reflect her longing for her husband's affection: for instance, Simeon, "the LORD heard that I am hated,"

8. Leon R. Kass, *The Beginning of Wisdom: Reading Genesis* (Chicago: University of Chicago Press, 2006), 407.

and Levi, "Now this time my husband will be joined to me" (Gen. 29:33, 34). Rachel is loved but is envious of her sister's fertility (Gen. 30:1), and so—like Sarah with Hagar—Rachel has Jacob marry her slave, Bilhah, to have children for her, and she boasts of her vindication and victory over Leah (Gen. 30:5–8). Leah responds in kind with her slave, Zilpah. The pathos of the whole situation is illustrated painfully in an episode in which the sisters bargain for a night with their husband for goods, as their father bargained them for Jacob's labor. Rachel asks for some mandrake fruit that Leah's son has picked, to which Leah angrily responds, "Is it a small matter that you have taken away my husband? Would you take away my son's mandrakes also?" (Gen. 30:15). Rachel offers to trade the fruit for a night with Jacob. Leah informs Jacob of this obligation—"You must come in to me; for I have hired you with my son's mandrakes" (Gen. 30:16)—and Jacob submits, giving Leah another son. All three, and the women's slaves as well, are in a relational mess of competition and yearning, love and devaluation. And the mess extends beyond this marital situation. Leah's son Reuben sleeps with Rachel's slave, Bilhah, sowing further discord (Gen. 35:22).[9] Laban squeezes Jacob and his family for all they are worth, leading his daughters together to lament his lack of love for them (Gen. 31:14–15) and leading Jacob to flee from Laban and risk conflict.[10] Free of Laban, Jacob must lead his family in flight from his brother, Esau, whose wrath Jacob still fears. And Jacob continues with his children the favoritism modeled by his parents and reinforced in his marriages, favoring Joseph and predisposing Joseph's brothers to plot his murder (Gen. 37:3–4).

Sin wreaks havoc on relationships, both when we consciously and willfully choose it and when even our most faithful decisions are only between imperfect options. But there is redemption. God works through and over the

9. This act by Leah's son can be read as an act of aggression against Rachel, who used Bilhah's womb to compete against Reuben's mother. Compared with a similar act by David's son, it can also be read more as an attempt to usurp his father (see 2 Sam. 16:21–22). Genesis only makes clear that Reuben's act is wrong and displeases Jacob (Gen. 49:2–6).

10. Laban's daughters lament that he has "sold" them in marriage and now counts them as "outsiders" (Gen. 31:14–15 NABRE), yet Laban accuses Jacob of robbing him of his daughters and grandchildren as his, not Jacob's, property (Gen. 31:26, 43, 50). The legal difference in perspective is notable. Jacob is not legally a slave and, as shown by his autonomy in leaving Laban, did not see himself as such. But he was an outsider without his own holdings, a member of the community only under the aegis of Laban, and he might have been considered *like* a slave, in which case his wives and children born while with Laban could be considered Laban's property (cf. Exod. 21:4). See Gerhard von Rad, *Genesis*, OTL (Philadelphia: Westminster, 1973), 299–300.

fallenness in which his people participate to bring blessing. Esau will not bear the worldwide blessing of the Redeemer, but God does grant Esau's line a share in the land near Israel (cf. Deut. 2:22; 23:7; Josh. 24:4). God confirms the line of salvation through Jacob after and despite his tricking Esau (Gen. 28:12–15; 35:11–12). He continues it through Joseph, not killed but sold into Egypt by his brothers, and through Joseph's plight he delivers Israel and other nations amid a famine (Gen. 45:5–8; cf. 50:19–21) and allows Jacob's family to grow and multiply (see Gen. 46:3–4; Exod. 1:6–7). Indeed, God blesses Joseph in his sufferings not only with his own children but personally with the virtue of charity, such that he forgives and brings deliverance for those who rejected him, a prefiguring of Jesus (see Acts 7:9–16).

One can see God's mercy and redemption amid the mess and competition of Jacob's wives as well. Ultimately, Leah and Rachel, with Bilhah and Zilpah, give Jacob a daughter and twelve sons, each becoming a matriarch of the nation of Israel. God hears Rachel when she cries out in despair, and she becomes the mother of Joseph, the Christ-figure. But in God's mercy, it is *Leah*—unwanted by her father and not preferred by her husband—through whom God chooses ultimately to bring *the* Christ, whose ancestry traces back through Joseph to David and to Leah's son Judah (cf. Gen. 29:35; Matt. 1:1–17).

God works his purposes of mercy and salvation in and despite the brokenness of Jacob's family. As with Abraham, we can also see God come to Jacob in his imperfections and challenge him to greater faithfulness. After Jacob and Rebekah trick Isaac into blessing Jacob and he flees from Esau's wrath, God is not content merely to let Jacob bear the line of blessing by procreation. Rather, God calls him in a dream to an ongoing personal relationship, promising to be with Jacob and disclosing his promise of descendants, land, and blessing for the world through him (Gen. 28:12–15). Jacob wakes and worships God, but with some apparent hesitancy: "If God will be with me, and will keep me in this way that I go . . . , so that I come again to my father's house in peace, then the LORD shall be my God" (Gen. 28:20–21). Jacob's response is not wholly impious; he wants from God what God has promised to him, yet he does seem to be "hedging his bets."[11] He will give himself to God if God favors him in his journey *and* sees him safely home to his birthplace in Canaan. God does grant favor to Jacob in his sojourn with Laban, which Jacob acknowledges, and God's continued presence is mani-

11. Kass, *Beginning of Wisdom*, 417.

fested to Jacob through angels (Gen. 31:5–13, 42; 32:1; 33:11). But, while God promises afresh to be with Jacob on his journey back to Canaan (Gen. 31:3), Jacob's piety seems to grow even before his second condition is entirely fulfilled. Jacob continues to cling to God even when he believes God is causing Rachel's barrenness (Gen. 30:2). When he runs in fear of Esau, he prays humbly and without conditions in continued reliance on God's merciful aid: "I am not worthy of the least of all the steadfast love and all the faithfulness that you have shown to your servant" (Gen. 32:10). As a kind of penance for deceiving Esau (and as a peace offering to save himself from destruction, no doubt), Jacob sends a large gift to the brother he once robbed. Jacob is broken, but he is growing, and he clings to God's promise of blessing despite his trials. This is encapsulated in the episode in Genesis 32, where Jacob, waiting in fear for Esau, encounters an angelic being and wrestles with him, insisting, "I will not let you go, unless you bless me" (Gen. 32:26).[12] Jacob will cling to God's blessing, and over the course of his story we can see him seek it less and less by trickery and more with piety and even self-giving. Jacob receives forgiveness and is reconciled with Esau. Indeed, in that moment, Jacob says that seeing Esau is "like seeing the face of God," the face of his forgiver (Gen. 33:10). Jacob worships God often and commands his people to put away the idols that he apparently had formerly allowed (Gen. 33:20; 35:2–3, 7, 14; 46:1). Finally, although he arrives home to bury his father with Esau (Gen. 35:29), he obeys God when told to go to Egypt to become a great nation *there*. This is perhaps not as stark a call for faithfulness as God's test of Abraham, but it is similarly counterintuitive: Jacob must now lead his family *out* of the promised land to die elsewhere in order for his descendants to inherit it later (Gen. 46:3–4).

The story of Jacob's family showcases God's mercy and faithfulness in and despite the mess of human sin and brokenness—God's mercy to individuals in their plights, and God's mercy to the world in continuing his promise of the coming Christ. It also shows individuals—especially Jacob—reaching out and clinging to God with dogged hope rather than despair in their difficulties.

12. As earlier with Hagar (Gen. 16:13), Jacob understands himself to have seen "God" (Gen. 32:30). This being has sometimes been understood as a manifestation of the preincarnate Christ, the person of the Godhead who reveals God visibly (e.g., Tertullian, *Against Praxeas* 14). Differently, Augustine insists on angelic interpretations of Old Testament theophanies—since, apart from the incarnation, the Godhead (even the Son) has no body with which to wrestle, no voice box with which to speak, and so on (see *On the Trinity* 2; cf. Origen, *Homilies on Genesis and Exodus* 3.2). The interpretation of Jacob wrestling with an "angel" is explicit already in Hosea 12:4.

The natural consequences of their sins remain—Jacob's favoritism breeds competition and hatred among his wives and children. Yet, even as they reap those fruits, they are called to turn again and again to God in greater faithfulness and receive his blessing. God will repeat this call again to the tribes of Israel in their journey from Egypt to the promised land.

Forgiveness, Mediation, and Penance: Israel's "Baptism" and the Wilderness

The children of Israel dwell in Egypt for around four hundred years. God had foretold this to Abraham already (Gen. 15:13; Exod. 12:40). He had also foretold that he would bring "judgment" on that land, whose rulers would ultimately oppress Israel (Gen. 15:14). And God does bring judgment upon them. The plagues sent upon Egypt and the destruction of Pharaoh's armies at the Red Sea are "great acts of judgment" (Exod. 7:4). As we have seen elsewhere, God's acts of judgment against Egypt are not devoid of mercy or a desire for life. In the plague of hail, for instance, God has Moses not only foretell the hail but also plead that the Egyptians and their livestock come inside so that they may not be harmed, and he willingly accepts Pharaoh's imperfect contrition and stops the plague (Exod. 9:19–21, 27–30).[13] God's acts against Egypt are meant not only to bring Pharaoh to let Israel go, but to show God's divinity and power to Israel *and* to Egypt (cf. Exod. 9:16; 10:2; 12:12; 14:4, 17–18), bringing Israel to follow God and many others to join with God's people as they set out for the promised land (cf. Exod. 12:38; 18:10–11; Josh. 2:10; Neh. 9:10).

But God's judgments of Egypt also function as a warning for the children of Israel. The people have seen God's power to save them and should trust this God with their future. And they must know also that the same power can also be used to discipline and judge even Israelites who rebel against him (see, e.g., Pss. 105–106). The same goes for Christians too. In the New Testament, the life of Christians after baptism is likened to the life of Israel after being delivered from Pharaoh at the Red Sea. Paul even describes Israel's experience explicitly as a type of "baptism" (1 Cor. 10:1–2). It is the beginning of Israel's new life with God through water, a break from the past and deliverance from

---

13. Turning the Nile into blood, likewise, is presented as a show of power rather than as intended to kill the Egyptians, as it is only water from the Nile that becomes undrinkable. They are merely forced to seek other springs (Exod. 7:24).

the enemy that kept them back from going out to serve God, parallel to deliverance from the power of sin and death (Rom. 6:1–23). But Israel struggled to trust and obey God as God led them through the wilderness, and those who rebelled against God did not reach the land for which they had been redeemed. According to Paul, Christians should think on these narratives as examples that warn Christians to be repentant and not rebellious after baptism (1 Cor. 10:1–12). This makes them noteworthy for us as we consider the sacrament of reconciliation.

The introduction of the explicit law code at Sinai brings about another parallel to Christian life as well as a difference from God's people in the time of the patriarchs. God brings Israel through the Red Sea to Mount Sinai, and a divine voice speaks the Ten Commandments to the people from the mountain and gives the rest of God's law through Moses (Exod. 19–24). The core of the law covenant is a continuation of the relationship between God and Abraham's family promised earlier: "I will take you as my people, and I will be your God" (Exod. 6:7; cf. Gen. 17:7–8; Lev. 26:12–45), a union the prophets compare to a marriage (e.g., Jer. 2:2; Hosea 2:2, 16; cf. Song 6:3). But, like a marriage contract, the law ratifies their union and defines it with stipulations for faithful behavior. The Lord is their God, so they must worship no other gods, must not misuse God's name or neglect to worship God as he desires, and must treat their neighbors as God—who also created and redeemed their neighbors—stipulates (cf. Exod. 20:1–17; 34:11–27; Deut. 5:4–21). If they obey and honor God as their God, he will honor and protect them as his people, guarding and delivering them from their enemies by his mighty power. Indeed, in the ark of the covenant and the tabernacle, God will "dwell" with them, his presence and power in their very midst (Exod. 29:45–46). If they choose not to act as the people of this God, flouting his ways or following other gods, their transgression will be punished.

With the giving of the law, Israel has *explicit* direction and knowledge of God's commands and the consequences stipulated for fidelity and infidelity. Before Sinai, of course, a general moral law is assumed—Cain is wrong to murder Abel whether anyone has uttered an explicit command about it or not, and Joseph's brothers know that selling their brother and hiding it from their father is immoral and punishable (Gen. 42:21–22). But in many instances, while Genesis shows us natural consequences of imperfect behavior among the patriarchs, the characters are only fully culpable if they transgress a direct command—if, for instance, Abraham had not prepared to offer Isaac (Gen. 22) or Jacob had refused to move the family to Egypt (Gen. 46). In Exodus, too, before Israel receives the law at Sinai, they grumble against God about their lack of food on the journey. This is wrongful and indignant behavior, a lack of trust in the God who just delivered them. But, the law not yet being given, God chooses to "test them" with a command, to see "whether they will walk in my law or not" (Exod. 16:4 ESV). So he gives them the "manna," bread from heaven, and gives explicit instructions as to how they must receive this gift with faith and obey God's prohibition of gathering on the sabbath. When the law is given, it comes to function as a "testimony" or "witness" against the people, putting them on notice from now on as to what God requires and pronouncing penalty for transgression (Deut. 31:26; cf. Rom. 7:7–12).

Unlike Christ's New Covenant, the Sinai covenant sets God's ways in writing but does not yet inscribe them in human hearts as the Holy Spirit will by grace in the baptized (see Jer. 31:31–34; Ezek. 36:25–27; 2 Cor. 3:1–18). Yet under both the Old and the New Covenants, those who have passed through the water are given instruction as to how they "ought to live and to please God" (1 Thess. 4:1). Christians, too, are culpable for willingly sinning against the God who saves them. It is therefore especially instructive to consider instances of Israel's sin after their "baptism" in the Red Sea to see how the texts characterize *sin*, God's application of both *forgiveness* and *penance*, and the role of God's *mediators* and priests. We can consider these especially in three episodes: the golden calf apostasy, the unfaithful spies and Israel's forty-year penance, and Korah's rebellion.[14]

Sin and Reversing Redemption: The Golden Calf

After Israel's covenant with God is ratified by sacrifice, Moses and the elders of Israel ascend the mountain, and God calls Moses farther up the mountain alone to receive instruction for forty days, God's glory remaining visible there atop Sinai in cloud and fire (Exod. 24:12–18). But in Moses's absence, the people complain that they have no leader—or at least no faith that Moses will return—and ask Aaron, "Make gods for us, who shall go before us" (Exod. 32:1). Aaron complies, takes the people's gold, melts it, and fashions from it a golden calf, saying, "These are your gods, O Israel, who

14. There are other episodes, particularly in the book of Numbers, that we could consider. The apostasy at Baal-Peor is remembered often in Scripture (cf. Num. 25:1–9; Josh. 22:17; Ps. 106:28; Jude 11). Another, which will be noted later, is the episode of the bronze serpent (Num. 21:4–9; John 3:14).

brought you up out of the land of Egypt" (Exod. 32:4). The people bring burnt offerings and sacrifices and then follow their worship with indulgence and, as Moses sees later, wild dancing and celebration (Exod. 32:6, 18–19, 25).[15]

Moses describes this as a "great" sin (Exod. 32:21, 30). It is a clear violation of at least the first commandment not to worship other gods or to make graven idols to worship.[16] It is also an affront to the God who powerfully and faithfully delivered them from Egypt. In the words of Psalm 106:20–21, they not only "exchanged" the "glory" of the living God for an idol; they "forgot the God who had saved them" (NABRE). The nature of sin, the sin of idolatry but all sin in a way, is put on display here. It is a *forgetting* of God's past faithfulness and God's power, as well as a forgetting of God's commands and warnings and his track record for punishing infidelity. This is why Deuteronomy, along with many psalms, explicitly calls people to "remember" the Lord and his kindness and his severity (e.g., Deut. 8:1–20; Ps. 95). Moreover, we see in this text a depiction of grave sin as acting to *reverse our redemption*. God led Israel out of Egypt *so that* he might "be their God" (Lev. 26:45; cf. Exod. 6:7). God's command to Pharaoh, likewise, shows that God's goal was not merely to free Israel from serving (Hebrew *'avad*) Pharaoh but so that Israel might serve (*'avad*) him as God: "Let my people go to serve me in the wilderness" (Exod. 7:16 NABRE; cf. 3:12). But coming into the wilderness, they have complained and intimated that they would prefer to have died in Egypt (Exod. 16:3; 17:3). Now, precisely while their saving God's power is visible on the mountaintop, the people exchange the glory of the living God for a lifeless image of gold. This is the nature of willful, "great" sin. Although

15. The last verb in Exod. 32:6 ("revel") is derived from the same verb, *tsakhaq*, as the name Isaac is ("laugh," "play"), but it may have functioned as a euphemism for sexual play as well (translated "fondling" in Gen. 26:8).

16. There is some question as to what precisely is requested and given here. The name for the singular *God* of Israel is characteristically rendered with the plural noun *'elohim*, but with singular verbs and adjectives. The people ask Aaron to make *'elohim* to go before them—either "God" or "gods." Aaron makes a single calf and says that they will celebrate a "festival to the Lord," with the explicit name YHWH ("the Lord") indicating the one God of Israel (Exod. 32:5). This might suggest that they are requesting a single "god" (as the NABRE translates 32:1), using the calf as a symbol for the Lord, or that Aaron secretly hopes to lead them back to the one God. But their request and Aaron's reply use *'elohim* with plural verbs and adjectives, requesting and granting "gods," and the God who gave the Decalogue is hardly honored by the graven image or by the festivities that ensue. Two such calf-idols were, however, used to worship Israel's God among the northern tribes under Jeroboam I, a practice condemned by the prophets (see 1 Kings 12; Hosea 8:5–6), and the memory of these may have influenced the phrasing in the final text of Exodus. Compare Brevard S. Childs, *The Book of Exodus: A Critical, Theological Commentary*, OTL (Philadelphia: Westminster, 1974), 558–67.

one might not say outright that one no longer wants the benefits and blessings that God promises, to willfully return to grave sin—which is servitude to the power of sin—is to reject what one was redeemed *for*.

God responds initially to this idolatry by threatening the full penalty, to allow their rejection of the living God to bear its full fruit in their death, wiping out the entire people and remaking the nation afresh through Moses. But Moses intercedes for the people, appealing to God's past acts of redemption and his promises to Abraham, and God stays his hand.[17] There is still penalty for the nation, though not the final destruction deserved. Moses grinds the calf down to powder and forces the people to drink the gold in punishment, and the Levites slaughter a select number of people—around three thousand—out of zeal for the Lord.[18] Moses begs God to forgive the people and intercedes for Aaron as well (Exod. 32:32; Deut. 9:20).[19] He even demands to be removed from God's heavenly ledger and counted with the sinners, if God will not forgive, rather than be made a nation in place of Israel.[20] One should not miss Moses's valiance; he "stood in the breach" before God as an intercessor (Ps. 106:23), pleading that God would not only forgive the people but asking God to lead and protect them on the way to the promised land (Exod. 34:9). We should also not miss the revelation of God's character here: he will not leave sin without punishment or penalty, but he shows himself "slow to anger" (Exod. 34:6). God does go with Israel and lead them into the land, knowing

17. As in other places, God is described as becoming regretful or heeding second thoughts about the punishment (with the Hebrew verb *nakham*), often translated as "changing his mind" or "repenting" (Exod. 32:14; cf. Gen. 6:6; Ps. 90:13; Jon. 3:9). For an exegetical and theological discussion, see Gregory Vall, *Ecclesial Exegesis: A Synthesis of Ancient and Modern Approaches to Scripture*, Verbum Domini (Washington, DC: Catholic University of America Press, 2022), 43–71.

18. The text does not identify a criterion for why the Levites killed only certain people. Since God insists in this passage that "only" the one who sins will be condemned (Exod. 32:33), and given the discourse on God's pedagogical justice in Wis. 12:2–18 and the distinctions in penalty in other rebellion narratives (cf. Num. 14:36–37; 16:32), the slain may have been ones who led the apostasy or rejected Moses's rebuke. Differently, John Goldingay reads the slaughter as a less discriminate "pruning" in which a "representative punishment of some people can avail for the whole" (*Old Testament Theology*, vol. 1, *Israel's Gospel* [Downers Grove, IL: InterVarsity, 2003], 418–19).

19. Some interpretations read Aaron very sympathetically here (e.g., Pseudo-Philo, *Biblical Antiquities* 12.2–3), but our consideration of sin and divine mercy should not miss the note in Deut. 9:20 that Moses had to intercede for Aaron lest he, too, be destroyed.

20. Heavenly ledgers recording names and deeds—the righteous being in God's "good books," as the phrase goes—is a common ancient image in Israel and elsewhere. See Carol Meyers, *Exodus*, New Cambridge Bible Commentary (Cambridge: Cambridge University Press, 2005), 261–62.

that his people will be stubborn and rebellious, and he renews the broken covenant for the benefit of Israel and, looking ahead to the coming of Christ, for the world. He is, furthermore, an all-powerful God who nevertheless invites and delights in the intercession of his mediators who "have found favor" before him, even when they intercede for those in great sin (Exod. 33:12–17).

Forgiveness and Penance: The Unfaithful Spies

God remains with the people and continues his faithfulness to them. They stay at the mountain for around two years (Num. 1:1; 9:1), with the canonical narrative halting after their worship of the calf to detail laws regulating worship of the living God and communal purity in the final chapters of Exodus and the book of Leviticus. The book of Numbers resumes the wilderness narrative as the people set out from Mount Sinai for the promised land. The book begins with census data—literal "numbers"—that highlight God's faithfulness to multiply Abraham's family into a great nation. The family of about seventy who had moved to Egypt now numbers more than six hundred thousand, counting only men of age for military service and not counting the tribe of Levi, who are to be noncombatants (Num. 1:44–54; cf. Gen. 46:26–27; Exod. 1:5). God's presence goes with them in the cloud over the tabernacle and the ark of the covenant and leads the people from the mountain and toward the promised land.

But even though they had seen God's wonders, they continue to grumble against God and against Moses at the hardships of their journey. Moses, too, complains at the difficulty of caring for the people. God responds with temporal penalties, but he remains with them and distributes the charism of divine leadership and prophecy to others to aid Moses (Num. 11–12). Finally—and fairly quickly in the canonical narrative—they reach the edge of the promised land, in which the Canaanites currently dwell. This is the fulfillment of God's promise to establish Abraham's family as a great nation in this land. At God's direction, Moses sends out twelve spies, representatives from each tribe, to scout out the land so that they may prepare to move in and take it. And they return with a good report! The land "flows with milk and honey" just as God had told them (Num. 13:27). But ten of the spies report fearfully that the people and cities will be too strong to be dispossessed. Despite words of hope from the two other spies—Caleb and Joshua—despair spreads through the people, and they lament their own fate and that of their children (Num.

13:30–14:9). While Moses and Aaron fall down to do penance, Joshua and Caleb insist that their God is powerful enough to fulfill his promise despite any fears or obstacles. They plead with the people, "Do not rebel against the LORD" (Num. 14:9)—but the people do rebel. Again desiring to undo what God had redeemed them for, they try to appoint a chief to lead them back to Egypt, and they threaten to stone Caleb and Joshua (Num. 14:4, 10).

As at Sinai, God responds by threatening to disown and destroy the people and make a nation out of Moses. Moses begs God to "pardon" them, appealing to God's promises, God's name, and God's character demonstrated in his pattern of forgiveness (Num. 14:13–19). God's response is to decree both pardon and penance for the nation, and it is worth quoting at length.

> I do forgive, just as you have asked; nevertheless—as I live, and as all the earth shall be filled with the glory of the LORD—none of the people who have seen my glory and the signs that I did in Egypt and in the wilderness, and yet have tested me these ten times and have not obeyed my voice, shall see the land that I swore to give to their ancestors; none of those who despised me shall see it. . . . But your little ones, who you said would become booty, I will bring in, and they shall know the land that you have despised. But as for you, your dead bodies shall fall in this wilderness. And your children shall be shepherds in the wilderness for forty years, and shall suffer for your faithlessness, until the last of your dead bodies lies in the wilderness. According to the number of the days in which you spied out the land, forty days, for every day a year, you shall bear your iniquity, forty years, and you shall know my displeasure. (Num. 14:20–23, 31–34)

God "forgives" the people. This forgiveness means that he will not carry out the full and final penalty of their sin. But it does not mean that there will be no consequences.[21] Instead, God assigns a fitting penalty: forty years of wandering for the forty days in which the spies saw the good land but refused to trust God's power to grant it to them. The generation that rejected the promised land will not inherit it, while the children for whom they despaired will inherit the land. This is both a *punishment*, imposing a partial penalty

---

21. The notion of forgiveness (here Hebrew *salakh*) "does not necessarily refer to the remittal of all penalty, but does allow for a mitigated one" (Jay Sklar, *Sin, Impurity, Sacrifice, Atonement: The Priestly Conceptions* [Sheffield: Sheffield Phoenix, 2005], 84). Compare Mary C. Moorman on temporal punishment and indulgences, in which "a certain nonequivalent and 'proportionate' justice is put into effect" (*Indulgences: Luther, Catholicism, and the Imputation of Merit* [Steubenville, OH: Emmaus Academic, 2017], 218).

for a past sin, and also a kind of *penance* through which individuals can make amends and grow in their faithfulness toward God in the future. God does not disown or abandon Israel, and they have an opportunity to renew their trust in the Lord as they wander and continue to receive the manna, continue to receive instructions to obey (or choose to disobey), and worship God year in and year out in feasts that commemorate his faithfulness. And their children have all the more opportunity to learn faithfulness as they wander and prepare to inherit the land.

Compared with the sacrament of reconciliation, we see figured here the forgiveness of the eternal punishment due to sin and a fitting temporal penance assigned. Here, too, the penance is not only an imposed judicial punishment but also *medicinal*—though surely, like many medicines and treatments, unpleasant. Deuteronomy later characterizes these penalties as "discipline" or "instruction," as having a remedial and instructive function for the nation and for individuals who will accept these penalties with hope and with a repentant heart (Deut. 8:5). God will continue such disciplines as the people continue to struggle to trust God's provision in the wilderness, but God will not abandon them. Indeed, the numbers again show us God's provision to make Abraham's descendants fruitful amid the punishments and deaths of many individuals along the way. After their wanderings, as the next generation prepares to enter the promised land, they still number more than six hundred thousand fighting men (Num. 26:51).

The Importance of Mediators: Korah's Rebellion

One last rebellion in the wilderness worth noting is narrated in Numbers 16–17. It is led by Dathan and Abiram, from the tribe of Reuben, and by Korah and others with him from the tribe of Levi. As elsewhere, we can see in their rebellion a rejection of their redemption. Dathan and Abiram even accuse Moses of bringing them *out of* "a land flowing with milk and honey to kill us in the wilderness" (Num. 16:13), identifying *Egypt* as the promised land and God and Moses as their destroyers, not their saviors. But their discontent is highlighted alongside the particular ingratitude of the Levites led by Korah. The Levites accuse Moses and Aaron of lording it over the rest of the people illegitimately: "You have gone too far! All the congregation are holy, every one of them, and the LORD is among them. So why then do you exalt yourselves above the assembly of the LORD?" (Num. 16:3).

They are complaining over the grades of mediation and holiness that God has set up among the people.[22] When Israel had first arrived at Mount Sinai, God proclaimed, "The whole earth is mine, but you shall be for me a priestly kingdom and a holy nation" (Exod. 19:5–6; cf. Deut. 10:14–15). Among all the nations of the earth, it is with Israel that God dwells, and Israel as a nation has a priestly role to mediate God's blessing and to witness to the living God's justice and favor by their worship and obedience (see Deut. 4:5–8). But *within* the nation of Israel, the holiness of God's dwelling among the people in the ark and tabernacle require further mediation. The Levites are holy to God among God's holy nation, charged with a higher degree of purity so that God's wrath might not break out among the people because of misuse or defilement of the sanctuary (Num. 1:50–53). They have charge of the tabernacle and its equipment. Further, among the Levites, the priests from Aaron's line have a yet higher requirement for holiness—with the high priest having higher requirements than other priests (e.g., Lev. 21)—and so can handle the holy things and present sacrifices, which the Levites cannot (Num. 4:15, 20).[23] All Israel is holy, but not all are Levites; not all Levites are priests, and not all priests are high priests. This mediation is good and meant to be a gift, both a symbol of the holiness of God and a real protection against unlawful contact with the consuming fire of God's holiness, for the protection of people and of the Levites (Num. 8:19; cf. Exod. 33:4–5).[24]

Korah is correct that all Israel is consecrated to God, but he is wrong to infer that this democratizes mediation and the priesthood. Moses accuses Korah and the Levites of ingratitude and insubordination to God: "Is it too little for you that the God of Israel has separated you from the congregation

22. See, among others, Phillip Peter Jenson, *Graded Holiness: A Key to the Priestly Conception of the World*, JSOTSup 106 (Sheffield: JSOT Press, 1992).

23. Moses is, likewise, unique among Levites as a leader and mediator between God and Israel, such that God punishes Miriam for grumbling, with Aaron, against Moses's leadership (Num. 12:1–15). And Moses is himself held to the highest standard of faithfulness—barred from entering the promised land for one act of disobedience (Num. 20).

24. Some interpret the restriction of the priesthood to Aaron's line as a punishment for the golden calf apostasy, before which every Israelite was a priest. That incident may explain why the zealous Levites, in particular, are chosen as the ministerial and priestly tribe (Exod. 32:25–29). But the nation being a "priestly kingdom" before this incident hardly negates distinctions in holiness or liturgical responsibilities. Indeed, before the calf, when they arrive at Sinai, all must purify themselves, but only some are allowed on the mountain lest they die. And when the people hear God's voice and ask Moses to mediate for them lest they hear God directly again, they are told that this is the correct response: God's unmediated voice was a "test" to see if they feared God and recognized the need for a mediator (see Exod. 20:18–21).

of Israel, to allow you to approach him in order to perform the duties of the
LORD's tabernacle, and to stand before the congregation and serve them? He
has allowed you to approach him, and all your brother Levites with you; yet
you seek the priesthood as well!" (Num. 16:9–10). Moses and Aaron intercede
for the people, and an ordeal is set up to allow God to reveal who is in the
right in this confrontation: Korah and the disgruntled Levites bring censers
to offer incense to God, and Dathan and Abiram stand at their tents. God,
through Moses, tells the people to get away from them—it is not God's desire
that the people die unnecessarily—and then sends clear punishment on the
rebels and those who still stand with them. The ground opens up to swallow
up the rebels, and fire burns those offering the incense (Num. 16:31–35).

This should suffice to show the people that God truly does mean the Levites
to keep their position as ministers but not as priests, as God's further laws
and the memorial to be made from the rebels' censers are meant to reinforce
(Num. 16:36–40; 17:1–18:32). But the day after the rebels had been swallowed
up by the earth, "the whole congregation of the Israelites rebelled against
Moses and against Aaron," blaming them for what had happened: "You have
killed the people of the LORD" (Num. 16:41).[25] God again announces the full
penalty of destruction on the community, but Moses and Aaron intercede. A
deadly plague of divine wrath breaks out among the people, and Moses tells
Aaron to make atonement for their sin with his own incense offering. Aaron
takes his censer and runs into the midst of the assembly and offers incense on
their behalf, and the plague that swept through the people assembled there
stops where Aaron is. "He stood between the dead and the living; and the
plague was stopped" (Num. 16:48). It is striking to picture Aaron, standing
with his censer to intercede and stop the further spread of sin's punishment,
as an image showing both divine wrath against sin and the power of atonement and intercession.

The very community that complained at the mediatory office of Moses and
Aaron, imperfect though they are as human beings, is saved by their exercise
of that very same office. As Wisdom 18:21 recounts it, Aaron "hastened to be
their champion, bearing the weapon of his special office, prayer and the pro-
pitiation of incense" (NABRE). In regard to the sacrament of reconciliation,
this passage calls the Church to give thanks for the mediatory sacramental
role of its priests, despite their imperfections and even great sins—we must

25. In Bibles that follow versifications from the Hebrew Bible, this story occurs in Num. 17.

not forget Aaron's with the calf—as conduits of divine mercy. For in the New Testament as well, as we will see, the whole of Christ's people are made holy and granted a mediatory role as a "holy priesthood" for the world (1 Pet. 2:5), yet here too only certain persons are consecrated *within* the Church to administer the sacraments and pronounce forgiveness authoritatively in Jesus's name (cf. 1 Cor. 12:27–30).

In Israel's exodus from Egypt and wandering in the wilderness, we can see God's merciful and provident guidance of the people. Then, after the giving of the law, we can see more explicitly the way in which God responds to his people's sin. He forgives Israel, not exacting the full and final penalty and not withholding his care and guidance as their God. Through divinely appointed mediators, he imposes penalties for sin in such a way that, both for the people as a whole and for individuals among the people, these penalties can become occasions for repentance and strengthening in faithfulness toward God. We will see this continue in the period of the kings, as the prophets accuse Israel and announce the Sinai covenant's greatest penalty for the nation—exile—and as they also announce God's merciful call to repent and be saved.

4

Rebuke and Promise for Israel

Kings and Prophets

> Return, O faithless children,
> I will heal your faithlessness.
> —Jeremiah 3:22

God provided for the children of Israel throughout their forty years in the wilderness, as the generation that left Egypt died and a new generation learned to depend on God. God continued to shower the gift of manna upon them day after day, defended them from the attacks of other nations (see Num. 21–24), and brought them finally to the promised land to take possession of it. As they prepared to enter the land, Moses retold the story of God's gracious deliverance and of their failures, and he reiterated to them the terms of the Sinai covenant to remind them of what was expected of them in this new land.[1]

---

1. The reiteration of the covenant and laws in Deuteronomy includes some alterations in view of their new situation. Formerly, while the whole people followed the tabernacle in the wilderness, all meat was to be slaughtered in sacrifice at the tabernacle (Lev. 17:3–4). As they prepare to possess the land, this regulation is lifted, since the one God will have one shrine in the land—the ark's home in the tabernacle, at Shiloh, and later in the Jerusalem temple—and most would live too far away to eat meat lawfully under the old rule, though they must still make pilgrimages to the shrine (Deut. 12:1–27). Regulations for future kings are given (Deut.

He called them to *remember* the Lord, God's track record for both mercy and sternness (Deut. 8:1–20; 11:1–7), so that they might stay faithful in this land in which they will grow into the "great nation" promised to Abraham, the nation through which the Savior would be born.

Israel does take possession of the land under Joshua, after Moses's death. Beginning with Saul and David, the nation grows into a monarchy with kings and princes, as God had foretold (Gen. 17:6, 16). However, they struggle and ultimately fail to remember the Lord. Moses had told them that their obedience to the law would be a sign of God's wisdom, justice, and faithfulness to the pagan nations (Deut. 4:5–8). Instead, the nation and its leadership overall perpetrate *greater* evil than the pagans (2 Kings 21:11). For this, they will not be allowed to retain the blessing of the land and will be exiled. Far from home in exile, they will have to learn to trust God again in a new kind of wilderness, and from there they will be redeemed and restored.

In God's responses to Israel's sin throughout the time of the kings and the exile, we see God's character as one who is merciful and just. He patiently but sternly calls for repentance. He punishes sin and forgives the penitent, and he applies his punishments in a way that trains his people for greater faith and hope. In this chapter we will review the people's sin and the prophetic call to confession and repentance, and we will see God's mercy and justice as it is applied to individuals and to the nation.

Israel's Sins and the Kingdoms' Fall

As discussed above in chapter 3, the covenant made at Mount Sinai joins God and Israel together in mutual faithfulness. "I will be your God, and you will be my people" (Lev. 26:12 NABRE). God will show faithfulness and loyalty to them, as almighty God and protector, and they must show loyalty and obedience to him as his dependents.[2] They must worship their creator; care

---

17:14–20), as are new laws enjoining charity toward the Levites, who will now depend on hospitality from other tribes when they are not on duty at the shrine (Deut. 18:1–8).

2. The form of the covenant is often compared to treaties between powerful lords or emperors and their vassals, who will receive land or protection or privilege from their lord and must in return offer loyal support and maintain their subordinate role in the alliance. See Klaus Balzer, *The Covenant Formulary* (Philadelphia: Fortress, 1971). With an emphasis on the primacy of the lord's (or Lord's) favor in initiating and maintaining this relationship, see Robert D. Miller, *Covenant and Grace in the Old Testament: Assyrian Propaganda and Israelite Faith*, PHSC 16 (Piscataway, NJ: Gorgias, 2012).

for God's creatures and treat them with justice; heed God's laws and love him with their minds, hearts, and strength; and ensure that each new generation learns to do the same (Deut. 6:1–15; 10:12–22). As they enter the land, Moses warns them sternly not to imitate the pagan nations around them and to avoid submitting themselves to customs or leaders that will lead them to forget the true God and his ways.

If they are faithful, God will maintain their position in the land he has given to them, grant rain for crops, protect them from attacks, and grant them peace. All of these are gifts of God, and it is in God's prerogative and power to give them—it was hardly Israel's own strength that freed them from Egypt or sent them manna in the wilderness or drove out the nations from the land. But if the nation as a whole is unfaithful, God will remove these protections and blessings as a "chastisement" or "discipline," to punish the proud and call them to repentance (Lev. 26:18–19). If they repent and turn again to God, blessings will be restored. If they do not, God will continue to call them to repentance. He will send greater, more severe rebukes and blights and will allow them to see how they fare without his divine help against opposing nations. He will send prophets to rebuke the people's sin, diagnose their malady, and prescribe the medicine of repentance. But if they continue to act as God's enemy, God will act like theirs and come with increasingly harsh rebukes. God, we are told, promised Israel this land and led them to conquer it in part to end the wickedness of the nations who had lived there—including oppression, immorality, bloodshed, idolatry, and child sacrifice to the god Molech. God will not abandon Israel because of his promises to Abraham. But Israel, too, will be besieged and exiled from the land if they imitate those nations' wickedness (Lev. 26:27–35; cf. 18:28).[3]

This is, however, precisely what happens. The book of Judges highlights repeated unfaithfulness among the twelve tribes immediately after they conquer the land. The people turn to follow after foreign idols and unholy, unjust practices, and God responds by allowing their enemies to subjugate them. Then, when they realize their God is their only hope, they cry out to God, and God raises up a deliverer to restore them to blessing. But then they forget the Lord's kindness and power again, and the cycle repeats itself (Judg. 2:10–19).

---

3. Those who read the passages referenced in parentheses will notice in Lev. 26:29 and elsewhere the punishment that people will eat their own children (or vice versa in Ezek. 5:10). This is an image of the worst fate of a city under siege. As the enemies cut off supply lines and food runs out, people despair of survival and turn to cannibalism.

The book of Judges sounds the note that a king will be able to unite the tribes and guide them in piety (Judg. 17:6; 18:1; 19:1; 21:25). As we learn, though, that all depends on the king's faithfulness and on whether the people obey him (cf. Sir. 10:2). Under Saul and David, the people's first kings, we already see rivalry between the northern and southern tribes. David is able to unify them, and he does lead the people well. He centralizes the people's worship in Jerusalem, exhorts them to remain faithful, and achieves some political peace and stability (2 Sam. 6:17–19; 7:1). But David's personal sins create competition among his children and advisers, leading to a painful rebellion led by one of his sons. David is succeeded by his son Solomon, who receives great wisdom from God and builds the temple. Through his alliances and many political marriages, however, Solomon not only comes to allow worship of idols but even worships them himself—building altars to numerous idols and even to Molech, who was worshiped by child sacrifice (1 Kings 11:1–8).[4]

God allows a revolt under Solomon's son Rehoboam, and the kingdom splits in two—the northern tribes against the southern kingdom "Judah," which housed God's temple and the ark in Jerusalem. The northern tribes, often called "Israel" or "Ephraim," start poorly under their first king, Jeroboam I. While initially he is depicted as following God's plan to split the kingdom as a temporary measure (1 Kings 11:31–39), he quickly seeks to secure the ongoing independence of his kingdom by setting up separate northern shrines, with a non-Levitical priesthood, with alternate feasts, and with idols of golden calves by which to worship Israel's God in the north so that his people would not send tithes or make pilgrimages to Jerusalem (1 Kings 12:25–33). As is frequently reiterated, this sin is not Jeroboam's alone; it is one that he, in his role as king, "caused Israel to commit" (e.g., 1 Kings 14:16). Use of the idol-shrines and other "high places" reinforces a plurality of liturgical spaces that encourages worship of a plurality of gods. The kings chase after the favor of other nations and other gods for security and prosperity, and violence and social injustice ensue (e.g., 1 Kings 21:1–26; 2 Kings 15:16; Hosea 1:4). God

---

4. The Deuteronomistic perspective in Samuel–Kings draws out Solomon's sin most explicitly in the case of this idolatry. Less explicitly, the narrative seems to show Solomon breaking nearly every law laid down for kings in Deut. 17:14–20: he amasses gold and horses for himself (1 Kings 4:26–28; 10:14–29), amasses wives (1 Kings 11:1–8), and allies himself with Egypt by marriage (1 Kings 3:1). Solomon does lead Israel in prosperity, but he also comes to be seen by many in Israel as a harsh taskmaster, conscripting forced labor from non-Israelites in the land and burdening many Israelites with a similar "heavy yoke" to build the temple and his palace (1 Kings 5:13–18; 9:15–23; 12:3–4). Humanly speaking, this is the cause of the revolt and split of the kingdom (1 Kings 11:27; 12:1–20).

sends prophets and droughts and allows military and political loss to rebuke the nation (cf. 1 Kings 17:1; 2 Kings 10:32–33), but they do not repent, and ultimately the northern kingdom is defeated and exiled by Assyria in the late eighth century BC (2 Kings 17).

With God's temple and the Davidic king reigning there, it might seem that the southern kingdom would be more likely to maintain faithfulness (cf. Ps. 78:67–72; Hosea 1:6–7; 4:15). The southern kingdom does last longer and has some pious kings. But ultimately "Judah also stumbles with" Israel (Hosea 5:5) and becomes even "more corrupt than they" (Ezek. 16:47). They do not learn from God's punishment of Israel (Jer. 3:6–10; Ezek. 16:44–52), and their possession of the temple and the Davidic dynasty makes them presumptuous, assuming that God would never allow them to fall (Jer. 7:1–7). After Solomon had the temple built, people continued to worship Israel's God and other gods at unauthorized "high places," a popular practice that continued nearly uninterrupted throughout Judah's history. As in Israel, kings seek security in foreign alliances rather than in God, social injustice is rampant, pagan liturgical practices become common in Jerusalem, and child sacrifice is reported as well (cf. 1 Kings 14:22–24; 2 Kings 16:1–4; Jer. 7:31; 32:35; Ezek. 16:21). Pious kings' attempts at reform are overturned by their successors or have little effect on the populace: Hezekiah destroys worship sites at high places, but his son Manasseh rebuilds them and adds pagan altars in the temple; his son Josiah reforms the temple and makes the law of Deuteronomy the law of the land, but he cannot reform the hearts or habits of the people, and the law becomes slack or "numb" and ineffective (Hab. 1:4).[5] God promised not to abandon Judah or the Davidic line through which the king and Savior, Christ, would be born (2 Sam. 7:5–16). Yet God's wrath is kindled no less against the sins of Judah, and it will not turn back until Judah's crimes are punished (Jer. 30:24). Ultimately, Babylon conquers and exiles Judah in the early sixth century.

With regard to confession and penance, the fall of the kingdoms certainly highlights the problem of sin among God's people and its just penalty. The history of the kingdoms also invites us to see God's efforts to call his people back especially through the prophets, whose words show us God's patience and even God's pleas for the sake of his people, as well as the tragedy of their prideful refusal to confess.

---

5. Jeremiah 8:8 also adds an accusation of serious scribal corruption of the law.

The Prophetic Call: Confession, Repentance, and Hope

The covenantal promises in Leviticus and Deuteronomy show a kind of progression in God's work to prompt people to repentance. God will continue to send rebukes, increasingly harsher ones if necessary, to call the people back before their sin finally requires exile (Lev. 26:14, 18, 21, 23, 27; cf. Deut. 28:15–62). Essential in God's call to repentance is the work of the prophets, who announce it explicitly. In one image, prophets are set as "sentinels" or "watchmen" (cf. Jer. 6:16–17; Ezek. 3:17; Hosea 9:7–8), warning the people of coming calamity and interpreting present calamities as divine rebukes. In a more legal image, the prophets are witnesses or spokesmen for God when God accuses Israel. God is depicted often in the prophets and elsewhere as the almighty *accuser* of sin in his people, confronting them with their sins against him and calling for redress, like an injured party in a civil suit.[6] Consider, for instance, this example from Hosea:

> Hear the word of the LORD, Israelites,
>   for the LORD has a dispute
>   with the inhabitants of the land:
> There is no fidelity, no loyalty,
>   no knowledge of God in the land.
> Swearing, lying, murder,
>   stealing and adultery break out;
>   bloodshed follows bloodshed.
> Therefore the land dries up,
>   and everything that dwells in it languishes:
> The beasts of the field,
>   the birds of the air,
>   and even the fish of the sea perish. (Hosea 4:1–3 NABRE)

Hosea announces God's "dispute," God's legal *contention* and *accusation* against Israel. He accuses them of their sin: faithlessness toward God and neighbor. And he announces the current penalty, agricultural distress, as a sign of God's wrath and rebuke, calling them to wake up and turn from their sin in repentance. "But as for you," Hosea calls, "return to your God, hold fast to love and justice, and wait continually for your God" (Hosea 12:6).

6. See, e.g., Kirsten Nielsen, *Yahweh as Prosecutor and Judge: An Investigation of the Prophetic Lawsuit (Ríb-Pattern)*, trans. Frederick Cryer, JSOTSup 9 (Sheffield: JSOT Press, 1978).

Such accusation of sin is a main task God sets for the prophets in times of unfaithfulness: "Announce to my people their rebellion, to the house of Jacob their sins" (Isa. 58:1). This is an important part of the "trial" proceedings of God's dispute. The righteous creator will not leave sin that mars his creation unpunished or unaddressed. But he is also not interested in simply bringing destruction from heaven just for the sake of punishment. God is interested in his people's *life* and *betterment*, so he patiently restrains his punishment and calls Israel and Judah to repentance. "As I live, says the Lord GOD, I have no pleasure in the death of the wicked, but that the wicked turn from their ways and live; turn back, turn back from your evil ways; for why will you die, O house of Israel?" (Ezek. 33:11). God confronts the people with their crimes in order to show them how far they have fallen and to call them to repent and be restored to God's blessing and friendship. The goal of confronting them with accusations is, ultimately, *reconciliation* between God and his people.[7]

> Come now, let us argue it out,
>   says the LORD:
> though your sins are like scarlet,
>   they shall be like snow;
> though they are red like crimson,
>   they shall become like wool.
> If you are willing and obedient,
>   you shall eat the good of the land;
> but if you refuse and rebel,
>   you shall be devoured by the sword;
>   for the mouth of the LORD has spoken. (Isa. 1:18–20)

God offers absolution if Israel will just repent and heed his commands. Their former disobedience will be forgiven, washed away and purified, and they will be restored to God's favor and friendship. But they must humble themselves and repent.

In one sense, a basic paradigm of how people should respond to God's call to repentance is found not among God's covenant people but in Assyria, in the city of Nineveh (see Luke 11:29–32). God does not want the Ninevites

---

7. For the legal goal of reconciliation to restore justice between contending parties, before it is imposed by judicial punishment or warfare, see Pietro Bovati, *Re-establishing Justice: Legal Terms, Concepts and Procedures in the Hebrew Bible*, LHBOTS 105 (Sheffield: JSOT Press, 1994), 120–23.

to die, but to live, so he sends Jonah (who does not share God's goodwill for the Assyrians) to accuse them of sin and warn them of God's judgment (cf. Jon. 1:2; 4:2, 11). They respond with a show of sorrow over their sins and a desire to amend their ways—with fasting and sackcloth and lamentation—and God does not send the disaster threatened (Jon. 3:1–10). God extends the same promise to Israel. "Yet even now," God invites them, "return to me with all your heart," that they may be spared judgment and receive blessing (Joel 2:12; cf. Amos 5:14–15). God threatens punishment because he wants them to live, not die. Indeed, this is true even *after* a point of no return has been reached and God has decreed that Babylon must overtake Jerusalem. Jeremiah announces to King Zedekiah what God commands for the present moment: Surrender to Babylon and "your life shall be spared" (Jer. 38:17). They will not be able to keep the city and must go into exile, but people will not die needlessly under siege if they surrender peacefully, and God will bless them *in* their exile as they obey him and will return them to the land (Jer. 29:4–19).

But perhaps the greatest problem in Israel's relationship with God is their refusal to acknowledge their sins. As with Adam and Cain, though far more urgent and direct, the prophetic accusation is an *invitation to confess*, to repent of sin and turn to God. The accusation focused on the past is aimed at healing Israel's present and future relationship with God. Isaiah proclaims, "Your iniquities have been barriers between you and your God, and your sins have hidden his face from you so that he does not hear" (Isa. 59:2). If it is their sins that have ruptured their relationship and separate them from communion with God, the first step toward reconciliation on Israel's part is to acknowledge their sins and lay them before God's mercy. With sins confessed and forgiven, they may press forth to amend their lives in renewed relationship with God. But they do not. Sometimes confession is blocked by *presumption* or *pride*. They think that God cannot see their sins, that God will be appeased by sacrifice without true repentance, or that their God would not actually punish his beloved people (cf. Isa. 2:11–18; Jer. 3:5; Ezek. 8:12; Hosea 7:10; Amos 5:21–25; Mic. 2:6; Zech. 7:1–14). And they have plenty of false prophets and leaders reinforcing such ideas (cf. Jer. 23:9–40; Ezek. 13:1–16). But the result is that they show no shame for their crimes, and this blocks their ability to repent and provokes greater judgment (Jer. 6:15; 8:12). "I am bringing you to judgment for saying, 'I have not sinned,'" says the Lord (Jer. 2:35).

Sometimes, in what appears to be the opposite of presumption, the people do not confess not because of presumption but because of *despair*. They see their sins and hear of God's wrath, but they despair of being reconciled. "Hopeless!" they cry—it is useless to repent (Jer. 2:25; 18:12). This, too, leads them not to confess or to approach God for his mercy or reconciliation. Their "wound is severe," and they will bear it in despair rather than hope (Jer. 10:19). But a wound that we refuse to show the physician is a wound that has no hope of healing, and despair leads us to turn away from God rather than toward him. Indeed, such despair can be another manifestation of pride, if we believe that God forgives and heals but that *our* sin is somehow beyond God's abilities.

Both despair and presumption are contrary to hope.[8] Repentance, on the other hand, "is an act of hope."[9] We hardly approach someone to confess our sins if we think that person will simply push us aside or berate us: "No one can repent to good purpose unless he hopes for mercy."[10] Israel must have hope that God will forgive, that God will be willing and able to heal. The prophets underscore God's faithfulness and his promise to accept Israel's confession and repentance. He is a merciful and patient God. And he is entirely capable of healing their sin, of restoring his people, even of defeating the greatest armies of their enemies. He extends this offer earnestly to his people through the prophets. "Return, O faithless children, I will heal your faithlessness" (Jer. 3:22). "I will not look on you in anger, for I am merciful, says the LORD; I will not be angry forever. Only acknowledge your guilt, that you have rebelled against the LORD your God" (Jer. 3:12–13).

Models of Repentance among Wicked Kings

The prophetic call is a call to confess sin and to repent, to turn from sinful ways and to receive God's mercy and walk anew in God's ways. Overall, as noted above, the story of the northern and southern kingdoms is one of decline and unrepentance. But God's call to repentance does not remain merely theoretical in this literature. Even when the nation as a whole is in decline and being punished, God will not overlook repentance in individuals, even when the temporal consequences of others' sins affect them in the form of famine or conquest. One's past righteousness will not avail once one has turned from it to wickedness, but one's past crimes will not block God's mercy when one

8. CCC 2091–92.
9. Walter Brueggemann, *Theology of the Old Testament: Testimony, Dispute, Advocacy* (Minneapolis: Fortress, 1997), 436.
10. Pseudo-Ambrose, *Concerning Repentance* 1.1.4 (NPNF[2] 10:329).

repents, even if natural or necessary consequences for sin remain (cf. Isa. 48:17–22; Jer. 34:8–20; Ezek. 18:1–29; 33:12–16; Mic. 2:7; Zeph. 2:3). Before considering God's work to punish, forgive, and restore the nation as a whole after exile, it is worth meditating on some examples of repentance among individual kings. We will consider the repentance of David in the following chapter. Here we will consider the examples of Saul, Ahab, and Manasseh, who committed serious sins that bore serious consequences, but whose repentance God awarded with mercy.[11]

Saul's Rejection and Repentance

Saul is not remembered as a good king. A majority of the book of 1 Samuel is spent recounting his failures, his jealousy, and his angry pursuit of David. Indeed, knowing the story from its end in David's God-willed accession to the throne, it is difficult not to read Saul as a negative figure even from his first introduction as a tall and handsome man of means, in contrast to the ruddy, less-regal shepherd David (cf. 1 Sam. 9:1–2; 16:4–13). But Saul was the first divinely ordained king over the twelve tribes. He is explicitly revealed by God to the prophet-priest Samuel as the first king in response to Israel's request for a king, an appointment confirmed by divine signs and military victory (1 Sam. 9–11). However, after Samuel reiterates to the people—now together with their king—that they and their king must remain faithful (1 Sam. 12:6–18), Saul begins to show signs of arrogance and disobedience. He takes it upon himself to offer sacrifice when Samuel is delayed, against Samuel's command, at which point Samuel announces that God will raise up another king, David (1 Sam. 13:10–14).

Saul's final rejection as king comes when, after a victory, he takes plunder and spares the lives of captives upon whom God pronounced the death penalty (1 Sam. 15:1–23). Samuel accuses Saul and again announces that God will give the kingdom to another. However, whereas earlier Saul frequently demonstrated pride, here he responds to Samuel with contrition: "I have sinned; for I have transgressed the commandment of the LORD and your words, because I feared the people and obeyed their voice" (1 Sam. 15:24). He confesses his sin and even admits the reason for his sin, that he wrongly feared the opinion

---

11. Hezekiah is also noted for repentance in 2 Chron. 32:24–27, which reports that after his pious life and miraculous healing he became arrogant, was stricken, repented, and received a reprieve.

of the people instead of fearing God. And he asks Samuel, "Now therefore, I pray, pardon my sin, and return with me, so that I may worship the LORD" (1 Sam. 15:25). If Samuel returns with him, it will be a sign, to Saul and to the others there, that Saul is being restored to God as an acceptable worshiper. Samuel, at first, refuses to go with him, and when Saul grabs hold of Samuel, Samuel reiterates that God is going to remove Saul from his role as king. But Saul confesses and pleads again for Samuel to return with him so that he might worship God and be rid of his public shame. And Samuel does. "Samuel turned back after Saul; and Saul worshiped the LORD" (1 Sam. 15:31).

For his sins, Saul will not be allowed to remain king. His actions and choices bear temporal consequences for his royal office. Yet we should not read political kingship as his soul's salvation; his rejection as king is not his damnation. Moses's disobedience, in the end, meant that he was not able to enter the promised land—the new generation would not take over the land under the leadership of one who saw God's wonders intimately and yet failed to trust and sanctify God before the people (Num. 20:1–12). But this did not mean that God refused to favor Moses ever again in other ways. Saul's story comes out poorly in the end, with his own suicide in battle (1 Sam. 31:1–10), quite different from Moses's peaceful death on the mountain with God (Deut. 34:1–8). Yet in this moment, God, through his mediator Samuel, appears to accept Saul's confession—even if his contrition is imperfect and motivated more by shame than true devotion. He has sinned but repents, and those sins are forgiven. Will he commit more sins? Yes. But those will be judged and forgiven as he repents or does not repent of them. Here, when Saul pleads to be forgiven and restored to communion with God, he receives it. He will lose the kingship in punishment for his sins, but he does not lose God's love and is not irretrievably rejected from friendship with God. In that moment, through God's priestly mediator, the contrite Saul is restored.

Ahab and Jezebel

If Saul's character can admit of a mixed or complex depiction in Scripture, this is not the case with Ahab, ruler of the northern tribes, and his wife, Jezebel. The two of them, together, commit grave social injustices, set up altars to foreign gods, and seethe with threats and antipathy against God's good prophets. After they perpetrate a premeditated murder in order to steal land from a citizen, the prophet Elijah announces God's condemnation: every male from the line of Ahab will be cut off, and dogs shall devour Jezebel (1 Kings 21:20–26).

However, despite their unity in so much evil, the couple's responses to this condemnation differ. Jezebel does not repent but continues to practice and promote idolatry (2 Kings 9:22). She dies and is picked clean by dogs, as prophesied (2 Kings 9:30–37). But Ahab, when confronted with this condemnation, "tore his clothes and put sackcloth over his bare flesh; he fasted, lay in the sackcloth, and went about dejectedly" (1 Kings 21:27). His inner sorrow for his sins is visible both from his demeanor and from the outward expressions of penance in his dress and in fasting. Despite all Ahab's wickedness, God accepts this penitence. God says to Elijah, "Have you seen how Ahab has humbled himself before me? Because he has humbled himself before me, I will not bring the disaster in his days; but in his son's days I will bring the disaster on his house" (1 Kings 21:29). Because of Ahab's repentance, God says, he will not bring the disaster foretold—the full end of his line—in Ahab's lifetime. That line will end, and Ahab's dynasty will no longer get to reign over Israel; these are temporal consequences for that family's sins against God and the people they were to govern. But as a mercy toward Ahab for his penitence, God will delay this until after Ahab's death (2 Kings 9–11). Ahab does not, one should note, show anything approaching admirable piety after this; he is still reluctant to seek God's counsel through good prophets and even threatens them for prophesying woe (1 Kings 22:8–9, 26–27). Yet, as we saw with Cain, God is ready to honor even imperfect contrition with mercy, mitigating the punishment deserved. Such small examples, says John Chrysostom, should galvanize believers to hope. "For such is the loving-kindness of God. . . . For even should any one not manifest complete repentance, he does not pass by one which is small and insignificant, but assigns a great reward even to this."[12]

The Repentance of Manasseh

A final example comes in Manasseh, one of the last kings of Judah before the exile and in many respects the worst of them. The books of Kings, written after the exile to show the immorality and impiety that were its cause, remember him only badly. He rebuilt the illicit shrines his father destroyed, practiced divination and child sacrifice, built pagan altars into the Jerusalem temple, and shed much innocent blood (2 Kings 23:2–16). Indeed, the sins

---

12. John Chrysostom, *Exhortation to Theodore* 1.6 (NPNF[1] 9:95).

Manasseh committed and encouraged mark a point of no return in God's punishment, a guilt that requires exile (2 Kings 23:26; 24:3–4).

The books of Chronicles were written after or during the rebuilding of Judah to underscore God's work and plan for the Davidic dynasty (and highlighting punishment and mercy for sin and repentance). Chronicles also lists Manasseh's great sins and their effects (2 Chron. 33:1–10, 19, 22–23), but it includes a significant turnaround.[13] Manasseh's crimes are punished when he is captured and deported. But there Manasseh repents. He receives this punishment as a discipline prompting him to turn toward God. Manasseh "entreated the favor of the LORD his God and humbled himself greatly before the God of his ancestors," and "God received his entreaty, heard his plea, and restored him again to Jerusalem and to his kingdom. Then Manasseh knew that the LORD indeed was God" (2 Chron. 33:12–13). According to the Chronicler, after his restoration, Manasseh tried to restore some proper worship of God in Judah, though his son Amon did not follow the better aspects of his father's example (2 Chron. 33:14–25).

Manasseh led his people into many evils, and this bore public, national results that his personal repentance could not reverse. This should remind us of the seriousness of sin and the consequences that it bears. But the same example should also show us the beauty of God's forgiveness and the redemptive nature of his punishments. Manasseh does not repent merely at a word from a prophet like Ahab or Saul. He persists until punishment comes upon him. But he receives the punishment as a call to repentance and lets it work its salutary medicine in him. So he is remembered not only for his crimes but also as a model of repentance.[14] An early Jewish prayer speaks in Manasseh's voice of how God "appointed repentance as the salvation for sinners," confessing his unworthiness and beseeching God's kindness. "For you are God of those who repent, and in me you will manifest all your grace; . . . you will save me according to the multitude of your mercies."[15]

---

13. The differences in audience and intention between Kings and Chronicles introduce questions about episodes in Chronicles that paint Judah's kings in a more sympathetic light, but the Deuteronomistic account in Samuel–Kings should not be accepted merely because it is more one-sidedly negative. Canonically, both *accounts* (regardless of what historical facts they occlude or illuminate) are inspired for the edification of believing readers (Rom. 15:4).

14. In the rabbinic Mishnah (tractate *Sanhedrin* 10:2), Manasseh is listed as one of three kings who have no share in the world to come, but Rabbi Judah's correction is recorded, that Manasseh was saved by his repentance.

15. *Prayer of Manasseh* 7, 13–14. The translations here follow Charlesworth's (in *OTP* 2:635–37) for text-critical reasons, though I have smoothed out his "God of the repenters" (Greek *ho*

Forgiveness, Purification, and the Penance of Exile

Ultimately, both kingdoms must undergo the penalty of exile. God has sent them prophets, but they have refused to listen (Isa. 30:9–11; Jer. 25:1–7). God has sent blights that prohibit sacrifice and show the emptiness of their presumptuous offerings (Joel 1:13; Amos 4:6–10). God has shown them favor and care, preserving them mercifully and promising love to them. Yet they have not responded rightly either to God's punishments or to God's favors.[16] Social injustice, sexual immorality, priestly corruption, and idolatry abound and increase (e.g., Jer. 2:8–13; 5:7–9, 26–29; Amos 2:6–8; Mic. 3:1–12). God's people have become like Sodom in Abraham's day: the outcry against their sins has risen beyond the power of intercession, and there are not enough righteous individuals for whose sake to spare national punishment (Jer. 5:1; 15:1–4; Ezek. 14:12–20).

The exile is a punishment for the people's sin. Nonetheless, God will not destroy the people utterly. "I will by no means leave you unpunished," says God, "but I will not make an end of you! I will chastise you in just measure" (Jer. 46:28). Sin must be punished, and idols must be destroyed (cf. Isa. 10:21–22; 27:9–11; 65:1–7). But the exile is not the end of the story or of God's relationship with his people. He punishes them in faithfulness to his covenantal promises at Sinai (Jer. 32:24; Bar. 1:20–22), and for the sake of the same covenantal promises to Israel—and, in Christ, to the whole world—God will continue to care for and discipline the people in their wanderings. Though individuals will perish at the hands of foreign armies, to be sure, for the nation even the exile becomes not an end but a "transitional phase," a discipline by which God's people can be purified and grow in faithfulness to God (cf. Lev. 26:40–45; Deut. 30:1–10).[17] It is a punishment but also a "threshing" or "purification," removing evil and calling for faithfulness in a new way from the remnant that survives.[18] It will be like a new wilderness experience (Jer.

---

theos tōn metanoountōn) in v. 13. The *Prayer of Manasseh* found liturgical use particularly in the Eastern Church. Though Jerome did not translate it, it was also included in an appendix in several editions of the Vulgate (including the Clementine of 1592), often as an addition to 2 Chronicles, and is cited as such in Aquinas's discussion of confession (*Summa Theologiae* III, q. 84, a. 5).

16. See the rehearsals of this point in, e.g., Jer. 2:2–9, 29–32; Ezek. 16:1–43; 20:1–26; Hosea 11:1–7; Amos 4:6–13; Mic. 6:1–5.

17. The quotation is from Frederick Vinzenz Reiterer, *Gerechtigkeit als Heil:* צדק *bei Deuterojesaiah; Aussage und Vergleich mit der alttestamentlichen Tradition* (Graz: Akademische Druck- und Verlagsanstalt, 1976), 91 (my translation).

18. See Isa. 1:25–28; 4:2–6; 48:10–11; 65:8–9; Jer. 24:1–10; Ezek. 22:20–22; 24:12–14; Amos 9:8–10; Zeph. 3:8–12.

31:2; Ezek. 20:34–38). Without the trappings of national security, the allure of prosperity through politics, or now even the temple that led many to presume on God's blessing, God's people will be forced to trust him anew.

As with Manasseh, it will take the punishment of deportation to wake the nation up. But like Manasseh, their hearts will be turned toward God in their captivity, and they will be forgiven and restored. *There*, in the "wilderness," God will "speak tenderly" to Israel, his bride, and espouse her to himself again (Hosea 2:14–15). *There*, in exile, the faithful will repent and cling to God, even while suffering the punishment decreed for the nation, and will receive pardon. "I will purify them of all the guilt they incurred by sinning against me; I will forgive all their offenses" (Jer. 33:8 NABRE; cf. Isa. 33:24; Jer. 50:20; Mic. 7:18–20). The people will again learn God's ways (Jer. 31:31–34; Bar. 2:31; Ezek. 11:17–21), the nation that was formerly arrogant will lament its sins (Ezek. 36:31–32), and those who were covered in shame will be clothed with righteousness and glory (Bar. 5:1–2). Their debt will be paid, and God's wrath will then turn against the nations to punish their sins and to rescue Israel (cf. Isa. 10:24–26; 33:1).[19] And the new wilderness experience will give way to a new and even greater *exodus*, as God leads his people out of exile to return to the promised land (see Isa. 35:3–10; Jer. 16:14–15).

This shows us again the realities of God's response to sin. God desires the life of his people, yet he will not let sin go unpunished. So God directs the punishment due for sin to become itself a vehicle for redemption, calling the people to accept it and receive it as an opportunity to grow in faith and cling to God. The exile shows us also something of the experience of repentance. Those who repent in exile must be patient to see the results of God's favor. Those who were pious and suffer exile because of the rest of the nation's sins, too, must endure this and maintain their hope in God. God decrees seventy years of exile under Babylon for Judah (Jer. 29:10). This is a requisite consequence for the nation's sin, and the faithful in exile must endure it. The prophets, speaking for the faithful and serving as a kind of paradigm for them, give voice to this patient, penitent longing for God's deliverance. "I will wait

---

19. A major reason for God's defeat of the nations who defeated Israel is, of course, God's favor for Israel and his promises to Abraham. Other rationales are provided as well in God's punishment for sin. God used the nations against Israel to punish Israel's sin first, but the nations were arrogant about it, unjustly merciless in carrying out the exile beyond the punishment decreed, or simply contemptuous of God and his people, so they also will deserve punishment after God disciplines Israel. Cf. Isa. 10:12–26; 40:2; 47:6; 61:7; Jer. 50:15, 29; Ezek. 28:2, 26; 35:12–15; Obad. 8–14; Nah. 2:11–12; Zeph. 2:8–11.

for the LORD, who is hiding his face from the house of Jacob, and I will hope in him" (Isa. 8:17; cf. Mic. 7:7–10). The prophet wails in Lamentations after the exile, "I am one who has seen affliction under the rod of God's wrath. . . . I have forgotten what happiness is" (Lam. 3:1, 17). But while he does not hide his pain, neither does his confidence falter:

> The steadfast love of the LORD never ceases,
>   his mercies never come to an end;
> they are new every morning;
>   great is your faithfulness.
> "The LORD is my portion," says my soul,
>   "therefore I will hope in him."
>
> The LORD is good to those who wait for him,
>   to the soul that seeks him.
> It is good that one should wait quietly
>   for the salvation of the LORD.
> It is good for one to bear
>   the yoke in youth . . .
> to give one's cheek to the smiter,
>   and be filled with insults.
>
> For the Lord will not
>   reject forever.
> Although he causes grief, he will have compassion
>   according to the abundance of his steadfast love. (Lam. 3:22–27,
>   30–32)

God's mercies are ever new, even for one already suffering punishment for sins. Indeed, the experience of that suffering is itself a mercy, training one for even greater patience and repentance that is pleasing toward God. To give one's cheek willingly to the "smiter," when the smiting is a divine punishment for sin, is an act of *hope* in the God who punishes sin and who promises mercy on the other side of judgment. It is embodied in the words of the Suffering Servant, who suffers innocently with and for sinners:

> The Lord GOD opened my ear;
>   I did not refuse,
>   did not turn away.
> I gave my back to those who beat me. . . .

> The Lord God is my help,
>> therefore I am not disgraced;
> Therefore I have set my face like flint,
>> knowing that I shall not be put to shame. (Isa. 50:5–7 NABRE)

To accept punishment with faith and hope is not the opposite of confidence in God's love, but the opposite of rebellion. It is rather an act of submission and trust in God, an act of *faith* by which the pious will have life (Hab. 2:4).

God's love and forgiveness do not mean the immediate removal of all penalty, individually or corporately for God's people. But the prophetic rebuke highlights for us once again God's way of making even serious punishments remedial and healing for the faithful. The people's blessing is blocked by their refusal to acknowledge their sin, and God uses various means—even, ultimately, exile—to call them to turn to him in repentance and hope. In the sacrament of reconciliation, too, Christians must humble ourselves to confess and name our sins and to be willing to accept a penance as we receive God's forgiveness. But we do it because we believe and hope in the God who reconciles us in Jesus Christ and speaks to us through his mediators. We humble ourselves before God because we know that he promises to give grace to the lowly (Prov. 3:34). In the sacrament, as for Israel, we should see our penances— far lighter than siege or famine or exile—as opportunities to grow by turning in prayer to the God from whom our sin has separated us and to live anew in friendship with him. We will see further examples of this as we consider Israel's return from exile in chapter 6. But in the next chapter we will reflect more on penance in the everyday life of God's people—in exile or not—in the Psalms and the Wisdom literature.

5

Confession, Restoration, and Penance

Psalms and Sages

> How great is the mercy of the Lord,
> and his forgiveness for those who return to him!
> —Sirach 17:29

God's response to the sin of Israel paints on a large canvas a pattern of human sin and divine rebuke. God calls the people to repentance and promises restoration; if they refuse to return to the Lord, God warns of further rebukes and greater punishment. This pattern is encoded in the covenant that God and Israel made explicitly at Mount Sinai, and the fall of the kingdoms and the words of the prophets put it on full display.

In the Psalms and Wisdom literature (particularly Proverbs, Job, Sirach, and Wisdom), we learn that the same basic pattern applies not only on the national-covenantal level but also in the lives of individuals, though in different ways. God "disciplines" and "chastises" people for their sin (cf. Ps. 39:11; Prov. 3:11), not necessarily with national calamities but by prompting their consciences toward repentance by his commands or by other means. The faithful who sin and feel God's rebuke—whether in physical suffering or simply in pangs of conscience—are exhorted to respond with confession and penitence in order to be forgiven and restored.

This chapter will allow us to see that pattern play out in the exhortations of the sages and the prayers of the psalmists, whose voices afford a perspective on confession and repentance that is at once more theoretical and more personal. They offer a more theoretical perspective in their direct descriptions of how God responds to sin in the world and how it works out in the lives of human beings, and they offer a more personal perspective in that they allow us to hear the voices of individuals in their sin pleading for mercy and praising God after they have received it.[1] Considering the sacrament of reconciliation, we will be able to see in the Psalms and Wisdom literature the pattern of the sacrament's actions—confession, contrition, absolution, and penance—and the logic that orders them.

Have Mercy on Me: The Example of David

It will serve us well to begin by treating the most famous of the "Penitential Psalms," Psalm 51 (Ps. 50 in the Septuagint and Vulgate's numbering).[2] It is recited weekly in the modern Liturgy of the Hours, and at some points in history it was recited at least once daily. "No other psalm has been so central to the complex history of Christian penitential devotion, nor to the great doctrine of atonement."[3] Many psalms confess sin, ask for deliverance, or praise God for having granted mercy. But Psalm 51, especially when read against its canonical backdrop, "offers *a model* for actual confession."[4] While not every aspect of confession and penance is contained in this psalm, the penitent's

1. To read the psalms for what they say about God's work with individuals is not to read them as *individualistic* rather than as communal texts. National ("we") psalms are meant to be affirmed by individuals and form them in piety, and psalms from the perspective of one individual ("I") can speak for the whole nation or for every righteous person; even in royal psalms the king is representative. Compare Sigmund Mowinckel, *The Psalms in Israel's Worship*, trans. D. R. Ap-Thomas, 2 vols. (Oxford: Blackwell, 1962), 1:225–27; 2:1, 133–41. Indeed, it is partly by this individual-personal interplay that God's people can see in the Psalms the figure of Christ, the righteous Davidic king, and also hear the voices of suffering, faithful sinners who are righteous in Christ.

2. Traditionally, the "penitential psalms" are Pss. 6; 32; 38; 51; 102; 130; and 143. They are not all identical in structure or in whether they contain an explicit confession. Samuel Terrien classifies them, with most of the Psalter in fact, as "supplications" more broadly (*The Psalms: Strophic Structure and Theological Commentary*, 2 vols., ECC [Grand Rapids: Eerdmans, 2003], 1:43).

3. Bruce K. Waltke and James M. Houston, with Erika Moore, *The Psalms as Christian Worship: A Historical Commentary* (Grand Rapids: Eerdmans, 2010), 446.

4. Walter Brueggemann, *The Message of the Psalms: A Theological Commentary* (Minneapolis: Augsburg, 1984), 98.

response to his own sin and God's rebuke show a basic structure or model that we can follow as we consider confession and restoration in this chapter.

The psalm's superscription sets it in David's life, when God sent the prophet Nathan to confront David about his sin. David had remained in Jerusalem when his armies went to war, leaving many women temporarily husbandless in the city, and he sees a woman and lusts after her. She is the wife of Uriah, one of David's mighty companions and the aide of David's army commander, Joab (2 Sam. 23:39). Her name is Bathsheba. David learns who she is but still sends men to bring her to him, and he takes her to his bed and impregnates her (2 Sam. 11:1–5). When David learns that she is pregnant, he attempts to cover up his crime by sending for Uriah on the pretense of wanting news from the battlefield, hoping that Uriah will sleep with Bathsheba while at home and later think the child is his own. Uriah comes and stays a few days, but, out of solidarity with his men still far away on the battlefield, he refuses to go home—even when, as a last-ditch attempt, David gets him drunk. David, changing plans but still calculating, sends Uriah back to the army with a sealed letter commanding Joab, the commander, to send Uriah to the front lines of the thickest fighting and let Uriah die (2 Sam. 11:6–15). Joab complies. Uriah dies, and David receives the report with some self-satisfaction. Bathsheba laments her husband, but when her set period of mourning is over, David sends for her again and makes her his wife (2 Sam. 11:16–27).

One can see sin at work in David's desires and in the way he heeds them here. As James puts it, "Each person is tempted when he is lured and enticed by his own desire. Then desire conceives and brings forth sin, and when sin reaches maturity it gives birth to death" (James 1:14–15 NABRE). David feels attracted to the beautiful Bathsheba, which in one sense is natural. But his attraction becomes desire to have her. Rather than resist his desire, he leans into it. He chooses to take one step toward gratifying a lust that he knows is sinful, then a bigger step, then a bigger step. He sees Bathsheba, inquires about her, makes the choice to have her brought to him, and then makes the choice to lie with her. Then, in an attempt to cover it up, he acts connivingly, gets Uriah drunk, and plots and commands his death—misusing the royal authority that God gave him to administer justice. Through it all, he conceals his sin and presses forward to get what he wants: to possess Bathsheba. Whether marrying her was an attempt on David's part to do right by her or merely another way to get what he wanted all along, David's action was evil in God's sight (2 Sam. 11:27).

As God responded to the nation's sin by sending prophets to accuse them, so God sends Nathan the prophet to David. God brings an *accusation* against David through Nathan. He accuses David of ingratitude for the other blessings God has given him, that he should have so much and yet covet and take Uriah's wife and then take Uriah's life. He charges him with injustice—specifically, theft and murder—and he pronounces a *judgment*: the adultery and murder that David sought to keep secret will have public consequences as his own children emulate their father (2 Sam. 12:1–12).

David could respond by continuing to cover up his sin, killing God's prophet as other kings do. But David, though he has sinned greatly, hears God's accusation and judgment and *repents*. In the narrative of 2 Samuel, a single sentence conveys his confession: "I have sinned against the LORD" (2 Sam. 12:13). In Psalm 51, we hear the king pour out his confession and plead for divine mercy.[5]

> Have mercy on me, O God,
>   according to your steadfast love;
> according to your abundant mercy
>   blot out my transgressions.
> Wash me thoroughly from my iniquity,
>   and cleanse me from my sin.
> For I know my transgressions,
>   and my sin is ever before me.
> Against you, you alone, have I sinned,
>   and done what is evil in your sight,
> so that you are justified in your sentence
>   and blameless when you pass judgment. (Ps. 51:1–4)

Rather than maintaining his innocence, David acknowledges his sin. He confesses, and he acknowledges the justice of God's word of judgment against him. Knowing how far from God he has fallen, he asks to be restored to God's favor and blessing. He asks for this using several images for sin and its removal.[6] He admits his *transgressions*—misdeeds, infractions of God's law—and begs God to *blot out* or erase them from his record, asking God

---

5. In Bibles that follow versifications from the Hebrew Bible, the psalm's prayer begins at v. 3.

6. On metaphors used for sin generally, see Joseph Lam, *Patterns of Sin in the Hebrew Bible: Metaphor, Culture, and the Making of a Religious Concept* (Oxford: Oxford University Press, 2016).

not to hold this sin in remembrance against him. "Hide your face from my sins" (Ps. 51:9). He asks God to *wash* him of the guilt and impurity that now taint his soul before God, to cleanse him in the way that sin offerings brought purification (Ps. 51:7).[7] And he begs that, so purified, he would be renewed in spirit and "restored" to God (Ps. 51:10–12).

In the Levitical sacrificial system, the kind of purification David requests is usually achieved through animal *sacrifice*, which is both an expression of contrition and a plea to be purified by its blood. Premeditated murder, however, is not a sin to be atoned for by such means (Num. 35:30–34). David's sins are worthy of death, crimes incurring bloodguilt (Ps. 51:14).[8] David offers God a sacrifice, but he is convinced that what God wants from him instead of an animal is sincere and humble *contrition*: the sacrifice David brings "is a broken spirit; a broken and contrite heart, O God, you will not despise" (Ps. 51:17). Many other psalms offer God a sacrifice of *praise*, promising to praise God publicly and tell others of his mercy (cf. Pss. 50:14, 23; 116:12–19). David offers this too. Even before receiving forgiveness, he promises that he will give God public "praise" and proclaim God's just mercy for sinners in return for God's pardon (Ps. 51:13–15).

The psalm lets us see the psalmist's prayer but not God's response. We can, however, see God's response by returning to the narrative in 2 Samuel. David, confronted by the prophet Nathan, confesses sin (2 Sam. 12:13). In the very next sentence, Nathan pronounces forgiveness in God's name: "The LORD has put away your sin; you shall not die" (2 Sam. 12:13). In response to David's contrition, God grants forgiveness through the word of a mediator. The full

7. In v. 7 the first verb David uses is *khata'*, which in the *qal* stem means "to sin" but in the *piel*, as here, refers to making a sin offering (a *khatta't*) or specifically to the cleansing that the sin offering effects. David is asking to be purified, in language that implies sacrifice and atonement. Sin offerings (or "purification" offerings) purified especially the sanctuary and holy things when they had been defiled by the people's sin or by impurities that were more ritual than moral. However, similar to the psalm's (here moral) use of the image, the Levitical ritual seems also to purify not just the holy things but the sinner as well. See Joshua M. Vis, "The Purgation of Persons through the Purification Offering," in *Sacrifice, Cult, and Atonement in Early Judaism and Christianity: Constituents and Critique*, ed. Henrietta L. Wiley and Christian A. Eberhart, RBS 85 (Atlanta: SBL Press, 2017), 33–57.

8. In Ps. 51:14, David asks to be rescued from *damim*—literally, "bloods." "Blood" (Hebrew *dam*) can refer to blood itself or to violence and bloodshed, and in English translation this verse sometimes sounds like a prayer to be delivered from violent enemies. But *dam* and the plural *damim* are common shorthands for bloodguilt, either guilt *deserving* death (Lev. 20:16) or guilt *incurred* for murder or for what American jurisprudence calls "wrongful death" (see Exod. 22:2–3; Deut. 19:10; 22:8). Compare Marvin E. Tate, *Psalms 51–100*, WBC 20 (Waco: Word, 1990), 6–7, 26.

and final penalty of death will not be visited upon him. He has confessed and asked for God's mercy, and he will receive it.

There are, nonetheless, temporal consequences. One is a natural consequence or effect of a father's sins on his children. David's sinfulness will still affect his children, who will themselves become involved in sexual sin and murder as Nathan foretold.[9] Another consequence is imposed by God: Bathsheba's child will not survive (2 Sam. 12:10–12, 14). David pleads with God for the life of their child, humbling himself with fasting and prayer. But what David wants is not God's will for this child's soul, and the child dies. David, having received an answer from God, goes to the temple to worship the Lord, and God grants him and Bathsheba another child, Solomon, who will become David's divinely chosen heir and successor as king (2 Sam. 12:15–23). David's return to the temple indicates that he did receive the divine purification for which the psalm begs, and his restoration to God's favor is indicated in the narrative also by the gift of their new and blessed child.

This psalm, read against its canonical setting in David's life, is rightly prized for what it models for us. Most importantly, it shows us that the faithful can sin greatly and that *God forgives even the greatest sin in those who repent*. Not all instances of sin, repentance, and restoration are like David's in every respect. But the pattern of divine rebuke, confession and penance, restoration and worship can apply after grave or light sins, as God calls all to deeper conversion and greater communion with himself. We can now look at the components of that pattern in turn and learn how they fit into God's merciful work in the Wisdom literature and the rest of the Psalter.

God's Discipline and the Call to Repentance

When David sinned, God accused him and called him to repentance directly through a prophet. As we have seen, God did the same with the nation and its kings. At the national level, likewise, we saw that God removed geopolitical blessings of prosperity (in agriculture, warfare, or politics) as a rebuke

9. Note these episodes in 2 Sam. 13: David's son Amnon rapes his half-sister Tamar, taking a woman unlawfully as his father had; her full-brother, David's son Absalom, vengefully commands his attendants to wait until Amnon is drunk and then kill him, acts which resemble David's treatment of Uriah. Later, Absalom usurps his father's throne temporarily and, as a public show of his takeover, sleeps with David's concubines publicly on a rooftop—which is where David first saw and lusted after Bathsheba (2 Sam. 16:21–22; cf. 11:2). Absalom ultimately dies in the rebellion.

to wake Israel up to their fallenness and call them back. But what about individuals to whom no prophet comes with a specific word from God? What witnesses do they have to their sin that prompt them to confession and repentance?

Psalm 39:11 states directly that God "chastises" or disciplines humans by rebuking them for sin. These disciplines can, on the one hand, be viewed as punishments exacting a penalty, but they are intended not merely to pay sinners back but to instruct them, to teach them the wrongness of their ways and turn them back to God. The Hebrew noun meaning "discipline" or "chastisement" is *musar*, derived from the verb *yasar*, meaning "instruct" or "direct." When people have done wrong, God instructs them to return to him by reproving them and calling them to repent of wrongdoing. Discipline can be imagined as mere punishment for past actions, but with God—as it *should* be with humans—any punishment required in discipline and instruction is calculated to redirect them to good behavior in the future. A human parent's discipline for a child can involve discomfort when the rebukes cause psychological shame and, when it involves corporal punishment, even physical pain (cf. Prov. 13:24; 22:15; 29:15). But humans are commanded not to discipline as though they are trying to destroy their children, but to use it to reprimand and redirect children to the path of life (Prov. 19:18; 23:14). God's discipline is not a capricious crushing of puny mortals, but a father's loving correction to wayward children: "The LORD reproves the one he loves, as a father the son in whom he delights" (Prov. 3:12; cf. Sir. 30:1; Heb. 12:7–8; Rev. 3:19).[10] God's discipline is patient, not visiting the full penalty of people's sins on them, but granting light penalties, offering them an opportunity for repentance, out of his mercy and love (Wis. 11:23–26). "Therefore you rebuke offenders little by little, warn them, and remind them of the sins they are committing, that they may abandon their wickedness and believe in you, Lord!" (Wis. 12:2 NABRE). Such discipline is to be loved and accepted by those who want to walk in truth and receive God's reward (cf. Ps. 50:16–17; Prov. 12:1; 15:10, 32; Sir. 21:6; 23:2–5).

God sends reproofs and disciplines little by little, so they are fittingly sent and experienced in a variety of forms and intensities. While most individuals

10. This seems denied occasionally by Job, who in his anguish accuses the eternal God of being petty for judging human sin (e.g., Job 7:17–21), but the progression of the dialogue within the book as a whole shows the ultimate inadequacy of Job's perspective. See Israel McGrew, "'What Is Enosh?' The Anthropological Contributions of Job 7:17–18 through Allusion and Intertextuality," *CBQ* 84 (2022): 404–23.

may not have an explicit, personal accusation delivered by a prophet, God has not left himself without witnesses. God's *commandments* themselves are a witness for God against sin, which one might hear—or simply remember— and feel convicted enough to repent. They are given to all, as warnings to teach people not to sin and as rebukes meant to make people aware of sins they have committed (Ps. 19:7–11; Prov. 6:23; Sir. 1:26–27). Such guilt pangs, experienced within, are taken by the pious as divine promptings to repentance. Ideally, consciences should be moved to repent by *example* as well, when they see others punished for their sins or rewarded when they confess (cf. Pss. 32:6; 51:3; Wis. 19:10; Sir. 23:27). Not all consciences are sufficiently moved by such witnesses, however. In many cases, various types of *suffering* are understood to be more direct confirmations of God's displeasure. In the Psalms, for instance, physical distress, public shame, and other calamities are interpreted as divine calls to repent (cf. Pss. 6:1–7; 38:1–12; 107:10–12, 17–18). Job (along with his friends) interprets his loss of prosperity, family, and health as divine rebukes visited upon him (Job 7:18; 10:6, 14; 13:19–28; 19:6; 27:2), although the book's narrator clarifies that God is only allowing what Job thinks God is intentionally doing to him.

Importantly, not all experiences of suffering are rebukes for specific sins. Jesus makes this point explicitly in John 9:1–3. God does "repay" all people "according to their work" (Ps. 62:12), and a life of wisdom and righteousness does bear fruit in blessing, but not always in obvious or conventional ways.[11] God allows some to suffer innocently in the mystery of his saving will. And the wicked do not always experience obvious ruin, and they are often blind to the ruin they do experience in their souls, as continued sinfulness hardens and blinds them against the truth. Even Ecclesiastes is convinced that God *will* bring every deed to judgment (Eccles. 12:14), but when and how God

11. At points, the Wisdom books appear contradictory here. In the canon they can be read complementarily, as reflecting both real confidence in God's justice and sovereignty and, simultaneously, the reality of innocents suffering and the wicked prospering. All of the books, perceiving this tension, press the reader to seek God's ways and wisdom more deeply. They also interpret one another toward a synthesis. To take one example: Prov. 16:31 says that gray hair is a mark of righteousness (i.e., the righteous live longer). Ecclesiastes and Job offer a correction: sometimes the good die young without conventional reward (e.g., Eccles. 7:15). A later sage synthesizes both truths by saying that a person's righteousness *is* their gray hair, interpreting the early death of the faithful as a sign of God's approval: they proved faithful through the trials of their (short) life, and God now grants them rest (Wis. 4:7–14). For a helpful survey of this literature and the emphases and perspectives of these books, see James L. Crenshaw, *Old Testament Wisdom: An Introduction*, 3rd ed. (Louisville: Westminster John Knox, 2010). See also the following note.

will do so, and whether it will be visible to others, is left to the mystery of divine justice and the way in which God will invite them to repentance.[12] But for all, suffering can be understood as a *test*, a moment in which one must decide whether to be faithful or to forsake God, a call to the wicked to turn to God and to the righteous to grow stronger in faith and endurance (cf. Jdt. 8:27; Ps. 11:5). "It is good for me that I was humbled, so that I might learn your statutes" (Ps. 119:71). God's commandments themselves can be understood as "tests," opportunities for the faithful to obey and so to grow in their relationship with God and their love for others (cf. Exod. 16:4; Ps. 81:7). Suffering, likewise, can be a "test" of faithfulness and friendship. Sirach suggests that humans should let friends prove their friendship in times of trial (Sir. 6:7). God's tests and discipline are opportunities to exercise and grow in faithfulness, wisdom, and "friendship with God" (Wis. 7:14; cf. Ps. 17:3–4; Sir. 4:15–19; 18:13–14). Even in the case of Job, God allows him to be tested because he is confident in Job's ability to endure it faithfully (Job 1:8, 12; 2:3, 6), and ultimately Job passes the test (Job 42:7–17). Those suffering innocently can view suffering as an opportunity to turn to God and learn to submit and hope faithfully in God—to be further purified, though not being punished as such (Wis. 3:5–6; Sir. 2:1–6). Suffering and various other trials are moments of decision for the innocent as well as for backsliders: Will I cling to God in hope in this moment, turning *toward* God even if in dismay, or will I turn *away* from God and seek other sources of blessing and happiness?

The Faithful Respond: Humility, Penance, Confession

God tests his friends, and he rebukes and disciplines those who stand against him so that they might be reconciled and become his friends. There will be a day when an individual's time of testing and opportunity to repent is over. The book of Sirach in particular exhorts people to think of their death and

---

12. Job's experience of innocent suffering and of seeing the wicked prosper is undeniable (Job 6:26; 13:1–2; 21:6–17; 24:1–17). Job's friends are wrong to insist that *Job's* suffering is a punishment for grave sin, but they do agree with many psalms and with the rest of Scripture about the general truth of God's punishment of the wicked and reward for the righteous, though it may be delayed within this life (cf. Job 20; Ps. 73). Job affirms this too—at least as a desire of what should be (Job 24:18–24; 27:8–23; cf. 13:10; 19:29). Later literature synthesizes these affirmations by pointing explicitly to the delay of rewards until *after* death (cf. Wis. 3:18; 4:20–5:13; Sir. 11:26; 18:24).

turn to God now: "Do not delay to turn back to the Lord" (Sir. 5:7; cf. 7:36; 28:6; 18:24; Eccles. 12:1–8, 14). God's "mercies never come to an end; they are new every morning" (Lam. 3:22–23). His mercy is renewed every day, and every "today" that one is alive is a day to turn to the Lord, to hear God's word and follow it (Ps. 95:7–8; Heb. 3:7–13). The faithful are called to turn to God every day and repent, in some moments accepting God's discipline for their sin and in others disciplining themselves so that they will not fall into sin, to submit themselves and their desires and their sinfulness to God. This is a call to penance and confession, and it is a call to *humility*.

Humility and Acts of Penance

One's response in a moment of trial can be characterized fundamentally as a choice between humility and pride. The proud—also called "scoffers" (see Prov. 21:24)—reject God's instruction and discipline, turning to themselves and their own imaginations or their own resources for blessing instead of God. Pride and self-satisfaction, if left unchecked, lead to a kind of spiritual "blindness," so that one does not feel the need to repent or even perceive God's rebukes as rebukes. This only leads one to continue in sin or to presume on God's favor (Ps. 73:6–9; Sir. 5:4–7; 10:12), or perhaps to blame God for one's failures (Sir. 15:11–20). It requires humility to acknowledge one's inadequacy and sinfulness, to acknowledge that one has sinned—as in the words of the confession at the opening of the Mass—"by *my* fault, by my most grievous fault." And it requires humility to seek the mercy and instruction of another instead of depending only on oneself. Humility is part of piety and faithfulness: "Those who fear the Lord prepare their hearts, and humble themselves before him" (Sir. 2:17; cf. 1:27; Prov. 15:33; 22:4). Humility is the disposition of those who ask for mercy and those who receive it (Ps. 25:9–11; Sir. 3:18).

God's rebukes are meant to call people to turn back to God—whether issued simply in the form of God's commandments or enhanced by suffering and punishment. Since pride blocks one from repentance, one of the goals of God's rebukes is to *humble* and bring low the proud. In Psalm 90, those who have been "humbled" by God's punishment pray for restoration: "Make us glad as many days as you have humbled us, for as many years as we have seen trouble" (Ps. 90:15 NABRE). Psalm 107, likewise, extols sinners whom God humbled and who then turned to the Lord and received mercy (Ps. 107:12–13).

Augustine on Humility, Confession, and Charity

For Augustine, humility is integral to one's reconciliation to God both for the sake of confession and forgiveness and for our own growth in love, since it works against our interior pride.

> Pride extinguishes charity; consequently humility strengthens charity; charity extinguishes offenses. Humility pertains to confession, whereby we confess that we are sinners. . . . Tell people what you are, tell God what you are, because, if you don't tell God what you are, God will condemn what he finds in you.[a]

a. Augustine, *Homilies on the First Epistle of John* 1.6 (trans. Ramsey, 27).

Humility submits oneself, one's past transgressions, and one's future blessing to the mercy of God. The humble turn to God in utter dependence on him, creatures looking to their creator. God's commands and rebukes, as well as God's power as creator over all, should make one bow the knee and submit to God.

Practices of penance such as fasting, almsgiving, and prayer are, in part, meant to express and enact such humility before God. *Prayer* expresses humility in that we turn to God to praise him (not ourselves) and acknowledge our dependence upon him (not on ourselves) in supplication (2 Chron. 7:14). Humble confession, likewise, submits our past transgressions and our future blessings to his mercy. *Fasting* is also a way of humbling or denying ourselves— "I humbled my soul with fasting" (Ps. 69:10; cf. Ezra 8:21). Fasting from food or other good things is a way of submitting our desires—from which temptations and sins arise, like David's—to God and God's commandments. Fasting is thus often connected directly with confession and repentance, part of one's turning from sin (1 Sam. 7:6; 1 Kings 21:27; Neh. 9:1). It is also done in petition and prayer, a sign—along with ashes—of human frailty and mortality, and a sign of submission and dependence, asking the creator's mercy for his creatures (Ezra 8:23; Esther 4:3). Likewise, *almsgiving* is an act of humility, acknowledging the unity of rich and poor under God (Prov. 14:31; 22:2) and submitting one's wealth to God and God's command to care for the poor (Sir. 29:11–12). It is an act of humble charity to make a gift of one's own resources—which are themselves gifts from God—in order to preserve and aid the life of others who cannot repay the gift.[13]

Such acts of submission and humility are called for in all the faithful, whether at particular moments (such as communal fasts) or as general practices of penance, as ways of continually submitting oneself to the Lord and disciplining oneself in faith. Penance in a way *anticipates* God's discipline and judgment, inasmuch as it is a way of disciplining oneself and training oneself against temptation or desire: "Before you fall ill, take care of your health. Before judgment comes, examine yourself; and at the time of scrutiny you will find forgiveness. Before falling ill, humble yourself; and when you have sinned, repent" (Sir. 18:19–21). Sirach's exhortation depicts penance not just judicially but also in terms of preventive medicine. One who is healthy, or relatively healthy, should exercise and nourish himself with good food in order to remain healthy and increase in health. It will pay dividends when illness attacks.

While the Levitical system did not provide for sacrificial atonement in the case of grave sins that required expulsion or death, lighter or inadvertent sins could be "covered" or "atoned for" (Hebrew *kpr*) by faithfulness and righteousness (Prov. 16:6; cf. Ps. 40:6–8). The book of Sirach holds that keeping God's law, acts of charity, and honor for one's parents have the value of sacrifices and sin offerings (Sir. 3:3, 14–15; 35:1–5). Anticipating Jesus's words in the Our Father, Sirach also teaches that the charitable act of forgiveness has such value as well: God will be forgiving to those who forgive, but not to the proud who refuse to be merciful (Sir. 28:2–5; Matt. 6:12). God calls for a "sacrifice" of praise and obedience from those who would seek his favor (Ps. 50:14–15), and prayer is itself a kind of sacrifice (Ps. 141:2). Psalmists also point to their acceptance of suffering as a sign of their fidelity (Pss. 17:3, 15; 116:10). Almsgiving is extolled especially as a counter to the effects of sin and as a kind of sacrifice—a sacrifice for which God will deliver one from past sins and which he will remember in one's favor after future sins (Tob. 4:7–11; 12:8–10; Ps. 41:1; Sir. 3:30–31; 29:12; 35:4; Dan. 4:27). To give alms to God's needy creatures, as Proverbs 19:17 promises, is a loan to God that God will "repay."

Sacrifice, fasting, alms, and even prayer are nothing, however, without true humility and obedience. God does call for sacrifice and prayer, even as signs of

13. The value of giving to those who cannot repay is emphasized later by Jesus (Luke 6:34–36). This element of almsgiving is underscored especially in Sir. 7:32–33, where it is connected with charity for the *dead* in funding burials.

repentance (e.g., Joel 2:12), but they must be signs *of repentance*.[14] Without true repentance, these are not in fact sacrifices, not acts of self-giving and submitting to God, but instead are like bribes that enrage the just judge (Sir. 7:8–10; 34:21–31; cf. Eccles. 4:17; Isa. 58:3–14). Sacrifices or prayers without penitence are an "abomination" (Prov. 15:8; 28:9). For one who has sinned, obedience and humility require true contrition and a desire to walk in true faithfulness toward God.

Confession and Contrition

For one who has sinned, turning *to* the Lord requires turning *from* sin. The goal of God's rebukes is to call sinners to return to him "with all your heart, with fasting, with weeping, and with mourning" (Joel 2:12). But if one fasts or sacrifices with no intent to turn from sin, God's call to repentance essentially remains ignored. One must not merely presume on God's favor in return for an offering. One who hopes for mercy should, rather, confess with contrition and an intent to amend one's life.

As in Psalm 51, turning from sin calls for explicit *confession*. "No one who conceals transgressions will prosper, but one who confesses and forsakes them will obtain mercy" (Prov. 28:13). Confession is a mark of one who seeks after God with humility and love for God's statutes. Readers may notice some psalmists who insist on their innocence and their own righteousness, or the stark contrast between "the righteous" or "wise" and "the wicked" or "fools," and get the impression that some viewed themselves to be completely sinless. But in many cases, psalmists who appeal to their innocence are appealing to their innocence in a particular matter or over against enemies, not claiming that they have no faults.[15] In Psalm 69, for instance, the psalmist appeals to his innocence against others, yet in asking for deliverance he states that God knows the psalmist's own "folly" and faults (Ps. 69:4–6). Another psalmist begins a plea for deliverance by stopping to ask that God not take his own sins into account (Ps. 143:2). Those who are righteous as opposed to wicked

14. God rejects worship and offering from the unrepentant "not as a rejection of sacrifice per se. Instead, he will not allow himself to be served in worship and will not serve people when commandment and life become detached from one another" (Reinhard Feldmeier and Hermann Spieckermann, *God of the Living: A Biblical Theology*, trans. Mark E. Biddle [Waco: Baylor University Press, 2011], 290).

15. For an in-depth study of such psalms, see Gert Kwakkel, *"According to My Righteousness": Upright Behaviour as Grounds for Deliverance in Psalms 7, 17, 18, 26 and 44*, OtSt 46 (Leiden: Brill, 2002).

are such because they seek God and repent when they sin, not because they never sin at all. The righteous err, but they "will not *wallow* in sins" (Sir. 23:12; italics added). Indeed, "the righteous falls seven times and rises again, but the wicked stumble in times of calamity" (Prov. 24:16 ESV). Everyone is called to confession. Some who fall from their righteousness such that they may be cast from God's presence, like David, must then be restored to their righteousness through confession. But those who remain righteous seek God by confessing and turning from sin as well. Sirach 39:5 says that the wise man rises early and asks for God's forgiveness, apparently daily. And one psalmist asks God's forgiveness from "hidden" transgressions of which he himself is not aware (Ps. 19:12).[16]

"Do not be ashamed to confess your sins, and do not try to stop the current of a river" (Sir. 4:26). To maintain one's innocence in all matters—including what we term venial sins and "sins of omission," where we know what is right and choose not to do it (James 4:17), and including "hidden" or unknown transgressions as in Psalm 19:12—would be anything but humble. But to confess sin is to lay one's wounds humbly before the God who heals. It is itself an act of righteousness, a mark of the wise who seek God with all their being. According to Augustine, for the sinner, confession itself is the beginning (or renewal) of righteousness. "The beginning of our righteousness is the confession of sins. When you have begun not to defend your sin, then you have started to be righteous."[17]

But confession, like fasting and sacrifice, can also be made emptily. The wicked can say "sorry" just to get what they want in an argument, intending all the while to continue their crimes (Sir. 19:25–28). So, too, one can confess to God to appear pious or to get forgiveness while fully intending to sin again. But God is hardly fooled. Confession must thus be made with *contrition* and an intention to turn toward God and *amend one's life*. Sirach emphasizes that God's mercy for the penitent is not a reason to be complacent and presume on God's mercy, and it exhorts people to pray and try to turn from sin toward God.

> Yet to those who repent he grants a return,
>   and he encourages those who are losing hope.

16. Indeed, even a lack of intentional, actual sins is no indication that one need not confess. One may act rightly only under compulsion or for lack of opportunity to do wrong (cf. Sir. 19:23–28; 20:4).

17. Augustine, *Homilies on the First Epistle of John* 4.3 (trans. Ramsey, 66).

> Turn back to the Lord and forsake your sins;
>> pray in his presence and lessen your offense.
> Return to the Most High and turn away from iniquity,
>> and hate intensely what he abhors. (Sir. 17:24–26)

As we have seen in several examples, God will accept contrition that is imperfect, motivated more by fear than simple love for God. Turning from sin is always an experience of struggle against the sinful desires that remain in us and the force of habits that must be broken. But even imperfect contrition must still be contrition, sorrow for having done what God "abhors," as Sirach says, and include a desire to do what God loves. External expressions of repentance like fasting or sackcloth cannot replace internal penitence (Joel 2:13). Many psalmists thus do not only ask for forgiveness verbally but also express sorrow for their sins: "I confess my iniquity; I am sorry for my sin" (Ps. 38:18). They promise to strive to be faithful in the future, to live in gratitude and tell others of God's mercy (e.g., Pss. 32:8–11; 51:13; 119:107–8). Some ask God to instruct and renew them, asking for mercy so that they will be able to trust and obey God (Pss. 51:10; 143:10). Further, in many cases they promise that they will make offerings of thanks and praise once they have been delivered, vowing that they *will* turn to God again in prayer (e.g., Pss. 79:13; 106:47). This is an expression of their contrition now as they ask to be restored to God, showing their desire to engage that relationship of worship anew once they have received mercy.

Reconciliation and the Response of Penance

God loves to hear confessions that are expressions of true repentance, turning toward the Lord and submitting oneself to God's mercy and guidance. When his people respond to his rebukes with repentance, God loves to forgive and heal those who submit their afflictions to him. Psalm 32 exults in the blessing of forgiveness for one who confesses:

> Happy are those whose transgression is forgiven,
>> whose sin is covered.
> Happy are those to whom the LORD imputes no iniquity,
>> and in whose spirit there is no deceit.
> While I kept silence, my body wasted away
>> through my groaning all day long. . . .

> Then I acknowledged my sin to you,
>   and I did not hide my iniquity;
> I said, "I will confess my transgressions to the LORD,"
>   and you forgave the guilt of my sin. (Ps. 32:1–3, 5)

When the psalmist refused to confess and kept silent in the face of his sin, he wallowed under God's rebukes and the pangs of his own conscience. But when he confessed, God granted him pardon and restored him to communion with himself.

This restored communion, restored relationship with God as God's friends, is what true confession seeks. Confession is not spiritual masochism or despairing self-hatred. We make ourselves low in confession in order that God may raise us up.[18] We acknowledge that we have behaved unfaithfully to our faithful God, asking him to restore us. And God does! He forgives iniquity, cleansing us and making us beautiful when our sins have made us loathsome, and he turns his face toward us not in wrath or rebuke but in welcome. A sign of this restored communion when one has fallen is often found in public worship and liturgy. David, restored to communion with God, pleaded for the life of his son with fasting and prayer, as he would for any other intention in his walk with God. When God's will for the child's fate was revealed, David put that prayer aside and returned to worship the Lord in the temple and offer other prayers. As we saw in the previous chapter, when Saul begged for mercy, returning to worship God with Samuel was the sign that his confession had been accepted.

As we have seen in many examples, of course, forgiveness does not mean that there are no *consequences* at all for the sin forgiven. Many temporal consequences for sin are simply natural. The evil that Manasseh committed and promulgated in Judah bore effects in the people he influenced to sin, even after he himself repented and received mercy. In David's case, the effects of his sins of lust and violence influenced his children after him even after his forgiveness. Other penalties, too, are imposed by God, as in the death of David and Bathsheba's first child. Nor does forgiveness mean that the penitent are freed from *obligation*. The penitent are spared the full penalty of their sin and restored to right relationship with God as God's friends. But God is friends with persons, not just with the forgiven parts of us. And we, as persons, with

---

18. See further Carol A. Newsom, *The Spirit within Me: Self and Agency in Ancient Israel and Second Temple Judaism* (New Haven: Yale University Press, 2021), 143–69.

all the good and bad baggage and formation that we have from our past, are called to live as God's friends. Our obligation is to live faithfully *now*, to act out of love and humility toward God in the present moment and in our present circumstances.

Psalmists, therefore, respond to God's mercy by praising God, by making offerings, and by fulfilling any vows they made as part of their pleas for mercy (cf. Pss. 54:5–7; 56:12–13; 106:47). "I will come into your house with burnt offerings; I will pay you my vows, those that my lips uttered and my mouth promised when I was in trouble" (Ps. 66:13–14). Psalm 107 recounts various persons distressed for their sins, crying out for mercy, and responding to God's forgiveness with praise and thank-offerings (Ps. 107:15, 22). Such actions, on the one hand, can have atoning value. Faithful behavior, praise, and offerings made in genuine gratitude do not simply return the sinner to a "blank slate" in God's judgment. They are themselves acts in which God delights, ones that God will remember in the person's favor. Likewise, internally, such faithful acts of love for God in response to mercy habituate one for further acts of love toward God. And they memorialize one's own experiences of God's rebukes and God's mercy, which one can remember against future temptations to sin or, after sin, to despair.

Further, within one's relationship to God, to repay God an offering of praise—paltry though it may seem compared to the mercy received—is an act of loyal and active *friendship*. Friends keep promises to each other, so penitents who make vows as pleas for mercy fulfill those vows out of love and fidelity for God. Likewise, even if one had not fallen and made such vows, acts of praise and gratitude are regular expressions of love and dependence on God.

> How can I repay the LORD
>   for all the great good done for me?
> I will raise the cup of salvation
>   and call on the name of the LORD.
> I will pay my vows to the LORD
>   in the presence of all his people. (Ps. 116:12–14 NABRE)

Thanks and praise are owed to the creator who gives us daily life and breath, for countless reasons. The same can be given in gratitude for mercy, in the specific case of sin forgiven. And when one has promised, as a sign of contrition, to make an offering—whether prayer or a particular vow or other kind of penitential act—to fulfill that promise is the act of a friend who keeps faith with God. The redeemed undertake such penances because they have been made God's friends.

God's mercy restores and heals us after a time of sin. What is more, God's mercy makes the forgiven into *witnesses* of his love and mercy for other sinners. If our sins, seen by others, can scandalize or lead others into sin, so too can the example of our repentance—especially when restoration is completed in readmittance to the public liturgy. David prays, in pleading for forgiveness, "I will teach transgressors your ways, and sinners will return to you" (Ps. 51:13). Psalm 32, quoted above, tells of the inner turmoil of stubbornly keeping one's sins bottled up and the blessing of forgiveness when one confesses. And the psalmist exhorts every faithful person to follow his example (Ps. 32:6). The penitent, when forgiven, become walking, talking, praying evidence of God's power to save, to cleanse, and to deliver the repentant from the full penalty of sin. "I shall not die, but I shall live, and recount the deeds of the LORD" (Ps. 118:17).

Psalms, Sages, and the Sacrament

The Psalms and Wisdom literature teach us much about sin and the call to repentance in God's wise and fatherly dealings with creation. And these books, the Psalter especially, let us hear the cry of penitence and the joy of deliverance from the mouths of humans.

In these books, further, we see the *pattern* of penance and reconciliation that is on display in the sacrament. People are made aware of their sin—whether small or great—in various ways, perhaps through their own consciences formed by God's commands, perhaps through the rebukes of others, or perhaps through suffering. Those who respond faithfully respond with *contrition*—perhaps joined to fasting—and *confess* their sin and *ask* for mercy. And they regularly offer some kind of vow or *penitential act* as evidence of their contrition, whether in the form of an offering, prayer or public praise, or other penances. And when they receive mercy from God, they fulfill that promise joyfully as a first step in their renewed friendship with God.

The basic framework of the sacrament of reconciliation is visible here, including in its more modern form of confessing not just grave but also venial sins. We can see in this literature also the *logic* of the final element of the sacrament: penance and satisfaction. Penance is offered or agreed to by the penitent before being absolved, and that penance is usually—in the sacrament's modern form—completed after the absolution. We have seen that God's forgiveness remits the fullest punishment of the sin (death in the case of grave sins in the Old Testament, which we thus call "mortal"), but other fitting but noneternal consequences can still be imposed in God's justice. In the Psalms, we see people *offering* a penance themselves, freely. Sometimes the penance is undertaken already when one confesses, praying for absolution while fasting in sackcloth. At other times it is promised as part of the plea for forgiveness—like a penitent in the confessional today agreeing to do penance after being absolved. Whether promised or undertaken already, this penance is a demonstration of one's contrition and desire to turn toward God as one asks for forgiveness.

We have also, in the Psalms and Wisdom literature, seen affirmations that such penitential acts can have a kind of atoning value. If God disciplines his children by humbling them with rebukes for sin, humbling oneself can function to obviate and anticipate such penalties so that they do not need to be imposed as a rebuke. Likewise, acts of penitence have the potential, at least, to counteract the more natural or social consequences of sin. If public sin influences others badly, public repentance can counteract such influence in those who are willing to learn from it. If secret sin causes one to be defensive, reclusive, or irritable toward others, the joy of forgiveness should—as one continues to walk with God—allow them to be more open and charitable. By God's grace, if we let it, such penance can even help reform our own habits and desires.

But even more fundamentally, the promise and fulfillment of penitential vows is an essential part of what confession and forgiveness are meant to *do*. Confession is not a request for a mere "clean slate," but a petition to be admitted to a restored and ongoing *relationship* with God. This is God's goal in rebuking sin: to reconcile us to walk anew in his friendship. This is what psalmists want when they confess and express contrition. The assignment of penance by a priest builds this aspect of renewed relationship into the rite of reconciliation. If I ask for forgiveness but *refuse* to accept a penance of prayer or Scripture reading or whatever else is assigned, am I treating God as a friend toward whom I want to turn or like a spiritual vending machine whom I can leave once I get the grace I want?[19] And if I accept the penance

---

19. If the first penance assigned in the confessional is not possible or highly impracticable, the penitent can ask the priest for a different penance. If the problem is genuine, this is not inimical to contrition; it is different than refusal to do any penance at all.

to receive forgiveness but later *refuse* to do it, refusing to turn to God for a couple of minutes of prayer, is that how one would treat even a human with whom one wanted real friendship? That would only add sin to sin, and it would be a prideful—not humble or grateful—way to respond. "God is not mocked, for whatever one sows, that will he also reap" (Gal. 6:7 ESV). God's goodness and forgiveness are a reason not to walk away from him but to turn with active love and reverence to the Lord who loves us: "There is forgiveness with you, so that you may be revered" (Ps. 130:4).

The logic behind the pattern of confession, absolution, and penance can get lost if we focus only on the priest or the setting, if we let our pride lead us to balk at the penance assigned as too little (*my* sin was bigger than that) or too much (*my* sin wasn't that bad), or if we come only wanting God's gift without wanting the Giver. But it is a logic of *friendship* with God. We come to the confessional for reconciliation, and penance builds into the sacrament our desire—or our willingness at the very least—to turn toward God and prescribes small steps by which to do so. God's forgiveness is a means by which he renews us in friendship with him, and our penances are, in this respect, ways by which we live out the reality of our reconciliation. As we close our reflections on the Old Testament in the following chapter, we will see Israel strive for faithfulness and confess their sins as they return from exile and hope for God's salvation.

6

Confessing in Hope, Awaiting the Messiah

I wait for the LORD, my soul waits,
and in his word I hope.

—Psalm 130:5

So far, we have seen the pattern of confession, forgiveness, and penance at both the national level and the individual level. In this chapter, which concludes our consideration of the Old Testament, we will see both again. And we will be able to highlight the hope that points ahead to the coming of Christ.

At the national level, we consider Israel's return from exile. God's people are returned, and the exile has purified the nation as promised. But the problem of sin remains. We will see the nation do penance and confess their sins, pleading for God's mercy upon them to be complete. We will also see examples of individual piety and faithfulness, extolled and encouraged by prophets and visible in exemplary characters such as Tobit and Daniel. These texts will show forth, once more, the association of confession and mercy with humility and acts of penance. They will also show how the ongoing problem of sin suggests a still-hoped-for redemption, pointing forward to the New Testament and the coming of Abraham's descendant, Jesus, who will "save his people from their sins" (Matt. 1:21).

Returning from Exile, Repenting in Hope

As we saw in chapter 4, God rebuked his people for their sins as he promised in the Sinai covenant. As they continually refused to repent of their idolatry and wickedness, God finally punished them with exile. The northern kingdom was wiped out by the Assyrian Empire, and Judah, the southern kingdom, was defeated and exiled by the Babylonians.

This punishment was not final, however. It was an act of chastisement and discipline, repaying the people for their sins and leading them to repent and call upon God. God sent them away from their home in the land, but he would not abandon them. God "did not choose the nation for the sake of the holy place, but the place for the sake of the nation" (2 Macc. 5:19), and loss of the land does not mean the destruction of Abraham's family or God's promises to be their God and bring blessing for the world through them. Further, God made a covenant with David promising to build David a "house," a dynasty, and that God's people would always be ruled by one from David's line (2 Sam. 7:7–16). God would chastise the nation and call them to repentance, but he would not let them be destroyed entirely or abandon them. The exile and the punishment of the many would atone for the nation's sins, purifying it of its "filth" (Isa. 4:4; cf. 1:25; 48:10). The remnant that survived Babylon's takeover, having been purified, would be pure: "The iniquity of Israel shall be sought, and there shall be none; and the sins of Judah, and none shall be found; for I will pardon the remnant that I have spared" (Jer. 50:20). Scattered abroad in exile, they would turn to God again in confession, prayer, and faithfulness. "In the land of their exile they shall have a change of heart" (Bar. 2:30 NABRE). They would remember and turn to the Lord, and God would remember his covenant with Abraham and bring the exiles home (Lev. 26:40–45; Deut. 30:1–5).

God does just that. Cyrus, ruler of the Medo-Persian Empire, defeats Babylon and allows exiled peoples, including the former inhabitants of Judah, to return and rebuild their nations as provinces under his empire (2 Chron. 36:22–23; Isa. 45:1–7, 12–13; Ezra 1:1–4). As the books of Ezra and Nehemiah narrate, the province of Judah, or "Yehud," is reconstituted under Zerubbabel, a descendant of David (2 Chron. 36:19). The temple is rebuilt around 515 BC, close to seventy years after Jerusalem was conquered (587 BC), as Jeremiah had predicted (Jer. 25:11–12; 29:10).

In one sense, this narrative would suggest that Israel's time of punishment and penance is over. Sin was the problem of exile, and if the exile has ended, that should imply that their sin has been dealt with. However, the people's duty to live in renewed friendship and faithfulness toward God remains. The remnant must "maintain justice, and do what is right" (Isa. 56:1) and "hold fast my covenant" (Isa. 56:4; cf. 48:17–18). But the human proclivity to sin remains in them. When Ezra, the priest and scribe, comes with a group of returnees to the land, he is shocked to find infidelity and impurity among the priests and others who, supposedly, had returned in repentance. He tears his clothes in lamentation and confesses that, while God had punished the nation's sins, God has not punished nearly so much as is deserved (Ezra 8:3–5, 13–15). The prophet Haggai, likewise, speaks of the returnees not repenting when God rebuked them during the rebuilding of the temple (Hag. 2:17). The people continue to return God's love poorly (Mal. 1:6).

The pious feel the ongoing problem of sin on an individual level, as they seek to respond rightly to God with repentance. It is felt also on a national level, as many see the blessings they hoped for not yet fulfilled—or at least not completely fulfilled. They are home, but they are still geopolitically subjugated (Neh. 9:36). Even after the temple was rebuilt, the province of Judah was still under the thumb of the Persian Empire, then under the rule of Greeks and Syrians—persecuted quite heavily by Antiochus IV Epiphanes, who tried to enforce pagan practices in an effort to assimilate the Jews (see 1 Macc. 1:1–61)—and then, after a brief period of independence, under Roman rule as the province of "Judea." For many, this suggested that they were still receiving divine rebukes as a nation and that even after the return they were still, in a way, in exile and in need of purification and forgiveness.[1] The people did not think that God had forgiven nothing; the very fact that they had been returned from exile, they confess, is owed to God's great mercy and kindness (Dan. 9:18). But, as 2 Maccabees 8:29 has it, they did not feel that God had been "*wholly* reconciled with his servants" (italics added).

The problem of sin remains among the people, and their political situation reminds them of this problem and of the need to repent and call out to God for mercy. The people are, thus, exhorted again to remember the Lord and to turn to him in renewed faithfulness. If the nation can have hope that God will never abandon them because of his promises to Abraham, then restoration

---

1. See, broadly, N. T. Wright, *The New Testament and the People of God* (Minneapolis: Fortress, 1992), esp. 268–79, 299–301. For a single book that engages Wright's thesis with appreciation and criticism, see James M. Scott, ed., *Exile: A Conversation with N. T. Wright* (Downers Grove, IL: IVP Academic, 2017).

to the land and the blessings of the Sinai covenant require confession and repentance.[2] Pious individuals, too, feel a need for continued repentance in relation to their personal sins as well as a need to participate in the repentance of the whole nation. Postexilic texts, thus, point readers to hope in God's sure mercy and call them to respond to God with humble repentance. Naturally, this includes many acts that express humility, obedience, contrition, and a desire to amend one's behavior (or the nation's behavior) in friendship with God. Repentant obedience can include temporary matters like rebuilding the temple (Hag. 1:9–11) or, generally, acting justly toward one's neighbors (Zech. 8:14–17). Likewise, especially when the distinctive identity and beliefs of Israel are threatened, we find emphasis on faithfulness to purity laws and resisting idolatry (e.g., Tob. 1:10–11; Jdt. 12:2, 7; Esther 14:15–19; 2 Macc. 6:18–20; Dan. 1:8–16; 3:1–18). Among these, the texts also highlight hopeful *confession*, *fasting*, and *almsgiving* among other acts of penance and obedience. We may look at a few examples of each.

Confession and Doxologies of Judgment

In Ezekiel, early during the events of the exile, God said that the remnant must turn from their sin, loathing their former sins and knowing God's justice (Ezek. 6:8–10). The wicked among them must "forsake their way" and "return to the LORD, that he may have mercy on them" (Isa. 55:7). And the righteous must continue to turn to God in faithfulness and praise.

The piety encouraged in this period, therefore, promotes praise of God and confession of sin, often both at once. We see this at both a national and an individual level. In the book of Nehemiah, the returnees renew their covenant with God. Ezra and the Levites read and explain the law to the people in a public forum, celebrate the Feast of Booths, and prepare to recommit themselves to the law of Moses.[3] They don sackcloth and ashes as gestures of penitence (Neh. 9:1), and, with the Levites leading them, they praise God with a public confession. They laud God's blessings in his election of Israel as well as his patience in not abandoning them when they erred (Neh. 9:5–25). But, they acknowledge, they rebelled still more greatly despite God's patient

---

2. See Richard J. Bautch, *Glory and Power, Ritual and Relationship: The Sinai Covenant in the Postexilic Period*, LHBOTS 471 (London: T&T Clark, 2009), here esp. 71–74.

3. Notably, when the people hear the law, they begin to weep (Neh. 8:9), presumably out of "remorse for failure adequately to observe the demands of the Law" (H. G. M. Williamson, *Ezra, Nehemiah*, WBC 16 [Nashville: Nelson, 1985], 291).

rebukes, ultimately being exiled for their infidelity. Now returned from exile by God's mercy, the remnant praises God's righteousness in his punishments: "In all that has come upon us you have been just, for you kept faith while we have done evil" (Neh. 9:33 NABRE). They praise God for being just and faithful to his promises to punish and not to abandon. In renewing the covenant, they put their trust in God's ongoing faithfulness and recommit themselves to obedience and fidelity.

We can see the same kind of piety embodied in the figures of Esther and Daniel as they pray for the people in exile. Esther afflicts her body and covers herself with ashes as she asks God's deliverance for the Jews in Persia (Esther 14:2). Esther does not confess any personal sin and indeed appeals to her own faithfulness and her distaste for her position as queen of a pagan nation in asking God to hear her prayer (Esther 14:15–19). But regardless of her own deeds, before asking for deliverance, she quickly acknowledges the justice of her situation: "And now we have sinned before you, and you have handed us over to our enemies because we glorified their gods. You are righteous, O Lord!" (Esther 14:6–7).[4] Clothed in sackcloth (Dan. 9:3), Daniel prays similarly in Babylon: "The LORD our God is right in all that he has done; for we have disobeyed his voice" (Dan. 9:14). He throws the whole nation upon God's mercy: "We do not present our supplication before you on the ground of our righteousness, but on the ground of your great mercies" (Dan. 9:18).

Praising God for the justice of God's punishment is often called a "doxology of judgment."[5] It is a kind of confession and an expression of humility. To persist in sin despite God's rebukes is a way of insisting, proudly, that what has gone wrong is God's fault, that God is the one who needs to change. Says God to Job, "Will you condemn me that you may be justified?" (Job 40:8). But to praise God's rebukes as just is to acknowledge one's own injustice as the

---

4. This prayer is part of the longer version of Esther known from ancient Greek texts and received as canonical in Catholicism and Orthodoxy. In most English Bibles that include them, the additions are marked by different chapter numbers, counting up from ten (which is the number of chapters in the Hebrew edition), as in the NRSV above. The NABRE marks the additions as lettered chapters, and some Bibles put them within the chapter and verse of the Hebrew version next to which they stand in the narrative and add a new letter for every added verse. For historical and text-critical reasons, there is unfortunately little consistency. The words above are versified differently in the NABRE (C:17–18), the Rahlfs-Hanhart Septuagint (4:17n), and the ESVCE (4:17r–s), and the *Nova Vulgata* has Esther's prayer starting at 4:17q but with a different version of Esther's words.

5. Also, e.g., Ezra 9:15; Pr. Azar. 4 [= Dan. 3:27]; Bar. 1:15; 2:6. More expansively, see the theological and liturgical emphasis on "doxological contrition" in Khaled Anatolios, *Deification through the Cross: An Eastern Christian Theology of Salvation* (Grand Rapids: Eerdmans, 2020).

reason for those good rebukes, to condemn oneself in the court of one's own heart and to thank God for intervening to call one back from sin. "I know, O LORD, that your judgments are right, and that in faithfulness you have humbled me" (Ps. 119:75). Such doxologies are also acts of *hope*. One who confesses and praises God's justice to punish sin also, implicitly, is professing hope in a God who will be merciful and rewarding to those who repent. If God rebukes because he desires repentance and life for his creatures, then praising God's rebukes for one's sin means also having confidence that God will forgive the penitent and guide them on the path of life.

As in the case of Esther, who was not herself guilty of the stubborn idolatry that caused the exile, doxologies of judgment do not always have to relate to specific personal sin. But they embody the humility that should characterize the faithful as they endure trials and turn to God for deliverance, whether the trials are a punishment for one's personal sin or not. If calamities can function as tests for the righteous as well as rebukes for the wicked, then the pious response in both cases is to submit to God in faith and hope. Suffering a personal calamity, Tobit embodies this kind of response. Exiled in Assyria, Tobit has suffered mockery and shame for his piety, and now he has suddenly become blind. He responds by confessing God's just rebukes against the nation and against any sins he himself has committed.

> You are righteous, Lord,
>   and all your deeds are just;
> All your ways are mercy and fidelity;
>   you are judge of the world.
> And now, Lord, be mindful of me
>   and look with favor upon me.
> Do not punish me for my sins,
>   or for my inadvertent offenses,
>   or for those of my ancestors.
> They sinned against you,
>   and disobeyed your commandments.
> So you handed us over to plunder, captivity, and death,
>   to become an object lesson, a byword, and a reproach
>   in all the nations among whom you scattered us.
> Yes, your many judgments are right
>   in dealing with me as my sins,
>   and those of my ancestors, deserve. (Tob. 3:2–5 NABRE)

Tobit is presented as a model of faithfulness in the text, as one who suffers for his righteousness and whose piety is now being tested (as we learn later: Tob. 12:13–14), not dissimilar to Job. Like Job, Tobit laments his life and prays for death (Tob. 3:6). Unlike Job, he holds God to be righteous over against Israel and even against himself, even for unintentional sins.[6] Tobit is a model of the penitent piety encouraged in the exilic and postexilic periods. As a later Jewish text summarizes it, "The righteous remember the Lord always, confessing and acknowledging the righteousness of the Lord's judgments. A righteous person will not make light when he is disciplined by the Lord. . . . The righteous falls and acknowledges the Lord as righteous; he falls and looks to see where his salvation will come from."[7] All are sinners, whether gravely or inadvertently. But among sinners, the righteous are those who acknowledge God's justice and, with penitent humility, seek his mercy. They submit themselves—their past sins and their future fate—to their righteous and forgiving God.[8]

Fasting and Humility

Along with confession, the people approach God by "humbling themselves" with fasting. In many of our texts, this is coupled with prayer and petition, especially in times of distress as a sign of penance (1 Macc. 2:14; 2 Macc. 3:13–23). Communal fasts are proclaimed in times of penitence or solemn prayer (Ezra 7:21–23; Neh. 9:1; Esther 4:16) and also in preparation for battle (1 Macc. 3:47; 2 Macc. 10:25–26). Nehemiah fasts when lamenting Jerusalem's breached wall (Neh. 1:4). Daniel fasts as he confesses Israel's sins and pleads for mercy (Dan. 9:3). When Judith's community is under threat, they "humble themselves" by donning sackcloth and fasting (Jdt. 4:9–13). Esther's bodily mortification is similar, and she also replaces her regal garments with those of mourning and sorrow (Esther 14:1–12). Such alteration of dress—such as rending one's garments or wearing sackcloth—is a gesture of self-denial and humility, putting off what might suggest pride (such as showy, regal garments) and lowering oneself in an appeal to be exalted by God.

6. Parallels and differences between Tobit and Job are numerous. For a recent consideration of some, see JiSeong James Kwon, "Meaning and Context in Job and Tobit," *JSOT* 43 (2019): 627–43.

7. *Psalms of Solomon* 3.3–5 (my translation).

8. See the survey of the *Psalms of Solomon* and other texts in Mikael Winninge, *Sinners and the Righteous: A Comparative Study of the Psalms of Solomon and Paul's Letters*, ConBNT 26 (Stockholm: Almqvist & Wiksell, 1995).

But fasting is not only a pious response to calamity. It is a salutary practice of the faithful's regular life of faithfulness and prayer.[9] Judith's regular fasting and prayer, for instance, are noted as a part of her exemplary piety (Jdt. 8:6; 9:1). Indeed, in the New Testament, we see that regular fasting is a pious Jewish practice continued, after the crucifixion, by Jesus's apostles and followers (cf. Luke 2:37; 18:12; Acts 13:2; 2 Cor. 6:5; 11:27). As the angel tells Tobit and his son, Tobiah ("Tobias" in Greek and Latin), "Prayer with fasting is good" (Tob. 12:8). Of course, fasting as a sign of repentance must be a sign of actual repentance. As Jesus will emphasize, it is a sign for God and should not be done to impress others (Matt. 6:16–18). Likewise, if one fasts but still willfully pursues wickedness, the value of this self-humbling is nullified (Sir. 34:31). Nonetheless, Jesus says that earnest fasting, like almsgiving, stores up "treasure" in heaven that God will "repay" (Matt. 6:18, 20).

Considering the act of fasting and its associations can help one understand its value. Associated with major feasts and liturgical fasts in the Jewish calendar (cf. Lev. 23:27; Zech. 7:5), fasting sets apart particular times or seasons for prayer and penitence. Associated with occasions of mourning (e.g., 1 Sam. 31:13; 2 Sam. 1:12), particularly when it is accompanied by ashes, fasting is a humble self-reminder of one's own mortality. As a gesture combined with prayer, it is an act of humility before the immortal creator. It also bears psychological value to help one's life of repentance and faith. Temporary self-deprivation reminds us that it is not first our own hands and pantries that sustain us, but the power and mercy of God, and such intentional reminders of God's power can "nourish" prayer in that way.[10] Fasting also points us to repentance, since remembering one's death and coming judgment can deter one from sinning (Sir. 7:36). Likewise, fasting exercises one's will and puts bodily desires into subjugation, so it is an ascetic mode of training in faithfulness. Noncanonical texts point to fasting, in this way, as freeing one from slavery to unhealthy desire or envy and as a means to "pursue self-control and purity with patience."[11] Exercising one's will to deprive oneself of good things, like food, prepares one to be able to resist giving into our desires when they tempt us to evil. Fasting, therefore, is upheld by many in

9. John Muddiman says that the practice saw a "marked increase" in the postexilic period ("Fast, Fasting," *ABD* 2:773–76, at 774). Regular fasting can be seen in various sects but also among nonsectarian Jews, such that Romans could stereotype Jews by the practice (e.g., Suetonius, *Claudius* 76).
10. Tertullian, *On Penitence* 9.
11. *Testament of Joseph* 10.2 (trans. in *OTP* 1:821); cf. *Testament of Simeon* 3.2–3.

the postexilic period not merely as a proper response to God's discipline after sinning—though it is that—but also as a mode of self-discipline and training in godliness.

Almsgiving and Charity

We mentioned the worth ascribed to almsgiving in Scripture in the previous chapter. The money one gives to the poor honors their creator (Prov. 14:31). And this kindness, though it might seem a waste to give to a human who cannot repay, is in fact a loan to God that God will repay (Prov. 19:17). To give alms away on earth is to store up "treasure" in heaven (Sir. 29:12; Matt. 6:18–20). Almsgiving is also upheld as a sacrifice that covers sins (e.g., Sir. 3:30; 35:3–4; Dan. 4:27). We also see a paragon of almsgiving in the figure of Tobit. Tobit is presented as a man who "walked in the ways of truth and righteousness," marked not only by his pilgrimages to Jerusalem or by keeping the food laws, but especially by his various "acts of charity" (Tob. 1:3). He gives cash and other goods above his regular tithe in support of priests and Levites, widows, orphans, and converts (Tob. 1:6–8). He also fasts and gives his food to the hungry, invites the poor to share with him when he feasts, and gives clothes to the naked (Tob. 1:17; 2:2). He also cares for those who cannot repay him by burying the dead, though he suffers for it (Tob. 1:17–20; 2:4).

Indeed, the book of Tobit not only provides an example of steadfast almsgiving but strongly promotes the value of almsgiving as an act of piety.[12] We hear it from three voices in the narrative. The narrator's introduction, summarized above, emphasizes Tobit's deeds of charity. In the book's rising action and in its conclusion, Tobit himself emphasizes it in his exhortations to his son, Tobiah, and to his eventual daughter-in-law. He calls Tobiah to honor his parents and honor the dead with burial and offerings (Tob. 4:3–4, 17; cf. 6:15; 14:10–13), to avoid fornication and debauchery, and to practice self-discipline (Tob. 4:12–15). But he particularly emphasizes the value of alms: give proportionately of your wealth, food, and clothing to the needy (Tob. 4:7–8, 16). This

12. We do not have space to recapitulate the entire narrative here about Tobiah, Sarah, and Raphael. But readers will note that one burden of the book is to answer the question of Tobit's wife in Tob. 2:14, when she implies that his suffering proves that his charity and almsgiving have been for naught. The dramatic irony revealed to the reader is that his acts of kindness are recorded in heaven (Tob. 12:12–14), and God has dispatched the angel to lead Tobiah on a journey that will result in wealth and healing for Tobit as well as deliverance for another pious sufferer, Sarah.

Works of Mercy: Corporal and Spiritual

Tobit's acts of mercy and care for others' bodies and lives match nicely the "corporal" works of mercy enumerated in Catholic tradition, alongside acts of mercy and care for others' spiritual well-being. As in Tobit, the Church emphasizes almsgiving as a "chief" act of love for one's neighbor.

> The *works of mercy* are charitable actions by which we come to the aid of our neighbor in his spiritual and bodily necessities. Instructing, advising, consoling, comforting are spiritual works of mercy, as are forgiving and bearing wrongs patiently. The corporal works of mercy consist especially in feeding the hungry, sheltering the homeless, clothing the naked, visiting the sick and imprisoned, and burying the dead. Among all these, giving alms to the poor is one of the chief witnesses to fraternal charity: it is also a work of justice pleasing to God.[a]

a. CCC 2447.

is a worthy "offering" in God's sight, a deposit in one's heavenly "treasury" against future trials (Tob. 4:9–11), for God will be merciful and kind to those who have shown mercy and kindness (Tob. 14:9–11). A heavenly character, the angel Raphael, also confirms the value of almsgiving: "Do good and evil will not overtake you. Prayer with fasting is good, but better than both is almsgiving with righteousness. A little with righteousness is better than wealth with wrongdoing. It is better to give alms than to lay up gold. For almsgiving saves from death and purges away every sin" (Tob. 12:7–9).

Almsgiving is not the only mark of Tobit's piety, of course. It is intimately connected with obedience to other divine commands, with prayer, and with fasting. Nor does almsgiving "purge sin" or store up heavenly "treasure" automatically without faithfulness to other commandments. It is "almsgiving *with righteousness*"—not without it—that the angel commends (Tob. 12:8; italics added). But it is a characteristic practice of the righteous (Pss. 37:21; 112:9; Prov. 21:26; Sir. 29:1). Indeed, almsgiving, as an act of love for God and neighbor, embodies the theological virtues. Almsgiving is an act of *faith*, *hope*, and *love*. It takes faith in God to submit oneself and one's resources to God's command to care for the poor. And giving to support their life and well-being is an act of faith in the creator who gives them life.[13] It takes hope in God's promised reward to give away resources that one could use to secure one's own well-being. Faithful almsgiving is also an expression of love, giving of oneself for the neighbor's sake and for the sake of God. Further, like fasting, almsgiving has psychological effects to reinforce our own wills to abstain from selfishness and material desire and to act intentionally for the good of our neighbor. With fasting and prayer, it is a medicine that fortifies sin-sick souls and trains one's mind and will in godliness, constituting "a way of life accommodated to the divine commandments."[14] As Jesus says, it stores up "treasure in heaven" (Luke 12:33).

Awaiting the Messiah

The exilic and postexilic periods were marked by explicit repentance and confession as the people submitted themselves to their faithful God. The survivors of exile were, according to the prophets, recipients of a great mercy from the God who would not abandon or utterly destroy Israel. And the pious lived in gratitude for that, praising God's just punishments and merciful forgiveness and committing themselves to humble acts of penance and obedience. "If you, O LORD, should mark iniquities, Lord, who could stand? But there is forgiveness with you, so that you may be revered" (Ps. 130:3–4).

As noted above, however, humble repentance was not merely reverence offered in thanks for salvation received. It was also an expression of hope in salvation yet to come. The problem of sin remained in God's people, as did the consequences of sin stipulated for the nation in the Sinai covenant. God's promises of deliverance and renewal were in process but, it seemed to many, not yet complete. As we conclude this chapter and prepare to transition to the New Testament, we may highlight some hopes for restoration and divine mercy that point us ahead to the coming of Christ.

Repentance and the Coming Judgment

God called for repentance before the exile from backsliders, during the exile from the chastened remnant, and after the exile from the returnees.

13. This and much more is underscored excellently in Gary A. Anderson, *Charity: The Place of the Poor in the Biblical Tradition* (New Haven: Yale University Press, 2013).
14. Augustine, *True Religion* 7.13 (in *On Christian Belief*, trans. Hill, 38).

God's wisdom calls all to draw closer to God, and that means turning from sin, heeding discipline, and humbling oneself. The "righteous" and "wise" are not without faults. But they respond to their fallenness with repentance, seeking God and casting themselves upon his mercy. The righteous who respond rightly will experience blessing and divine reward.

However, this promise to the penitent seemed to be contradicted by human experience: the righteous often do not appear to be blessed more than the wicked. In fact, many suffer *for* doing what is right or are overpowered by the wicked. And many who spend their lives rejecting God appear not to receive their just deserts in this life. Babylon, Persia, and Rome ruled over Judah, and even if Judah sinned by breaking God's commands, these empires' power was hardly a reward for their righteousness. The wicked ultimately receive the penalty of death, true, but so do the righteous. Ecclesiastes laments that, while wisdom and justice are certainly better than folly or wickedness, ultimately everyone dies (Eccles. 2:12–23; 7:15–17; 9:1–3). Job points to this problem as an impediment for suffering patiently: "If a man were to die, and live again, all the days of my drudgery I would wait for my relief to come" (Job 14:14 NABRE). That is, if the dead are raised, then he would bear his test from God all his days without complaint, hoping for reward in the next life. But if the dead are not raised, then why pursue righteousness when it hurts if it may not turn to a blessing before this life ends? Of course, there are interior blessings that faithful endurance works in us (Rom. 5:3–4), but the desire for suffering to be rewarded, even with earthly blessing and resurrection, is hardly unenlightened selfishness. In the New Testament, the apostle Paul agrees: "If for this life only we have hoped in Christ, we are of all people most to be pitied. . . . If the dead are not raised, 'Let us eat and drink, for tomorrow we die'" (1 Cor. 15:19, 32).

The message that Paul proclaims—that Christ has been raised to eternal life and so too will those in Christ—is anticipated already in the Old Testament. As people experienced the real suffering of the righteous *and* retained their conviction that God rewards good and punishes evil, many explained the tension by insisting that judgment was delayed. It could be delayed in this life, as it takes time for the consequences of one's actions to work themselves out (cf. Job 20; Ps. 73). Babylon was finally defeated by Persia, and many whose wickedness seems blessed come to ruin eventually. But reward could be delayed until one's experience of death, with degrees of blessedness and torment in the condition of one's soul (cf. Sir. 11:26; Luke 16:22–23). Beyond this, some grew to hope for resurrection to eternal life in new bodies: "Many of those who sleep in the dust of the earth shall awake, some to everlasting life, and some to shame and everlasting contempt" (Dan. 12:2). Indeed, those who follow God will "shine" and be like the eternal stars (Dan. 12:3). A life of repentance may end in squalor, persecution, or martyrdom. But that is not the final end, not for soul or, indeed, for body. The Wisdom of Solomon speaks of a righteous one who was persecuted and whose death was plotted and carried out by enemies. Though the wicked seemed victorious, they will have no consolation on God's day of judgment, "when their sins are reckoned up" (Wis. 4:20; cf. 3:18; Sir. 18:24). But the righteous who died are at peace and hope for a new life, resurrected to incorruptibility beyond the pain of mortal decay.

> In the eyes of the foolish they seemed to have died,
> and their departure was thought to be a disaster, . . .
> but they are at peace.
> For though in the sight of others they were punished,
> their hope is full of immortality.
> Having been disciplined a little, they will receive great good,
> because God tested them and found them worthy of himself;
> like gold in the furnace he tried them,
> and like a sacrificial burnt offering he accepted them.
> In the time of their visitation they will shine forth,
> and will run like sparks through the stubble. (Wis. 3:2–7)

This hope in judgment and resurrection is an expression of confidence in *God's justice and mercy*, that God absolutely will not let evil go unpunished or leave those who cling to him without blessing. He knows and records every tear shed in suffering (Ps. 56:8), every secret sin and act of love. God's justice does not sleep. God will bring to light every deed and every intention, and he will repay all at the judgment.

Belief in resurrection is also a hope for a *reversal of the effects of humanity's fall into sin*. The dust of Adam's family decays and dies. Ashes to ashes. But, with God, death is not the end of one's story, nor is it irreversible. In God's hands, ashes rise. If in Ezekiel's vision God's raising of the dead is an image for the national restoration of exiled and "dead" Israel (Ezek. 37:1–14), the same power of God extends to the resurrection of individual human beings. This is, as 2 Maccabees 12:45 says, a "holy and pious" belief. It is a belief that motivates prayer and almsgiving in honor of the dead, praying that their sins might be forgiven before the day of judgment and resurrection (2 Macc. 12:38–46; cf. Tob. 4:17). Centrally, it is a belief that motivates the faithful to endure even under torture and persecution, as when seven brothers are martyred for refusing the enforced paganism of Antiochus IV Epiphanes. One brother gladly offers his hands and tongue to be cut out, confident that God will give him new ones in the resurrection: "I got these from Heaven, and because of his laws I disdain them, and from him I hope to get them back again" (2 Macc. 7:11; cf. 7:9, 14, 23, 29).[15] Sin's effects will one day be reversed. God's judgment will set all things right, on the day when he will not merely record every tear but wipe them away, the day that God will "swallow up death forever" (Isa. 25:8).

Righteous Suffering and Reconciliation

Righteous suffering and confidence in God's reward pointed not only to a hope in life after death and in the ultimate reversal of the consequences of Adam's fall; they also pointed to the *value* of justice and penance in sacrifice for others. As in the quotation from Wisdom 3:6 above, righteous martyrs could themselves be described as sacrificial "offerings" accepted by the Lord. Prayer and praise, almsgiving, contrition, and obedience could be thought of in terms of sacrifice (cf. Pss. 40:6–8; 50:14; 51:17; Sir. 35:1–5). They are pleasing and acceptable to God when done in true faith, both as regular practices and as vows made in confession. Rather than pridefully rail against God or seek their own glory or preservation, the righteous respond to suffering and sin by turning toward God in humility and patience, bearing up under trials and submitting to God in hope of mercy. Such faithful acts are received as holy offerings that work to the benefit of the one offering them. But sacrifices could also benefit others. And in several texts, we see innocents accept suffering and even martyrdom in hope that their self-sacrifice will avail for the good of others, as appeals for God's forgiveness for the nation.

Isaiah's oracles about the Suffering Servant depict one who is himself innocent yet suffers with others because he is one of them. He commits himself to God, not fighting back when harmed but trusting that God will vindicate him on the other side of his suffering (Isa. 49:4; 50:4–9). Although others—even

---

15. The brothers also profess confidently that God will punish Antiochus (2 Macc. 7:14, 17, 19, 31, 34–36).

his own people—thought him afflicted and punished by God, he was in fact suffering for their sins, not his own. In his willing obedience to the path laid before him, his life itself became an offering that has the capability of bringing forgiveness to others and restoring them to righteousness (Isa. 53:1–12). Because he submitted to this suffering and death, he himself would see "light" and then receive the spoils of victory (Isa. 53:11–12).[16]

The Suffering Servant in Isaiah, from the perspective of the New Testament, points ahead to the perfectly innocent suffering and sacrificial death of Christ, though the passage itself leaves questions as to whether it is a vision of the prophet, a king, or someone else (Acts 8:30–35; cf. Luke 22:37; Rom. 4:25; 1 Pet. 2:22–24). But we should note that a belief that innocent suffering, accepted in piety and humility, can have value as an intercessory offering for others is not limited only to the Suffering Servant. Others see their own suffering and piety in the same light. In Daniel, when the three young men are cast into the furnace for their piety, they respond with confession for their people's sins and with a similar hope in God. In the fiery furnace, they praise God and acknowledge God's justice in causing the exile (Pr. Azar. 3–15 [= Dan. 3:26–38]).[17] Having no burnt offerings or goats to bring forth, they ask that they *themselves* would be received as an acceptable offering that might avail for the nation (Pr. Azar. 16–17 [= Dan. 3:39–40]). Likewise, when the seven brothers mentioned above are tortured and martyred for refusing to obey Antiochus IV Epiphanes, judgment and resurrection are not the only beliefs in which they profess hope. They also express a confidence that their self-sacrifice will fill up what is lacking in God's punishment for Israel. The Jews are being persecuted as a continued rebuke for their sin, even after the return, says one brother (2 Macc. 7:18). But God's wrath, as the nation experiences it, is only a temporary discipline: "And if our living Lord is angry for a little while, to rebuke and discipline us, he will again be reconciled with his own servants" (2 Macc. 7:33). There is an ongoing problem of sin in the people that the brothers believe is blocking the fullness of God's blessing, so that God is not yet *completely* "reconciled"

16. The prophet Micah speaks similarly in the voice of the righteous who will suffer exile, saying that he will "bear the indignation of the LORD" until, afterward, God vindicates him and brings him into the "light" (Mic. 7:9).
17. In many Bibles, this material is labeled as the "Prayer of Azariah," either printed separately from the book of Daniel or, in some Catholic editions, printed in its place in the narrative in Dan. 3. In others (e.g., NABRE), the material is numbered as verses of Dan. 3 without the separate label.

with Israel (2 Macc. 1:5; 8:29). So they endure their suffering willingly not just out of obedience but also as a prayer "appealing to God to show mercy soon to our nation" (2 Macc. 7:37). There is a greater forgiveness for which they still hope, one they expect will come through the atoning value of innocent suffering.

Forgiveness, the Spirit, and the New Covenant

The ongoing problem of sin points also to the need for God's promise of the New Covenant. In some of the prophetic books, God promises a covenant after the exile, a "covenant of peace" by which God will again dwell with the people (Ezek. 34:25–26). One might expect this solely to point to the renewal of the Sinai covenant by the returnees. But Jeremiah, the only prophet to speak explicitly of a "new covenant," contrasts the "new" with the old. "I will make a new covenant with the house of Israel and the house of Judah. It will not be like the covenant that I made with their ancestors when I took them by the hand to bring them out of the land of Egypt—a covenant that they broke" (Jer. 31:31–32). Rather, in the New Covenant,

> I will put my law within them, and I will write it on their hearts; and I will be their God, and they shall be my people. No longer shall they teach one another, or say to each other, "Know the LORD," for they shall all know me, from the least of them to the greatest, says the LORD; for I will forgive their iniquity, and remember their sin no more. (Jer. 31:33–34)

The New Covenant will bear major continuity with the Old Covenant. As we have seen, since God's calling of Abraham through Sinai and afterward, the covenant has been a uniting of God and his people: he will be their God, and they will be his people (Gen. 17:7–8; Exod. 6:7; Lev. 26:12). The same is promised here. The New Covenant will, likewise, involve God's "law." But the New Covenant will bring forgiveness of sins and, with that, an intimate knowledge of God that makes the people one with him again. The people of the New Covenant will know him and will walk in his ways, because God's law will not merely be a message on stone tablets but will be written on their very *hearts*.

Ezekiel conveys a similar promise. He does not call it a "New Covenant" explicitly (though he does speak of the coming "covenant of peace" mentioned above), but he, too, speaks of it as involving the forgiveness of sins and as bringing the people to an intimate and obedient relationship with God, here by a transformation of the people's hearts.

> I will sprinkle clean water on you, and you shall be clean from all your unclean-nesses, and from all your idols I will cleanse you. And I will give you a new heart, and a new spirit I will put within you. And I will remove the heart of stone from your flesh and give you a heart of flesh. And I will put my Spirit within you, and cause you to walk in my statutes and be careful to obey my rules. (Ezek. 36:25–27 ESV)

Ezekiel's promise lines up with Jeremiah's, with some illuminating differences in description. Rather than speaking of forgiveness, Ezekiel uses the priestly language of purity: God will wash the people clean of their idolatries by water. Rather than speaking of intimate knowledge of God, Ezekiel says that God will put his own spirit—the Holy Spirit—into the people to renew their hearts and bring them to obey his laws with joy (cf. Joel 2:28–32).

In response to the continued problem of sin, some texts present the need for confession and forgiveness in terms of the removal of divine wrath and the restoration of national blessings. This is in keeping with the Sinai covenant, whose terms focus on geopolitical blessings and curses, and it is hardly absent from Ezekiel or Jeremiah (e.g., Ezek. 36:28–30). But here we see the prophets point to an internal aspect of sin that God means to counteract, a hope that God will bring his people to be reconciled to him by being healed of the anti-God desires in their *hearts*. Sin is not only a matter of past misdeeds that block blessing until forgiven. The deeper problem is within, "the intent of our own wicked hearts" (Bar. 1:22). God's work of restoring his people, then, will focus not merely on forgiving past misdeeds but also on mending broken and rebellious hearts and minds. Longing for redemption means longing for this inner renewal as well. David asked not only for forgiveness and cleansing but that God would create a *new heart* in him (Ps. 51:12–13). In one of the poems that make up Psalm 119, the psalmist says that he longs for God's laws (Ps. 119:40) and yet also has to ask God to lead him away from self-interest and to choose obedience to those laws, whose fulfillment is beyond his mere ability without God's aid: "Turn my heart to your decrees, and not to selfish gain" (Ps. 119:36; cf. 141:4). God must not only teach and instruct through stone tablets; he must renew the hearts of his people from within if they are to be truly faithful. "Teach me your way, O LORD, that I may walk in your truth;

give me an undivided heart to revere your name" (Ps. 86:11). The prophets do not promise that the New Covenant will come with no obligations to obey or repent after being forgiven. They promise that God's ways will be written on the people's very hearts, that they will be restored by God's own Spirit, softened to hear God's call, repent of sin, and walk in obedience and friendship with God.

The Shepherd-King Who Comes with Justice

The problem of sin would be dealt with by God himself. God will judge and raise the dead. Before that day, God will forgive and restore those who cling to him by his own Spirit. The prophets also promise that, in bringing salvation, God himself will *come*. Isaiah speaks of the exile's end, with Israel's sins having been atoned, as news of God's own arrival. In the "wilderness" of their exile (Isa. 40:3), God will come to deliver them.

> Go on up to a high mountain,
>   O Zion, herald of good news; . . .
> say to the cities of Judah,
>   "Behold your God!"
> Behold, the Lord GOD comes with might,
>   and his arm rules for him;
> behold, his reward is with him,
>   and his recompense before him.
> He will tend his flock like a shepherd;
>   he will gather the lambs in his arms;
> he will carry them in his bosom,
>   and gently lead those that are with young. (Isa. 40:9–11 ESV)

Elsewhere, Isaiah again envisions God's arrival to save, with watchmen proclaiming the "good news" that the king is coming:

> How beautiful upon the mountains
>   are the feet of the messenger who announces peace,
> who brings good news,
>   who announces salvation,
>   who says to Zion, "Your God reigns."
> Listen! Your sentinels lift up their voices,
>   together they sing for joy;

> for in plain sight they see
> the return of the LORD to Zion. (Isa. 52:7–8)

God is depicted here as a mighty *king* and also as a *shepherd*. These images might seem quite different if one imagines a king only ruling and waging war and shepherds only as nurturing. But in the biblical imagination they are closely paralleled. David appeals to his experience as an actual shepherd as worthy preparation for battle: he would often have to chase off predators in order to care for the sheep (1 Sam. 17:34–36). When David is acclaimed king, it is said that he will "shepherd" God's people (1 Chron. 11:2; cf. Ps. 2:9). A shepherd's job is to nurture and protect, which requires both tenderness and toughness; when there are threats to the flock from within or from without, caring requires combat and correction. A good shepherd's "rod" is a comfort to the sheep, and God, the king of all, shepherds his people with correction and compassion (Ps. 23:4; Sir. 18:13). Thus the leaders of God's people—judges, priests, kings, and others—are often called "shepherds." They are to defend God's flock against enemies, nurture them, and lead them in justice, and they are themselves to seek God in humility and faith as they lead.

But Israel's shepherds failed at these tasks (cf. Isa. 56:11; Jer. 2:8; 25:34–37; Ezek. 34:1–6). The kings' failure was often not a failure to try to protect or secure their kingdom geopolitically; they waged war for land, sought alliances, and worked toward economic prosperity (some with less skill than others). Theirs was a failure to protect the people from *sin*. Kings allowed and introduced idolatrous practices and multiplied injustices among the people. Judges perverted justice for the sake of gain. And false prophets and teachers, rather than rebuking people and directing them in repentance and faith, encouraged presumption and impiety. These problems continue also after the return. "My anger is hot against the shepherds," God says through the later prophet Zechariah (Zech. 10:3).

The solution promised to this crisis is manifold. God promises many new shepherds for the people who will lead them in the right way. "I will give you shepherds after my own heart" (Jer. 3:15; cf. 23:4). At the same time, there is also a promise of a single shepherd. *God himself* will shepherd the people: he will gather them, protect them against attacks, care for them, and judge justly among the sheep of his fold (Ezek. 34:11–17; Jer. 3:10). Yet there will also be one human shepherd over them, the coming Davidic king, in whom God's covenantal bond with the people will be secured. "I will set up over them one shepherd, my servant David, and he shall feed them: he shall feed them and be their shepherd. And I, the LORD, will be their God, and my servant David shall be prince among them; I, the LORD, have spoken" (Ezek. 34:23–24). The king will come out of David's city, Bethlehem, and will "rule" and "feed his flock" with divine power and bring them peace (Mic. 5:2–4). He will rule over all the earth, "from sea to sea" (Zech. 9:10), and will bring peace and justice to all the nations. And the whole world will be drawn to seek his instruction and rest in his peace (cf. Isa. 2:1–5; 9:2–7; 11:1–16).

The shepherd who is coming will be the Lord God, who will deliver his people and direct them in righteousness. The shepherd who is coming will also be a descendant of David, who will rule, save, and bring peace. He will be a ruler, yet "humble" as he arrives (Zech. 9:9). If his coming brings redemption and peace, it will come also with the forgiveness and reconciliation many still hoped for after the return, a hope that involves the suffering of innocent penitents like the Suffering Servant (Isa. 53:5). Inasmuch as this shepherd will defend and lead his people against sin, his work will also be part of the outpouring of God's Spirit and God's ultimate defeat of death, counteracting people's internal inclinations to evil as well as sin's effects on one's body. These elements are not all clearly united in the texts, and the shape of this hope may have been unclear to many who affirmed it. Looking back from the New Testament, however, we can see this hope pointing forward to its fulfillment in the God-man, Jesus Christ. In him, God himself will come to his people, to bring salvation to Israel and call the nations to repentance. He will deliver those captive to the powers of sin and death. He, as the Good Shepherd, will give his life for his flock and inaugurate the New Covenant, bringing forgiveness and renewal for sin-sick hearts through his own Spirit. And this one Shepherd, both Davidic and divine, will appoint many under-shepherds over his people to administer his gifts of forgiveness and renewal in the "ministry of reconciliation" (2 Cor. 5:18).

7

Jesus and the Mission of Restoration

I have come to call not the righteous but sinners to repentance.

—Luke 5:32

God had promised salvation even at the very beginning, at humanity's fall, when he promised that a descendant of Eve would be an enemy of the evil serpent, and that her son (her "offspring") would be struck by the serpent but would crush its head and defeat it (Gen. 3:15). That promise continued down through the family of Abraham, through Isaac and Jacob, through the line of Leah's son Judah and his descendant David. That Savior would be the king, heir of David, through whom God would bless all the families of the earth. In him God's promises would reach their fulfillment: a shepherd-king who would lead his people against evil, the innocent sufferer who would die and rise for the forgiveness of many, one who would call God's people back to him and pour out the Spirit to reshape sinful hearts in the image of God's perfect love.

With this chapter we turn to the pages of the New Testament and the revelation of God's love for sinners in Christ. In the "fullness of time," the Savior came (Gal. 4:4). Sent forth into the world, and humbling himself to assume human form (Phil. 2:5–11), the Son of God came to do battle against sin and free God's people from its dominion. He makes atonement for sin and restores fallen humans to live again as God's sons and daughters (cf. Rom. 5:1–11; 8:12–17; 1 John 2:2). Throughout his earthly ministry, Jesus "confronts the forces of evil."[1] He opposes Satan's temptations and casts out demons. He forgives sin and frees people from guilt, and he calls all to repent and, following him, to be restored to the family of God.

Christ, the Sinless Penitent

The "archetypal image" of each sacrament is to be found in Christ.[2] Christ both consecrates the Eucharist in the upper room and *is* the bread by which the disciples are united to him (cf. Mark 14:22–25; John 6:53–58). Christ was not himself married, yet he is the consummate "bridegroom" of the Church (John 3:29; Eph. 5:22–33). So too with the sacrament of reconciliation. Christ does not himself have sins of which to repent and be forgiven, yet he stands in the place of the penitent. Indeed, he lived as "the perfect penitent," humbling himself before the Father and entrusting himself completely to him.[3] And those who are joined to him come to share in his righteousness.

In the incarnate Christ, as the Letter to the Hebrews insists, God became entirely like his children in order to redeem them (Heb. 2:10–15). He was even able to experience temptation by Satan. Yet he did not sin. He was "in every respect . . . tempted as we are, yet without sin" (Heb. 4:15 ESV; cf. 2 Cor. 5:21; 1 Pet. 2:22; 1 John 3:5). And because he suffered willingly, because he lived in penitence not for his own sins but joining in what was deserved for *others'* sins, he "became the source of eternal salvation for all who obey him," not simply as a victim but as a divine priest making atonement for sin by offering his own life for others (Heb. 5:9). We can highlight Christ's own life of penance in three aspects: his baptism, his fasting and temptation, and his humble obedience.

Jesus's Baptism

Jesus's own submission to baptism is a penitential act. The baptism he received was not of the same character as baptism in the Church after Pentecost,

---

1. Jean-Philippe Revel, *La réconciliation*, Traité des sacrements 5 (Paris: Cerf, 2015), 203; see further 201–6.
2. Adrienne von Speyr, *Confession: The Encounter with Christ in Penance*, trans. A. G. Littledale (New York: Herder & Herder, 1964), 22.
3. Von Speyr, *Confession*, 22–23.

which confers forgiveness and the gift of the Holy Spirit (Acts 2:38–39).[4] He received the baptism of John the Baptist, which was "a baptism of repentance for the forgiveness of sins" (Mark 1:4). John called the people to repent and prepare for the coming of the Messiah and the return of God to his people, and when people came to John for baptism, they confessed their sins (Mark 1:5). John's baptism was a rite of penitence, and Jesus underwent it.

According to Matthew, John questioned why Jesus would submit to his baptism of repentance. John says that *he* should be baptized by Jesus, not the other way around. But Jesus responds that John must baptize Jesus, "for thus it is fitting for us to fulfill all righteousness" (Matt. 3:15 NABRE). Jesus's answer does not emphasize the utter necessity of his baptism, but its *fitting-ness*. It is "fitting" or "proper" to the situation, to the people involved, and to their goals. What is that goal? "To fulfill all righteousness." In Matthew, "righteousness" is regularly related to acts of justice and piety, doing what is right in the sight of God (cf. Matt. 5:20; 6:1). It can also have a broader sense of things *being* right or, when they are wrong, being set right. It is in this way an attribute of the "kingdom of heaven" that Jesus brings, God's reign as king and how things are (and should be) under him, within which people must do acts of righteousness and true piety (Matt. 5:20; cf. 5:10). Those who "hunger and thirst for righteousness" (Matt. 5:6) await God's promised kingdom and their own place in it.[5] Jesus commands his followers to seek "the kingdom of God and his righteousness" before all other things (Matt. 6:33).

Jesus's baptism fills up righteousness in both ways. It is, on the one hand, an act of piety and righteousness: Jesus characterizes John's call to repentance as one of "righteousness" (Matt. 3:2; 21:32), which Jesus here fulfills. When God's call is repentance, the correct response is to humble oneself and sub-mit to the kind of penitence that God commands—here through confession and baptism. It is how one walks on the way of righteousness as opposed to continuing in wickedness. To spurn God's call is to reject God's will. Luke characterizes submission to John's baptism as a pious doxology of judgment:

4. John's baptism did not confer the Spirit, but it does point forward to Christian baptism, especially in the Spirit's descent onto Christ in his baptism, to which baptized Christians are joined (cf. Mark 1:7–8; John 1:33; Acts 1:4–8; 19:1–7). According to an early explanation, Jesus's baptism allows his later crucifixion to sanctify the waters, which, by the work of the Spirit, would have saving power after Pentecost (Ignatius of Antioch, *To the Ephesians* 18.2).

5. W. D. Davies and Dale C. Allison Jr. point to the fulfillment of God's will as promised in Scripture here, so that Jesus's submission to baptism is a righteous act and also brings righteousness in the fulfillment of God's promises (*The Gospel according to Saint Matthew*, 3 vols., ICC [Edinburgh: T&T Clark, 1988–2004], 1:325–27).

sinners "acknowledged the justice of God" by being baptized by John, while those who refused to be baptized "rejected God's purpose for themselves" (Luke 7:29–30). Jesus submits himself to God in humility and in obedience to God's call for Israel to repent, giving his "unrestricted Yes to God's will."[6]

Moreover, by responding rightly to God's rebuke of the nation, Jesus's baptism is also part of God's righteousness and God's kingdom being realized in the world. We have seen in previous chapters that pious people such as Daniel and Esther submitted to God by acknowledging God's justice and confessing their people's sins, even when their own personal sins were not the cause of God's punishment of Israel. We have also seen that, when the righteous submit to God's rebuke and punishment of the wicked, their penitence can have a representative and atoning value for others. The Suffering Servant in Isaiah is innocent, yet he willingly submits to God's punishment for the sinful nation, maintaining his righteousness and humility rather than pridefully refusing to endure it—he offers himself in sacrifice for the people (cf. Isa. 50:4–9; 53:1–12). The seven martyred brothers and Daniel's friends in the fiery furnace, likewise, suffer with a hope that God will accept their suffering in sacrifice for the sins of the nation (2 Macc. 7:33, 37; Pr. Azar. 16–17 [= Dan. 3:39–40]).[7] So too the sinless Jesus identifies himself with sinners, the perfect Son of God standing in the place of God's wayward children. As such his baptism is part of "filling up" the righteousness of the kingdom that will pay the "ransom" price of the world's redemption (Mark 10:45).[8] Jesus's sinless acceptance of what is owed to sinners continues through his crucifixion, where he "ransoms" sinners at the price of his life (Mark 10:45). Here, as the Son, he shows his love for the Father (John 14:31). And in his sinless acceptance of what is owed to sinners, he offers the life of righteous love and obedience that humanity owes to God. "Jesus's submission to baptism is the beginning of this process of filling up all righteousness, which he

---

6. Benedict XVI, *Jesus of Nazareth: From the Baptism in the Jordan to the Transfiguration*, trans. Adrian J. Walker (New York: Doubleday, 2007), 17. Similarly, von Speyr, *Confession*, 36–39.

7. There are also several ways in which Christ, the Father's beloved Son, is depicted as willingly offering himself as a new Isaac, whose willingness to be sacrificed (though he was not, in fact) was understood to atone for Israel's sins (e.g., *Canticles Rabbah* 1.14.1). For an Isaac typology in Jesus's baptism and elsewhere, see Leroy A. Huizenga, *The New Isaac: Tradition and Intertextuality in the Gospel of Matthew*, NovTSup 131 (Leiden: Brill, 2009).

8. Nathan Eubank takes this to be the sense of "fulfilling" (i.e., "filling up" a treasury of righteousness) in Matt. 3:15. See Eubank, *Wages of Cross-Bearing and Debt of Sin: The Economy of Heaven in Matthew's Gospel*, BZNW (Berlin: de Gruyter, 2013), 124–31.

accomplishes through the acts of humility and obedience, especially through the cross."[9]

Jesus's Prayer, Fasting, and Temptation

Jesus's life as the sinless penitent is visible in many other respects as well. Jesus obeys the law of Moses, though at the same time claiming authority over it as its "Lord" and as the authoritative interpreter of the law's intent (cf. Matt. 5:17–48; Mark 2:28; 10:5). Though he does not carry the funds for himself and his band of disciples, he as their leader was apparently accustomed to give alms (John 13:29). He prays frequently (e.g., Luke 6:12; 11:1), and his agony in the garden shows him praying in humble submission to the Father and their shared divine plan (Matt. 26:36–46). Jesus also fasts. He very definitely feasts, and he calls his followers to feast while he is with them (Mark 2:18–20). His life is not one of constant abstinence and fasting like John the Baptist, whose call is primarily to prepare people for Christ in penance (cf. Matt. 11:18–19; Luke 1:14–17). Christ is the bringer of the joy of God's redemption, which the Gospels highlight in his feasting. But he does fast, it appears.[10]

The Gospels emphasize Jesus's fasting at a signal moment at the beginning of his public ministry, in which he does battle with the tempter. After his baptism, and before calling his disciples, Jesus fasts for forty days in the wilderness. Jesus's fast continues the representative penitence we saw in his baptism, and it prepares him also to endure temptations as he disciplines his body. According to Matthew and Luke, the devil brings three principal temptations against Christ to throw him off from fulfilling all righteousness (Matt. 4:1–11; Luke 4:1–13). He pokes at Jesus's power and prerogative as God's Son. "If you are the Son of God," the devil begins, turn some stones into bread so that you can eat! Jump down from the temple and prove it,

9. Isaac Augustine Morales, *The Bible and Baptism: The Fountain of Salvation*, CBTS (Grand Rapids: Baker Academic, 2022), 84.
10. Jesus's temptation is the only explicit depiction of him "fasting" (Greek *nēsteuō*). Did he fast otherwise? Jesus is presented as obedient to the Torah and as making regular pilgrimages to observe prescribed feasts (John 2:23; 5:1; 7:14; 10:22–23; 12:12); one assumes that he would have kept the "great fast" required at Yom Kippur (Lev. 23:26–32). Jesus commends voluntary fasting in secret (Matt. 6:16–18; cf. Mark 2:18–20), though it is possible to overread the "secrecy" element. Jesus's commendation of secret fasting no more contradicts communal fasting (when everyone would know everyone else was fasting) than his call to pray in secret (Matt. 6:6) contradicts his own practice of praying in a synagogue or aloud in public (cf. Matt. 19:13; Luke 11:1; John 11:41–42).

The Temptations of the New Adam

Many Church Fathers see in Christ's temptations a reversal of the temptations of Adam and Eve, who were tempted by the tree's appeal to their fleshly desire (taste), the longing of their eyes (covetousness), and their pride (wanting to become like God apart from God), the three temptations of the world mentioned in 1 John 2:16–17. Compare, for instance, Gregory the Great:

> If we look at the progress of his [Christ's] temptation, we see how great the struggle was that set us free from temptation. Our ancient enemy rose up against the first human being, our ancestor, in three temptations. He tempted him by gluttony, by vain glory, and by avarice. And he overcame him when he tempted him. . . . But the means by which he overcame the first man were the same ones which caused him to yield when he tempted the second.[a]

a. Gregory the Great, *Gospel Homily* 14 (trans. Hurst, 102–3).

since a psalm says that angels will catch and protect God's faithful! The devil tempts Jesus to prioritize the natural goods of food and protection over the plan of salvation. He also tempts him with glory and power: bow to me and I will give you all the kingdoms of the earth!

Food and protection from the Father are not bad desires in themselves. And Jesus, as the divine Son and Davidic king, is to be ruler and judge of all creation (John 5:22, 27; Matt. 25:31–46; Rom. 2:16; 2 Cor. 5:10). But all righteousness is fulfilled in the Son's submission to the plan of salvation through self-giving and humility. The devil tempts Christ to take these good things for himself, to take glory without suffering, to rule without serving. He wants him to be like Adam, who fell to the allure of the tree and its taste and the divine independence he thought it promised. But Jesus rebuffs the devil at every point. He quotes Moses's words about what Israel should have learned in another wilderness experience, as God fed them and sustained them throughout their forty-year journey: "One does not live by bread alone, but by every word that comes from the mouth of God" (Matt. 4:4; cf. Deut. 8:3; Luke 4:4). Jesus, who raises the dead, surely could turn stones into bread to feed himself. The devil's "if you are the Son of God" tempts him to do just that in the name of his relationship to the Father. But to break his fast in this way would be a violation of his unity with and his submissive dependence toward God the Father, who gives him everything through their unity in love (John 3:35; 5:19–23; 13:3; 17:2). God, Jesus responds, is not to be "tested" but is to be worshiped with devotion and obedience (Matt. 4:7, 10; Luke 4:8, 12), especially by those who are being tempted as Jesus is now.

Jesus's Humble Obedience

Jesus's fasting highlights the role of discipline in the fight against temptation. Fasting from food is a discipline that trains one to deny even good desires that might make us resist surrendering completely to God's good will. If it is true for the sinless Jesus, it is all the more true—and in more ways—for us.

But Jesus's fasting also gives us a kind of image of all the rest of his sufferings. Fasting, as opposed to simple hunger, is self-chosen or at least is willingly accepted in love for God and in self-denial, for the good of oneself or joined with prayer for others. This is the character of *all* Jesus's suffering. It is not utterly necessary that Jesus be baptized, but he chooses it as a "fitting" expression of submission to God as he stands in the place of sinners. He *can* turn stones into bread, but he chooses not to. The same is true of the sufferings of his passion. He could have called down legions of angels to protect him, but he chooses to let the soldiers capture him (Matt. 26:53). He is nailed to a cross, yet his life is not something anyone can take from him: "No one takes it from me, but I lay it down of my own accord. I have power to lay it down, and I have power to take it up again" (John 10:18).[11] Just as he chose to abstain from food day after day in his fast, Jesus chooses the cross at every point, every step up the hill, and gives up his life of his own accord.

This is his chosen submission to the plan of God: "not as I will, but as you will" (Matt. 26:39 ESV). This is willing submission, not one imposed or forced upon him. And it is by this that he, as a human, gives to God the life of gratitude, obedience, and righteousness that is owed to the creator—the life that Adam and Adam's heirs have failed to render.[12] Jesus himself lived

---

11. According to Mark 15:39, it is when the centurion sees the *way* Jesus died (Greek *houtōs*, "in this manner") that he exclaims that Jesus must be God's Son. Even in dying, he chooses the moment of his own death, giving up his Spirit when all has been accomplished (Luke 23:46; John 19:30).

12. See Anselm of Canterbury, *Why God Became Man* 1.14, 19–25; 2.6–7, 9–10, 14–18.

and, in his humanity, grew in obedience and perfection through suffering (Heb. 2:10). "Although he was a Son, he learned obedience through what he suffered; and having been made perfect, he became the source of eternal salvation for all who obey him" (Heb. 5:8–9). His death perfects—that is, brings to completion—the life of obedience and love that he lived from the start, one that he exhibited in his baptism, his fast, and his life of righteousness and love. His entire life of self-offering is a perfect offering, one not needed for his own sins but offered for the salvation of others. And the offering of the eternal and ever-living Son avails for all time for those who call upon him and follow him in the path of self-denial and the cross.

Jesus against Sin, Death, and Satan

Jesus's opposition to Satan and to temptation is clear in his own penitence and fasting. Jesus also opposes Satan and sin in his healings and exorcisms, in which he does battle with the demonic and the effects of sin. He overpowers demons, undoes the penalty of sin by raising the dead, and restores the impure to health and communion with God.

The synoptic Gospels emphasize Jesus's opposition to the demonic in his exorcisms.[13] God's people are oppressed by demons in various forms, and Jesus sets them free by overpowering and casting out the demons. When Jesus encounters an unclean spirit, he casts it out. The crowds are amazed at Jesus's "authority" over the demons. For he overpowers them not with a show of might, nor by muttering incantations or prayers, but simply on his own authority and the power of his word (Mark 1:27). Indeed, his power over them is so great that demons come to submit themselves to him in fear, for they know that he has come to put an end to their reign. When Jesus teaches in a synagogue, a demon sees him and cries out, "Have you come to destroy us? I know who you are—the Holy One of God!" (Mark 1:24 NABRE). At another point, a man possessed by many demons sees Jesus from a distance and runs to him, falling down and imploring Jesus, "Do not torment me" (Mark 5:7).

Jesus's opposition to sin and Satan is connected also to his healings. Death and decay, the breakdown of human bodies God made for life, are

---

13. John's Gospel depicts the cross as a kind of exorcism loosing the devil's power over the world (John 12:31; 16:11), but it does not include individual exorcisms in its narrative.

results of the fall into sin. Illness and bodily breakdown, as anticipations of death, are therefore also results of the curse of sin. Jesus opposes sin and the power of death, as well as "the one who has the power of death, that is, the devil" (Heb. 2:14; cf. 1 Cor. 15:56–57). We see Jesus engaged in this work when he heals and purifies people of "unclean" spirits and frees them from the hold that sin and Satan have on their bodies. Indeed, after healing a woman who was crippled, Jesus states that he has healed her from being "bound" by "Satan" (Luke 13:16). The Gospels also highlight Jesus's ability to deliver people from diseases that rendered them *incurably impure* and kept them in a state of anticipated death.[14] Jesus cleanses lepers, whom he sends to be diagnosed and approved as "clean" by the priests so that they might be restored to the communal worship of God (Matt. 8:1–4; Luke 17:11–19). Jesus casts out otherwise insuperable demons—"unclean" or "impure" spirits that rendered the possessed unclean (e.g., Mark 1:27; 5:13).

In a remarkable episode, Jesus heals and cleanses a woman with an ongoing discharge of blood that no physician was able to treat. This feat is meant to strengthen a man's faith that Jesus can raise his dead daughter (Mark 5:21–43), that Jesus can not only cure anticipations of death but even death itself. This is a signal demonstration of Jesus's opposition to evil in his earthly ministry, his work to overpower the "last enemy," death itself (1 Cor. 15:26). He raises the man's daughter. He raises a widow's son and restores him alive to his mother (Luke 7:11–17). He raises Lazarus, dead four days already, in order to show his power as God's Son (John 11:14–15, 38–44). Jesus does not raise every corpse that he passes by, but we can see in these healings his reversal of the curse of sin and his own power to give life. As the Son, united to the Father, he has the power of life in himself (John 5:26), and he exercises that power publicly as the one who will defeat death by his resurrection (John 11:25–26).

Jesus's power over sin, death, and Satan is evidence that he is bringing the kingdom of God (Luke 11:20). Indeed, these acts are the beginnings of his reclaiming the world in righteousness. He is subduing the enemy so that he can plunder and take back those Satan had taken as his own (Mark 3:27). Christ came to bring liberty and "release to the captives" and to restore those who had been lost to the power of death and Satan (Luke 4:18).

14. See Matthew Thiessen, *Jesus and the Forces of Death: The Gospels' Portrayal of Ritual Impurity within First-Century Judaism* (Grand Rapids: Baker Academic, 2020).

Sin, Healing, and the Spiritual Sense

Christian tradition has often read Jesus's healings not only as teaching us about his power to heal the body or as prefiguring the resurrection, but as also pointing to forgiveness and spiritual healing. Thomas Aquinas, for instance, sees a figure of sacramental confession and forgiveness in Christ's healing of the leper in Matthew 8:1–4. The leper comes to Christ in hope but also in humility, as a penitent should approach God in the confessional. He presents his impurity to Jesus for mercy, as we do in confessing our sins. Christ, by his word, cleanses the leper, as he does through the mouth of the priest in absolution. Then Christ commands him to show himself to the priests in obedience to the law (and to be readmitted as "clean" to the worshiping community), which Aquinas reads as a kind of penance.[a]

a. Thomas Aquinas, *Commentary on the Gospel of Matthew*, chapter 8, lecture 1, §§680–90.

Christ Restores the Lost: Repentance and Forgiveness

Jesus's ministry works against the influence and power of sin. As Jesus teaches, however, sin is not just a power or enemy that oppresses us from outside. Deliverance from sin's external effects and anticipations of death must come also with forgiveness and healing within. Indeed, when Christ restores physical health to a man who suffers paralysis, he first pronounces forgiveness of the man's sin (Mark 2:1–12). And when he heals the man at the pool of Bethesda, after the healing, he tells him, "Look, you are well; do not sin any more, so that nothing worse may happen to you" (John 5:14 NABRE). The inclination to sin dwells in each of God's people, in their hearts and minds and the desires of their flesh. "For it is from within, from the human heart, that evil intentions come: fornication, theft, murder, adultery, avarice, wickedness, deceit, licentiousness, envy, slander, pride, folly. All these evil things come from within, and they defile a person" (Mark 7:21–23). In order to save humans from sin and death, Jesus's mission must also reach into the heart and mind of each person. He came to set the captives free from their debts and restore them to life with God (Luke 4:18–21). And he does so by forgiving their sins and calling them to repent.

One of the ways in which Christ depicts himself and his mission is as a shepherd seeking after lost sheep. He often sought out fellowship with people that others believed he should not associate with, "sinners" and "tax collectors" and others (e.g., Matt. 9:11; Luke 7:34). Once when he was criticized for this, he responded with a parable: a shepherd had one hundred sheep, but one went astray and became lost. Should the shepherd not go and bring back the lost one? Of course! And when he returns the lost sheep, he throws a party and asks those with him to rejoice with him (Luke 15:1–7). The parable emphasizes, against those who would have him treat the lost as lost and say "good riddance," that *none in the Good Shepherd's flock is expendable.* This shepherd does not comfort himself that he still has ninety-nine in the fold. He wants his pen full, with none lost. As a parallel passage in Matthew explains, "It is not the will of your Father in heaven that one of these little ones should be lost" (Matt. 18:14). The parable also rebukes any who would see themselves as not having gone astray and calls them to rejoice at the return of the lost. It may also hint to such people that, if they want to cause the Shepherd joy, they too should examine themselves and repent of their sins. Indeed, just as the lost sheep is not to be treated as expendable, neither are any of the ninety-nine. Jesus dined with sinners despite the judgment of others. And he also dined with those who judged him for it, calling them to repent of their presumption and judgment (Luke 7:36–50; 14:1–14).

The image of the shepherd presents a figure of Jesus, the Son of God and Davidic king who would "shepherd" God's flock, working to seek and save the lost (Luke 19:10). In his mercy, he takes the initiative to search out and save, and it is by his power that they are returned to the fold, carried on his shoulders. This is the drama of salvation from a God's-eye view: he comes, he finds, he brings us home. But our Shepherd saves not sheep but human beings, who have a mind and will, and returning them home is not a simple matter of relocating them but requires their change of heart to return to God in repentance and love. Christ's mission is not only a matter of seeking or calling sheep but of calling sinners *to repentance* (Luke 5:32). He summarizes the parable of the lost sheep in this way, that there will be joy in heaven "over one sinner who repents" (Luke 15:7). According to John Chrysostom, the sheep's return "represents to us nothing else than the fall and return of the faithful."[15] This return, on our part, involves repenting from our sin, confessing, and seeking to be brought home by our merciful Lord.

15. John Chrysostom, *Exhortation to Theodore* 1.7 (NPNF[1] 9:96).

Jesus tells a similar parable just after that of the lost sheep, the parable of the prodigal son (Luke 15:11–32), with which we opened this book. This parable highlights the repentance of the fallen and the wonderful mercy of God. The image of sin, of pride and carnal desire, is clear in the prodigal's request and departure. He asks for his share of his father's inheritance and, taking it, leaves his father's house for a "distant country, and there he squandered his property in dissolute living," full of lust and gluttony (Luke 15:13; cf. 15:30). The son wants to use the goods of his father's house without being in his father's house, without being under his father's authority or rules or care. However, outside the continued economy of his father's house, the prodigal's inheritance runs out, and he finds no help or generosity from others. Hitting "rock bottom," as they say, he comes to realize how far he has fallen and his need to be restored.[16] So he swallows his pride and goes home so that he can again have some kind of living. He does not hope for reconciliation, but only to be hired by his father as a servant. But his father is there waiting, and when the son is approaching the house from afar, the father runs out and embraces him. The son confesses that he has wronged his father and admits his unworthiness to be readmitted to the household. "Father, I have sinned against heaven and before you; I am no longer worthy to be called your son" (Luke 15:21). But before he can even ask to be hired as a servant, the father summons servants to make a public celebration that his son—not a servant but a son—has returned. And the son who had been reduced to nothing is bedecked with a ring, sandals, and a fine robe. For, the father says, "this son of mine was dead and is alive again; he was lost and is found!" (Luke 15:24; cf. 15:32).

The prodigal is restored to the life and relationship he rejected: he returns to be a member of the family, to be a son under his father, restored to communion with the rest of the household. But the elder brother is not pleased, and he refuses to join in the family joy. When the father notices this, he approaches the elder son. The son complains, "All these years I have been working like a slave for you, and I have never disobeyed your command; yet you have never given me even a young goat so that I might celebrate with my friends" (Luke 15:29). The father patiently assures the elder son, "Son, you are always with

---

16. Luke's Greek says that he "came to himself," using an idiom that often appears in contexts of realizing that something is or has gone wrong (cf. *Testament of Joseph* 3.9; Epictetus, *Discourses* 3.1.15). Here it indicates "the beginning of his repentance" and "a regret for his misconduct" (Joseph A. Fitzmyer, *The Gospel according to Luke (X–XXIV)*, AB 28A [New York: Doubleday, 1985], 1088).

me, and all that is mine is yours" (Luke 15:31). He has not left home and has not given up his place in the family. But for that reason he must join the family celebration, for the prodigal—your *brother*, the father emphasizes—has been restored (Luke 15:32).

Jesus's parable is in part a rebuke to those who complained that he welcomed "sinners" (Luke 15:1–2). If they would be part of the family, they must join in the celebration. Indeed, they must repent of their own sins and learn to be better sons. The elder brother never left home, but his words betray that he also wants to be treated like a hired servant: he complains that he has served his father like a "slave" but never been given a goat to feast on with his "friends." He, too, wants to get something from his father that he can enjoy without the father. The parable's final rebuke calls the elder brother to join his heart to his father's and participate in the family by rejoicing over the prodigal's return. He may not need to return to the household after leaving it. But he does need to be a better son and brother in order to take part in the life of the family.

There is mercy, *extravagant* and unexpected mercy, with God for sinners. It is offered both to prodigals and to elder brothers. God wants all his children to live as part of the family; he "desires everyone to be saved and to come to the knowledge of the truth" (1 Tim. 2:4). But all who would receive this mercy must humble themselves and, like the prodigal, acknowledge their fallenness and seek restoration. One who is blind but believes that he sees will not ask for healing, and he will not receive it (John 9:39–41). But humble penitence is the posture in which we receive God's mercy, and God will give mercy to those who confess and ask for restoration.

Jesus illustrates this in a parable contrasting a Pharisee and a tax collector (Luke 18:9–14). Both go up to the temple area to pray. But one approaches with pride and presumption, while the other comes with humility and contrition. The Pharisee thanks God that he fasts and that he gives a tenth (a "tithe") of all his income as alms. He does good things and, even more, rightly thanks God that he does them rather than acting as though he did them all of his own power. But he is a type of those "who trusted in themselves that they were righteous and regarded others with contempt" (Luke 18:9). He does not acknowledge any unworthiness or imperfection or ask God's aid. He speaks as one who has already arrived, as one who *is* already righteous. When it comes to sin, he only directs God's attention to the sins of others: "God, I thank you that I am not like other people: thieves, rogues, adulterers, or even like this tax collector" (Luke 18:11). He mentions sins, but not his own.[17] The tax collector, however, "beat his breast, saying, 'God, be merciful to me, a sinner!'" (Luke 18:13 ESV). Despite his sins, he is the one Jesus says went home "justified" or "righteous" in God's sight (Luke 18:14). The Pharisee did not present his wounds to the healer. But the tax collector confessed his sin with contrition, and he was forgiven and put in the right with God. Such is the humility that is required of those who would receive God's mercy in Christ: "All who exalt themselves will be humbled, but all who humble themselves will be exalted" (Luke 18:14).

Jesus calls all to humble confession and penitence—prodigals and elder brothers, Pharisees and tax collectors. And when they respond to him with such penitence, he grants them forgiveness and restoration. We can see examples of the realities taught in the parables discussed above at several points in the Gospels. Here, we will highlight four.[18]

The Penitence of the "Thief"

Our first example comes from the end of Jesus's ministry before his death and resurrection, in the story of the penitent "thief" in Luke 23:39–43. The Gospels all include the detail that Jesus was crucified alongside two others—Luke calls them *kakourgoi*, "criminals" or "malefactors" (Luke 23:32–33, 39). We are not told their crime in particular. They are often described as "thieves," popularized by the King James and Douay-Rheims translations of their description in Matthew 27:38, 44, and Mark 15:27. But we should not imagine either of them as being crucified for petty theft. Mere burglary or thievery "was not a capital offence" in Roman law.[19] The term used by Matthew and Mark is better rendered "brigand" or "bandit" (Greek *lēstēs*, not simply *kleptēs*), a term also employed to refer to anti-Roman revolutionaries such as Barabbas, whose brigandry included murder (cf. Mark 15:7; Luke 23:19; John 18:40).

What is striking here is Jesus's mercy toward the brigand who shows penitence and faith. Both criminals hang there beside Jesus. But Luke presents a

17. Jerome, *Epistle* 147.9: "Why is it that you disregard your own scars and try to defame others?" (*NPNF*² 6:293).

18. The discussion on sacramental penance and absolution in the *Apostolic Constitutions* 4.3.24, for instance, presents as models Matthew, Peter, Paul, and the sinful woman in Luke. I have replaced Matthew and Paul with the "thief" and Zacchaeus here.

19. Davies and Allison, *Gospel according to Saint Matthew*, 3:616n42.

contrast in their responses to Jesus.[20] One reviles Jesus and asks him, if he is the Messiah, to act with power and save them from crucifixion now. The other, however, rebukes him: "Do you not fear God, since you are under the same sentence of condemnation? And we indeed have been condemned justly, for we are getting what we deserve for our deeds, but this man has done nothing wrong" (Luke 23:40–41). Differently than the other, the second criminal accepts his coming death and its justice, knowing and admitting his guilt. Differently again, rather than demanding earthly deliverance from Jesus, he asks Jesus, "Remember me when you come into your kingdom" (Luke 23:42). Jesus promises in reply, "Truly I tell you, today you will be with me in paradise" (Luke 23:43).

Despite some popular uses of this passage, this is not an example of one who is saved by faith without repentance. The thief turns to Christ with expressions of penitence that are fit to his current circumstances.[21] He admits his guilt and accepts his crucifixion as a "just" punishment of it. He likewise turns to Christ not in a demand but in a humble prayer, in which he also implicitly expresses faith in Jesus's status as master of a "kingdom"—one whose reign includes and does not contradict the cross.[22] Had he continued to live after this, he would be called to the same life of obedience and repentance to which all Christ's disciples are called in their loyalty to Jesus as Lord and king (otherwise Luke 6:46 would apply). What this episode does depict is the extravagant power and mercy of Jesus; Christ's love is for all who turn to him in repentance and faith and acknowledge him as Lord. Christ's love covers even one who by his own admission deserved crucifixion, and his saving death and resurrection have the power to bring him to the "paradise" from which Adam was expelled. It is this same love that is shown in the other examples we will highlight here: the love of the Shepherd who wants all his sheep home, the love of the God who wants "all to come to repentance" (2 Pet. 3:9).

20. This contrasts with the depiction of the brigands in Matthew and Mark, who report only that they both derided him (Matt. 27:44; Mark 15:32).

21. For John Wesley, the criminal's salvation cannot nullify Christ's call for "repentance" and works or "fruits meet for repentance; which if we willingly neglect, we cannot reasonably expect to be justified at all." It shows, rather, that the response of faith in works is conditioned by "time and opportunity" ("Sermon XLIII: The Scripture Way of Salvation," in *The Works of John Wesley*, 3rd ed., 14 vols. [Grand Rapids: Baker, 1986], 6:48).

22. "According to Luke, the good thief acknowledges Jesus' royal messiahship but realizes that it is not for today and that it is not separate from death. He will be only too happy if on the other side of his suffering Jesus does not forget him" (François Bovon, *Luke 3: A Commentary on the Gospel of Luke 19:28–24:53*, trans. James E. Crouch, Hermeneia [Minneapolis: Fortress, 2012], 311).

The Salvation of Zacchaeus

A signal example of Christ's mercy for the penitent, one who has the ability to commit to a life of repentance after turning to Christ, comes in the figure of Zacchaeus in Luke 19:1–10. Zacchaeus is a chief tax collector, and by his own admission he was what most people expected of tax collectors: he cheated or "extorted" extra money from people to make himself rich (Luke 19:2, 7–8).[23] But he is moved with a desire to see Jesus. He climbs into a tree along a path where the famous "Jesus" he has heard about is supposed to pass by, hoping to see who this Jesus is (Luke 19:3–4). Like the prodigal who hoped to become a servant but was welcomed as a son, Zacchaeus gets more than he bargained for. Jesus stops and calls to him: "Zacchaeus, hurry and come down; for I must stay at your house today" (Luke 19:5).

Here we see Jesus seeking the lost, calling the prodigal "home"—calling him not to a physical house of Jesus's but to communion with God. Jesus invites himself into Zacchaeus's physical house, but spiritually he is inviting Zacchaeus to come "home" to God by responding rightly to Jesus. And Zacchaeus does: he welcomes Jesus to his home with joy (Luke 19:6), and his encounter with Christ moves him to repentance. Zacchaeus says, "Behold, half of my possessions, Lord, I shall give to the poor, and if I have extorted anything from anyone I shall repay it four times over" (Luke 19:8 NABRE). Zacchaeus repents of his greed and extortion, and he vows not only to give alms of his possessions but also to repay those he defrauded. At this, Jesus pronounces Zacchaeus's restoration both to God and to the family of God's people: "Today salvation has come to this house, because he too is a son of Abraham" (Luke 19:9).

Zacchaeus has sinned, but when Christ comes to him he responds with joy and openness to the Lord. He lets himself be moved to repentance by Jesus's invitation. We noted earlier that many psalmists willingly took up a penance or promised one as they sought God's mercy. Encountering the merciful Christ, Zacchaeus vows to amend his life and to offer reparation for his past

23. Tax collecting was hardly considered a noble profession, principally because of the very real likelihood of extortion, against which most commoners had little recourse. We miss the gravity of images of tax collectors being forgiven if we consider them only as unfairly stereotyped or ostracized. Jesus uses "tax collector" as an image of sinfulness in Matthew (Matt. 5:46; 18:17). In Luke, when tax collectors ask John the Baptist what they must do to repent and prepare for the kingdom, John tells them, "Collect no more than the amount prescribed for you" (Luke 3:13). When Jesus seeks out Matthew/Levi and other tax collectors, he says that he is calling sinners to follow him (Mark 2:15–17), not merely consoling the disliked.

wrongs. Presumably he will do so, though we do not see the aftermath of this episode in the Gospel. What we do see is that, when Zacchaeus encounters God, he responds with humble *contrition*, promises to do *penance* in amendment of his life, and is restored to *salvation* and *readmitted* to life in God's family.

The Forgiveness of the Sinful Woman

In another episode, in Luke 7:36–50, Jesus dines at the home of a Pharisee named Simon. A "sinful" woman in the city learned that Jesus was there (Luke 7:37). Like Zacchaeus, having learned where Jesus would be, she wants to see him. Unlike Zacchaeus, she comes intending to show her devotion. She enters the house with a flask of perfume oil and gets down at Jesus's feet, weeping. She washes his feet with her tears, wipes them with her hair, and then anoints them with the oil. Simon grumbles that Jesus is allowing such a woman to touch him. Jesus responds to him with an instructive, parabolic question. Two people owed a certain creditor. One owed ten times as much as the other, but neither was able to repay the debt (Luke 7:42). So the creditor forgave both. Which debtor will love the creditor more? Simon responds, "I suppose the one for whom he canceled the greater debt." "You have judged rightly," Jesus says (Luke 7:43).

Jesus's parable depicts two people who owe a "debt," a common metaphor for sin—a sort of debit in God's heavenly ledger.[24] Both are sinners, and one is a much greater sinner than the other. But neither, not even the one with the lesser debt, is able to repay it. We can think here of Simon and the woman, or of the prodigal and his brother, or of so many other examples. They have different kinds and degrees of particular sins, but both are sinners in need of forgiveness. And in Jesus's parable, the solution to forgive the debt of sin lies ultimately with the creditor, with God. As Psalm 49:7 has it, "no man can . . . give to God the price of his life" so as to be spared death (ESV). There are many ways to *petition* God for forgiveness in Scripture, of course, whether through sacrifices of animals or contrition or fasting. But in this conception of God as a divine creditor, none of these work automatically or mechanistically to cause forgiveness in themselves, even when they are described as

---

24. For a treatment of sin as debt in Luke particularly, see Anthony Giambrone, *Sacramental Charity, Creditor Christology, and the Economy of Salvation in Luke's Gospel*, WUNT 2/439 (Tübingen: Mohr Siebeck, 2017). In Judaism and early Christianity more generally, see Gary A. Anderson, *Sin: A History* (New Haven: Yale University Press, 2009).

having "atoning" value. God, as the creditor, must choose to have mercy and remit the debt.

One with greater debt will have greater gratitude and love for the forgiver. This is what is evidenced in this woman's behavior. If Simon indignantly thought her actions were presumptuous, daring with her defiled hands to touch Christ, Jesus reframes her actions as those of a penitent. She has come humbly to Jesus, not as a host and not as an equal, but as a servant, making herself lowly and washing his feet like a slave. Indeed, she honors Jesus more greatly than does Simon, who only honored Jesus as a "prophet" and "teacher" (Luke 7:39–40). She cries over her sin and submits herself to Jesus, lavishing care and love on the Lord she knows loves her. Because she has acted with "great love," Jesus says to Simon, her sins are forgiven (Luke 7:47).[25] Then he goes further, pronouncing forgiveness on her himself: "Then he said to her, 'Your sins are forgiven'" (Luke 7:48). Some guests balk at Jesus's presumption to forgive sins, of course, but it remains with the divine creditor to remit a debt. And the divine Christ does so, for sins large and great, to those who approach him in penitence and love. She is forgiven and saved, released from her debt of guilt. Jesus sends her off, now at peace with God, to begin her life anew: "Your faith has saved you; go in peace" (Luke 7:50).

The Tears and Hope of Peter

There are other examples of penitents forgiven and restored in the Gospels. But a final and important example comes in the person of Simon Peter, the "rock" whom Jesus appointed "first" among his twelve apostles (Matt.

---

25. There is an interpretive tension in the relation of love to forgiveness here. The parable, applied to the woman, seems to imply that her great love is a result of her having already been forgiven at some unknown point. The NABRE and NRSV interpret Luke 7:47 this way (she is forgiven and "hence" has shown love). In that case, Jesus's pronouncement of forgiveness in 7:48 would be more a word of assurance for her than a pronouncement. However, the term Jesus uses in 7:47 (*hoti*) means "because" and seems rather to suggest that she is forgiven because she loved, not the other way around. Further, the verbal form (*apheōntai*) he uses in 7:47—usually translated "have been forgiven" or "are forgiven"—is regularly used by Jesus not as a description of a past event but as an authoritative speech act *pronouncing* forgiveness. He pronounces forgiveness in 7:48 with the same phrasing, which people take to be him claiming divine authority to forgive sins (as in Luke 5:20–21). In the canonical text, overall, Jesus's explanation of the woman's behavior seems to add to or redirect the parable slightly, rather than tell a parable that mirrors the situation exactly. Jesus tells Simon that her sins are forgiven *because* of the love she has shown (7:47), and then he pronounces it directly to the woman after rebuking Simon (7:48). See Giambrone, *Sacramental Charity*, 99–104; Michael Wolter, *The Gospel according to Luke*, 2 vols., BMSEC (Waco: Baylor University Press, 2016–17), 1:325–26.

10:2; 16:18). Peter was one of Jesus's inner circle, one who was ardent in his love and zeal for the one he came to know as the Messiah. On the night Jesus was betrayed, when Jesus foretells that the disciples will abandon him, Peter insists that he will never do so (Matt. 26:33). But Jesus responds that Peter's loyalty and zeal will fail that very night: he will deny him before the rooster crows.[26]

Peter does deny Jesus three times that night. Jesus is being put on trial and mocked, and he keeps silent except to proclaim his divine sonship and power—saying only enough to get himself killed (Mark 14:60–64). Meanwhile, Peter does the opposite. Sitting outside, some of the bystanders question him and deduce that he is one of Jesus's followers. Peter denies it three times, even swearing an oath and invoking curses. Weren't you with Jesus the Galilean? "I do not know the man" (Matt. 26:74). Are you one of Jesus's disciples? "I am not" (John 18:17, 25).

The gravity of Peter's denial should not be downplayed out of respect for the "Prince of the Apostles." Denial of self for Christ is fundamental to Jesus's call to repentance. And public loyalty to him is fundamental to receiving his salvation. "Everyone therefore who acknowledges me before others, I also will acknowledge before my Father in heaven; but whoever denies me before others, I also will deny before my Father in heaven" (Matt. 10:32–33; cf. Mark 8:38; Luke 9:26; 12:8–9). Peter has seen Jesus raise the dead, he has heard Jesus's preaching and has preached the message himself, and he has seen Jesus's power. There is very little ignorance to which he can lay claim to mitigate his guilt. And he denies Jesus. Instead of denying himself, enduring suffering for the sake of Christ, he denies his Lord to save his own skin. Peter has, in this moment, dissociated himself from the one through whom he must be saved.

Appreciating the gravity of his sin, however, only makes his example all the more inspiring for sinners after him who have recourse to the same Savior. *Peter repented.* Just after denying Jesus the third time, when he hears the rooster and remembers Jesus's words, he feels remorse and *contrition.* He "went out and wept bitterly" (Matt. 26:75; Luke 22:62; cf. Mark 14:72). He is deeply contrite. Further, after his sin, he seeks to return to the communion of Jesus's disciples, the nascent Church. Peter drops out of the biblical narrative

---

26. The number of crows from the rooster differs in the best texts of the Gospels. Matthew, Luke, and John all have Jesus saying that Peter will deny Jesus before it crows once (Matt. 26:34; Luke 22:34; John 13:38). Mark has the rooster crowing twice (Mark 14:30, 72).

between his denial and Easter morning. But, after the crucifixion, he apparently had returned to the apostles: he is with the others to hear the women's good news at Easter, runs to the empty tomb, and later encounters the risen Lord (Mark 16:7; Luke 24:9–12, 34; cf. Matt. 28:7–8, 16; John 20:2–10, 19). This evinces not only that he was contrite but that he also had a desire to amend his ways and a *hope* that he could be restored. His hope stands out in contrast to the despair of Judas. According to Matthew, Judas also feels remorse when he sees Jesus condemned and realizes that he has "sinned by betraying innocent blood" (Matt. 27:4). He even throws back the money he received for betraying Jesus. But his is not true repentance, not a turning to submit his past sins and his future fate to God. Judas feels remorse and fear, but it does not lead him to seek again the company of the apostles, nor to make an offering for his sins, nor to pray, nor to wait and see if Jesus will truly rise as he had said. Judas despairs and hangs himself. But Peter weeps and returns, seeking life on the other side of his sin.

This episode was important in ancient debates about whether Christians who faltered in times of persecution could receive forgiveness. Peter denied the Lord, but repented and wept. And Peter is welcomed back and *restored*. He is restored to communion and friendship with Jesus. And he is restored to his vocation as chief of the apostles. In Luke, as Jesus foretells Peter's denial, he also foretells his return and role in leading and strengthening the others: "Simon, Simon, listen! Satan has demanded to sift all of you like wheat, but I have prayed for you that your own faith may not fail; and you, when once you have turned back, strengthen your brothers" (Luke 22:31–32). Peter, the "rock," will fall, but he will get back up. And when he "turns back" he will again lead the apostolic band and strengthen them. Indeed, Peter strengthens not only the apostles but also all of the Church under him. John 21:15–17 depicts Peter's restoration after Easter in a conversation that inversely parallels his denial. Earlier, bystanders asked three times if Peter was one of Jesus's followers, and he denied it. This time, Jesus asks Peter three times if Peter loves him. And Peter affirms his love for Jesus each time. It is painful for Peter—a fitting penance, perhaps—that Jesus calls him three times to profess his love, surely a reminder of his threefold denial (John 21:17).[27] But Peter accepts this and affirms his love

27. Peter's grief at being asked "the third time" is sometimes attributed to Jesus's use of a different Greek verb for "love," *phileō*, whereas Jesus's previous two questions had used *agapaō*. But Peter's answer that, yes, he does "love" Jesus features *phileō* in response to all three questions, which suggests that the two verbs can refer to the same kinds of loving in this context. Indeed,

and service to Christ each time. At each response, the Good Shepherd commissions Peter with the care of his universal flock: "Feed my sheep."

Beyond tax collectors and disreputable sinners, Peter's is probably the most significant example of repentance and restoration of a believer in the New Testament. Even Paul, according to 1 Timothy 1:13, might be excused for his crimes against Christ and the Church for acting "ignorantly in unbelief." Further, Paul's is a conversion from unbelief to faith, more akin in sacramental terms to the initial sacrament of baptism that he receives (Acts 9:18; 22:16), making him a walking sign of God's grace for one who had been the "foremost" sinner (1 Tim. 1:15–16). Differently, in Peter we can see an example of one who fell from an already close relationship with Jesus and was restored again. Sacramentally, Peter's repentance is more like that of a believer who falls and is restored through the sacrament of reconciliation. He falls, yet his knowledge of his Savior fills him with deep contrition and a desire to return to the communion of Jesus's disciples. Like the sinful woman, Peter's restoration involves both tears and love. Tearful, his repentance is received with mercy by the Lord. Forgiven a great debt, he affirms that he loves the Lord. And he amends his life, loving Christ and following him even to the point of being martyred (John 21:18–19). The one who denied Christ out of fear now, repentant and restored, willingly accepts death in the name of Jesus and encourages others to do the same.

Christ's Call to Repentance and Renewal

The greatest sinners are not beyond redemption in Christ. But all, whether runaway prodigals or elder brothers, must heed his call to repent and turn to be restored to the family of God. They must recognize their need and turn to the Lord in hope and submission. And those who have converted and been restored must then continue to live a life of repentance, turning from sin and seeking deeper communion with God. Time is running out, and all must repent or perish (see Luke 13:1–9). As we conclude this chapter, we may focus on three aspects of Christ's call to repentance: its comprehensiveness as a call to be reconciled to God by faith and penance, the importance of self-denial and amending one's life, and the call to respond to God's mercy by showing mercy.

John's Gospel uses both verbs for the same kind of loving elsewhere: for disordered love (John 3:19; 15:19), for the Father's love of the Son (3:35; 5:20), and for Jesus's love of the "beloved" disciple (20:2; 21:7).

Repentance and Faith

Mark 1:15 summarizes Jesus's preaching ministry with these simple words: "The time is fulfilled, and the kingdom of God is at hand; repent and believe in the gospel" (ESV). The time is "fulfilled" and the kingdom is at hand. The creator who made the world for life and righteousness is, in Christ, returning to reclaim it and set all things right. He has come in fulfillment of prophecy, bringing God's mercy to Israel and taking away the sins of the whole world (cf. Luke 1:54–55, 68–75; John 1:29). All who entrust themselves to him by faith will have eternal life (John 3:16).

Jesus's call is a call to *repentance* and *faith*: "Repent and believe." Sometimes this is taken to refer only to initial conversion, as a call to turn ("repent") from idolatry or unbelief to belief in Christ. For one who has not yet converted, that is certainly included. But the call to repentance continues after one turns from unbelief to Christ. Repentance is not only a turning to faith, but a characteristic of a *life* lived by faith.[28] In Acts, Paul summarizes his message to unbelievers as a call both to believe and to do the works of repentance: "I preached the need to repent and turn to God, and to do works giving evidence of repentance" (Acts 26:20 NABRE). Jesus's call is comprehensive, one that embraces one's entire life, calling all to realize their sin and imperfection and turn constantly to the Lord for mercy and grace.

Repentance and faith go together in the life of Christ's followers. On the one hand, faith and hopeful trust in Christ are necessary for repentant actions to have any worth. Christ does not call for sham penance, and he will not accept it. Like the prophets before him, he rebukes sternly those who observe a few commands or worship God while "their hearts are far from me" (Matt. 15:8; cf. Isa. 29:13). He rebukes many for "hypocrisy"—originally a Greek term for "playacting" or "putting on a show"—when they fast or give alms or pray desiring to show piety and gain religious honor from *other people*: "Beware of practicing your righteousness before other people in order to be seen by them, for then you will have no reward from your Father who is in

---

28. Martin Luther noted this correctly in his *Ninety-Five Theses*: "When our Lord and Master Jesus Christ said, 'Repent' [Matt. 4:17], he willed the entire life of believers to be one of repentance" (Thesis 1), and this "does not mean solely inner repentance; such inner repentance is worthless unless it produces various outward mortifications of the flesh" (Thesis 3; trans. Jacobs and Grimm, 25). Unfortunately, though one can understand his concerns, his de-emphasis of the *sacrament* of penance (in Thesis 2) misses the role the sacrament plays within one's life of faith and growth in the *virtue* of penance.

heaven" (Matt. 6:1 ESV; cf. 6:1–21; 23:5).[29] True repentance and penitent acts must be grounded in faith. Any who would hope for recompense from God must, at the very least, "believe that he exists and that he rewards those who seek him" (Heb. 11:6). One who would follow Christ on the way to God must believe that he *is* the way to the Father (John 14:6).

By the same token, if Christ does not call for sham penance, he also does not call for what James calls a "dead" faith (James 2:26). Empty works are not the only mode of hypocrisy. One might claim to have faith only as a show for others, for God, or just to reassure oneself of one's salvation despite a life of unrepentance. In Jesus's parable, this is like the son who was asked by his father to go and do some work on the property: "He answered, 'I go, sir'; but he did not go" (Matt. 21:30). He gave lip service to please his father but did not do his father's will. Jesus only approves the other son, who "repented" and *did* what his father asked (see Matt. 21:28–32). Christ will not accept professions of faith that are not followed by repentance. "Not everyone who says to me, 'Lord, Lord,' will enter the kingdom of heaven, but only the one who does the will of my Father in heaven" (Matt. 7:21). "Why do you call me 'Lord, Lord,' and do not do what I tell you?" (Luke 6:46). Such an empty faith is faith that proves "in vain," in Paul's terms (cf. 1 Cor. 15:2; 2 Cor. 6:1; Gal. 4:11; 1 Thess. 3:5).

Jesus emphasizes the need for faith to *bear fruit*, to become active in obedience and love. One who believes in him and his words comes to "abide" or live in him by that bond of faith, like a branch relying on and receiving life from a vine (John 5:38; 8:31; 15:1–7). But those who are united to this Vine must bear fruit, and they must do so if they are to continue to abide in the Vine and glorify God; otherwise, they will be cut off and burned (John 15:4, 6, 8, 16). "Whoever believes in the Son has eternal life; whoever does not obey the Son shall not see life, but the wrath of God remains on him" (John 3:36 ESV). Repentance and the works that befit repentance are means by which one receives and grows in life from the Vine. Good works are not the reason one receives the gift of conversion or of being grafted onto the Vine, but they are a necessary part of persevering and growing in Christ. The famous parable of the soils and seed bears the same message. Jesus depicts four types

29. There were understood to be good kinds of playacting, naturally. But in a negative sense, the term "hypocrite" came to mean "pretender" in some Greek philosophical contexts and particularly in Jewish literature. "Hypocrisy" is the opposite of "truth" (*Testament of Benjamin* 6.5). For a discussion of the term and its connotations, see Ulrich Wilckens, "ὑποκρίνομαι, κτλ.," *TDNT* 8:559–71.

of things that can happen when the "seed," the word of God, is "sown" in preaching. In one instance, it is simply not received and not believed. But in the other three, the word is received and believed, but with different results. In the second, the word is received, but its roots are unable to grow deep and strong, and those who receive the word in this way "believe only for a while and in a time of testing fall away" (Luke 8:13). In the third, the word is believed and takes root, but the believers "are choked by the cares and riches and pleasures of life, and their fruit does not mature" (Luke 8:14). According to Jesus's words in Luke, both of these "believe," in contrast to the first, but in both cases the planting proves futile.[30] Jesus praises only the fourth planting, "the ones who, when they have heard the word, embrace it with a generous and good heart, and bear fruit through perseverance" (Luke 8:15 NABRE).

Christ calls believers to persevere by letting God's mercy and his word grow within them to "bear fruit worthy of repentance" (Matt. 3:8) from the time of their first conversion and onward. Naturally, the life of repentance will involve different specific actions depending on one's station, circumstances, and capacities. The criminal crucified alongside Jesus confesses his sinfulness and Christ's innocence, and he prays to be received into paradise by Jesus, the king (Luke 23:39–43). His actions evince his repentance, but he does not live long enough to do more. John the Baptist gives different particular instructions to tax collectors and to soldiers when they ask what they must do to repent (Luke 3:10–14). Jesus accepts Zacchaeus's vow to give alms of half his wealth, while he calls another man attached to his possessions to sell them all for alms (cf. Mark 10:17–22; Luke 19:8–9). The master gives different amounts ("talents") to his stewards to do business with while he is gone (Matt. 25:14–30). But *all* are called to a life of repentance, of responding with submission to the mercy and call of God in Christ. The one who receives his master's talent and does not make use of it is cast out and not rewarded. Those who say yes

---

30. Sometimes John's Gospel is taken to teach that it is not possible for one who is united to Jesus to fall away, since no power can snatch anyone out of God's hand (John 10:28–29), such that one who appears to fall away must have never truly believed (cf. 1 John 2:19). John's emphasis on God's power to protect his people against other powers is clear, and surely some who appear to fall away were always secretly unbelievers. But John's emphasis that one who does not abide in Jesus will be cast off (John 15:2, 6), and the fact that Jesus must warn and reassure the disciples so that they will not fall away (John 16:1), suggests that John countenances the possibility of one choosing to dissociate from Christ (not being snatched away by another power against one's will). In biblical theology, we must also heed Jesus's explicit description of some "believing" and then falling away in Luke 8:13, and of course other warnings (e.g., Rom. 11:19–22; Gal. 5:2–4; Heb. 6:4–6).

to the king's invitation or to the divine bridegroom's call but fail to prepare themselves adequately will not be admitted (see Matt. 22:1–14; 25:1–13).

Self-Denial, Amendment of Life, and Love

The life of repentant faith and faithful repentance to which Christ calls sinners could be called a life of "faith and works," emphasizing the unity of the two. If we consider specifically one's duty to continue to reject sin as part of one's restoration to God, we could also call it a life of *penance*. Fundamentally, it is a life of self-denial. We are called to follow Christ's own example of service: "Whoever wishes to be first among you must be slave of all" (Mark 10:44). We are called to follow Christ's own pattern of penitence, taking up our crosses to have fellowship with him in his sufferings in the hope of sharing also in his glorious life (Phil. 3:10–11). "If anyone would come after me, let him deny himself and take up his cross and follow me" (Matt. 16:24 ESV). Christ's penitent submission to baptism received God's decree that he is his beloved Son, and by following the same we join Christ as his brethren, as daughters and sons of God with whom he is well pleased (Rom. 8:16–17; cf. Mark 1:11).

Self-denial is an important and necessary part of growing in righteousness. We noted Jesus's words earlier that it is "from within" the human heart that evil desires and lust and malice and pride flow (Mark 7:21–23). Those inclinations—what theologians call concupiscence—remain after one converts to Christ. Those who have received the word of God must then endeavor to let it take root and to cut away the thorns that threaten to choke it. Jesus offers the image of an exorcism: if an unclean spirit leaves a person, but later it returns and finds its former home "empty, swept, and put in order" (Matt. 12:44), the demon will return again and bring more demons worse than itself to this now empty house, and the person will be worse off despite having been exorcised (Matt. 12:45). Forgiven and cleansed by Christ—exorcised, in a way—Christians still possess all the metaphorical furniture to make home for evil again. We must seek to *amend our lives* after receiving mercy, denying our sinful inclinations, and let the love and mercy of Christ transform us within by grace. And we must remove, inasmuch as we can, those things that enflame our sin beyond our ability to resist—in other words, *avoid the near occasion for sin*. "And if your eye causes you to stumble, tear it out and throw it away; it is better for you to enter life with one eye than to have two eyes and to be thrown into the hell of fire" (Matt. 18:9).

Jesus commends particular practices of self-denial and calls his disciples to turn not just from sin in general but from specific kinds of sin and attachments to sin. Against pride, Jesus commends *humility*. When his disciples debate about greatness or request to be great, Jesus tells them to humble themselves like a child, to know their neediness and dependence (Matt. 18:1–4; 22:25–28).[31] He calls for humility even in the specifics of day-to-day interactions with others, such as taking seats of lesser honor at dinner parties (Luke 14:7–11). He calls for it especially in *prayer*. Indeed, according to Teresa of Ávila, humility is the "main practice" necessary for the way of prayer.[32] One recalls the parable of the Pharisee and the tax collector: "All who exalt themselves will be humbled, but all who humble themselves will be exalted" (Luke 18:14). Jesus's instruction on prayer calls for and inculcates such humility. By its very words the Lord's Prayer sets us under God's care for everything from daily sustenance to our own forgiveness and sanctification. And it begins by putting into our mouths, even before we voice our own needs, prayers for God's will and the realization of God's kingdom, and that God's name—not ours—be honored (Matt. 6:9–13; Luke 11:2–4). The prayer's own words, if we make them our own, bring us to pray humbly and confidently to our Father, and they shape our priorities and desires to God's will first, then to our own needs for life, forgiveness, and deliverance. They set us in the place of those Jesus blesses in the Beatitudes, poor in spirit, hungering for righteousness, and ready to deny ourselves for God's kingdom (Matt. 5:1–12).

Against our temptations to gratify our own appetites, Jesus commends *self-denial* and *charity*. He speaks rarely of fasting, though we have seen from the biblical tradition otherwise that it is commended as a means of humbling oneself. Against the temptation to make fasting into an occasion to impress others, Jesus commands that self-chosen fasts should be done secretly and directed to the attention of God, who sees all and will "reward" or "repay" (Greek *apodidōmi*) this act of righteousness (Matt. 6:18). More frequently he speaks of almsgiving. Jesus also critiques hypocritical ways of giving alms, calling his followers to give in secret (Matt. 6:2–4). But almsgiving receives much more attention as a means to rid oneself of sin and grow in faith, hope, and love. In Luke 12, Jesus tells a story of a rich man who stored up income

---

31. Though today children are often lauded for innocence or simple trust, becoming like a "child" in Jesus's context would have conveyed dependence and neediness or, as Jesus's command indicates, "humility." See the excursus in Jeffrey A. Gibbs, *Matthew 11:2–20:34*, ConcC (St. Louis: Concordia, 2010), 889–96.

32. Teresa of Ávila, *The Way of Perfection* 4.4 (trans. Kavanaugh and Rodriguez, 54).

only for himself so that he could enjoy a nice retirement rather than work. But he quickly dies and finds that he had been a fool. Not only was he unable to enjoy the fruits of his labor, but he gave none away and so finds himself rich only in the economy of this world but with no heavenly credit (Luke 12:21). Jesus then calls his followers to rely on God's provision: they should have faith in God's care for their bodies and souls, and they should therefore forgo and even give away earthly treasure in order to have heavenly treasure. "Do not be afraid, little flock," he comments, "for it is your Father's good pleasure to give you the kingdom. Sell your possessions, and give alms. Make purses for yourselves that do not wear out, an unfailing treasure in heaven" (Luke 12:32–33).

Almsgiving is an act of justice toward one's neighbor and extends a kind of heavenly line of credit, laying up "treasure" or making a loan to God that God will repay (cf. Prov. 19:17; Matt. 19:21; Luke 18:22). It also has a salutary effect internally, counteracting one's sinful attachments and restoring the giver to the dignity of God's children made for self-giving. Jesus points to the internal effects of almsgiving in a rebuke of the Pharisees when they disapprove of his eating with unwashed hands. He retorts, "Now you Pharisees clean the outside of the cup and of the dish, but inside you are full of greed and wickedness" (Luke 11:39). The Pharisees present themselves as devout and righteous by such washings and concern for ritual cleanness. But what is inside of them is greed and malice, and it is from within that one's moral uncleanness before God arises. Jesus prescribes a solution: "As to what is within, give alms, and behold, everything will be clean for you" (Luke 11:41 NABRE). "Cleanness through 'alms' surpasses cleanness through water," because it "purges" sin within (see Tob. 12:9).[33] That is, it will bring about "internal moral purity" as it counteracts or atones for their immorality.[34] Almsgiving is a way of denying oneself for the benefit of others, and, when practiced with faith and a willingness to be renewed in the love of God, it becomes a means to grow in virtue and sanctification. Jesus's sayings about the good or generous "eye"—contrasted

---

33. Wolter, *Luke*, 2:123.

34. David J. Downs, *Alms: Charity, Reward, and Atonement in Early Christianity* (Waco: Baylor University Press, 2016), 127; cf. John Nolland, *Luke 9:21–18:34*, WBC 35B (Dallas: Word, 1993), 664. The accusative *ta enonta* ("what is within") is sometimes rendered as an object of the command to "give alms," which results in translations like "give what is within *as* alms." But it seems odd to think that they are being commanded to give *as* alms their inner greed and malice, and Luke's clear emphasis on the problem of greed and the goodness and necessity of almsgiving directs one rather to see a command to actual charity here. Translating the phrase as an accusative of respect is preferable ("*with respect to* what is within" or "*regarding* what is within").

with the "evil" or greedy eye that begrudges and covets—likewise indicate the internal effects of genuine almsgiving: an eye that is generous toward others shines and illuminates the rest of oneself (Matt. 6:22–24; cf. Luke 11:33–36).[35]

Jesus calls for other forms of charity and penance, of course. And those mentioned above can take various shapes. As in Tobit, Jesus encourages alms-giving not solely in monetary gifts but in inviting the poor to dine in one's home (Luke 14:12–14), clothing and feeding the needy, and caring for other bodily needs (Matt. 25:31–46). But growth in charity requires self-denial. Indeed, that is ultimately the goal of self-denial: growth in Christlike *love*. Jesus's followers are called to put away anger and lust from our hearts, to put away passions for pleasure or a defensive need to avenge ourselves against others (Matt. 5:21–22, 27–28, 38–42). In Paul's words, we are to "put to death"—to mortify—the malice and greed that incline us toward selfishness against God and others (Rom. 8:13; Col. 3:5). Dietrich Bonhoeffer was not wrong to summarize Christ's call by saying, "When Christ calls a man, He bids him come and die."[36] But the call to die to ourselves is a call to "live to God" (Gal. 2:19). Saying no to our selfishness is meant to allow us to say yes to God and neighbor. Love for God and neighbor, Jesus says, fulfills the greatest commandment (Matt. 22:37–40). Truly loving one's neighbor, not harming them but seeking their good, fulfills the law of God (Rom. 13:8–10). Truly loving God brings one to obey him, to repent of sin, and to praise God with one's whole heart and seek God's face ardently. Love is self-giving, of-fering one's time or resources or one's comfort or even one's very life for the beloved, so that the greatest self-giving is the greatest love (John 15:13). The path to love is therefore a path of self-denial, one that Christ has walked most perfectly in his love for God. And we, in lives of faith and repentance, are invited to follow him on that path and to live out our lives as daughters and sons reconciled to God in Christ. "If you keep my commandments, you will abide in my love, just as I have kept my Father's commandments and abide in his love. . . . This is my commandment, that you love one another as I have loved you" (John 15:10, 12).

---

35. The "evil eye" as an idiom for a stingy or greedy disposition occurs several times in Scripture (cf. Prov. 23:6–7; 28:22; Sir. 31:13; Matt. 20:15; Mark 7:22), but for the sake of En-glish idiom it is often invisible in English translations. The connection between Jesus's sayings about the "eye" and mammon is lost, however, when the bodily metaphor is retained in Matt. 6:22–24 or Luke 11:33–36.

36. Dietrich Bonhoeffer, *The Cost of Discipleship* (London: SCM, 1948), 44.

Forgive and You Will Be Forgiven

"Jesus denounces sin ruthlessly."[37] But he calls for harsh treatment and rejection of our sins *in order that* we ourselves might be restored. It is because of his great love for sinners that he calls them to great repentance (see Mark 10:21). He is the shepherd calling the lost to return to life in the fold. He is the father welcoming the prodigal and inviting him to *live* again as his son and as a member of the family, to live in submission and love for his father and in service to the rest of the household. The call to penance and self-denial has its goal in reconciling us to God and restoring us to God's image and the truest dignity of humanity.

One last aspect of Jesus's call to repentance and love is worth highlighting as this chapter concludes: his *call to mercy*. The life of Jesus's followers, forgiven and cleansed of their sins, is a life grounded in the mercy of God. This mercy is fundamental to one's identity as a disciple. Jesus calls for corporal works of mercy, feeding the hungry, giving alms, and clothing the sick. He also calls for spiritual works of mercy, most especially in his call to forgiveness.

This is perhaps clearest in the Lord's Prayer, which he gives not to pagans or the unrepentant but to his disciples. He introduces the prayer with a command: "When you pray, say . . ." (Luke 11:2) or, in the more well-known version from Matthew, "Pray then in this way" (Matt. 6:9). In the petitions for one's own spiritual and physical needs, Jesus tells them to pray thus: "Forgive us our debts, as we forgive our debtors" (Matt. 6:12 NABRE).[38] Jesus's disciples, who have already repented and come to faith, are to ask God to forgive their "debts"—their "sins," in Luke's version (Luke 11:4)—as they forgive those who sin against them.

This petition shows us, on the one hand, that Jesus expects that Christians will sin while still being Christians. He calls us to seek perfection in our lives as disciples (Matt. 5:48). God will bring that work to completion in the end, when we are fully purified of all sin and transformed so that only good and life remain (cf. 1 Cor. 3:12–15; Phil. 1:6). But Jesus does not demand perfection in order to become a disciple. Nor does he require his followers to be perfected

---

37. Revel, *Réconciliation*, 202.

38. Matthew 6:12 uses the aorist *aphēkamen*, a tense form pointing prototypically to past action in the indicative mood, which might be translated "as we forgave" (cf. NRSV), though it can also be read more generally, as the manuscript tradition and the parallel in Luke (using the present-tense form) suggest. In any case, past, present, or future, "the issue is whether the forgiveness sought from God is mirrored in the attitude of those [who] pray" (R. T. France, *The Gospel of Matthew*, NICNT [Grand Rapids: Eerdmans, 2007], 250).

already in this life. Even the apostle Paul says that he has not already attained perfection; rather, he lives now in repentance, pressing onward toward the goal (Phil. 3:12–14). Part of that life of repentance, for one not yet perfect, is continually seeking God's forgiveness for our sins. Jesus prescribes that his disciples beseech the divine creditor for forgiveness just as regularly as they ask for daily bread.

On the other hand, the gift of repeated forgiveness requires repeated forgiving. The petition builds a spiritual work of mercy into this prayer: "Forgive *as we forgive.*" The prayer brings with it a condition and command for those who will take it upon their lips: in asking for forgiveness, we agree to forgive. Augustine even speaks of our entering into a kind of "contract with our God" every time we pray this.[39] And Jesus emphasizes its importance, as this is the only petition of the prayer that Jesus immediately stops to reiterate and clarify in Matthew. "For if you forgive others their trespasses, your heavenly Father will also forgive you; but if you do not forgive others, neither will your Father forgive your trespasses" (Matt. 6:14–15). He repeats the same at various points, warning his followers to be on their guard against sin by forgiving their neighbors even repeatedly in the same day if they sin and come back to ask forgiveness (Luke 17:3–4). He even calls us to an internal act of forgiveness for others *every time* we pray, "so that" God will forgive us our trespasses (Mark 11:25).

The value of mercy and forgiveness toward others can be described in various ways. On one hand, there is a kind of "credit" or "grace" involved. To refuse to avenge oneself against others, to pray for one's persecutors and enemies, and to forgive trespasses are a kind of spiritual alms, joined in Jesus's teaching with generous giving and love for those who will not likely be able to repay (Luke 6:27–36). Like alms, such spiritual works of mercy store up treasure or a kind of heavenly line of "credit" that makes one rich in God's economy (1 Pet. 2:19–20; cf. Matt. 5:46; Luke 6:35). Acts of mercy are also a kind of self-denial in the battle against our own pride, as we refuse to hold ourselves (also sinners) above others or to count their evils against us as greater than those for which we ourselves hope to be forgiven. If we are inclined to strictness, or inclined to exact for ourselves more immediate justice than God does, God will use the same measure back on us (Matt. 7:1–2).

But forgiveness is more than another type of penance that Jesus promises to reward. It is *fundamental to one's identity* as a disciple of Jesus. Jesus's

---

39. Augustine, *Homilies on the First Epistle of John* 7.1 (trans. Ramsey, 104).

parable in Matthew 18:21–35 spells this out. A slave owed his master ten thousand talents, an enormous sum. But when his debt was called and he should have been cast into debtors' prison, he begged for mercy and was, wondrously, forgiven. But, when he leaves, the man sees a fellow slave who owed him one hundred denarii. This is a considerable amount to one earning a living—over three months' wages for a worker—but it pales in comparison to the first slave's debt. It would take about six thousand denarii to equal one "talent."[40] Yet the man, having been forgiven the enormous debt, does not let the master's forgiveness change his own attitude toward his money or toward others. He accosts his fellow slave, demands his money, refuses to show any patience, and has the man thrown into debtors' prison. When the master finds out, he confronts the unforgiving slave. "You wicked slave! I forgave you all that debt because you pleaded with me. Should you not have had mercy on your fellow slave, as I had mercy on you?" (Matt. 18:32–33). This time, the master recalls his forgiveness and has the man thrown into prison. "So my heavenly Father will also do to every one of you," Jesus concludes, "if you do not forgive your brother or sister from your heart" (Matt. 18:35).

Disciples of Jesus are people who live by mercy, by forgiveness. It is the source of our life, as we are ransomed by God from sin and renewed to his grace. But if God's mercy is the source of our life, it must also govern and reshape the way we live with others. To refuse to be forgiving is to refuse to be part of the Church, the community of God's mercy; it is to be a prodigal who wants his father to forgive him but refuses to return home to live in his household. Mercy and patience are defining characteristics of God (Exod. 34:6; Ps. 145:8). God, the divine creditor, has the prerogative and ultimate authority to forgive all sin, since all sins incur debt before God. Inasmuch as others sin against us and owe us a "debt," though, we have the honor of *imitating God* in mercy and love. "Be merciful, just as your Father is merciful" (Luke 6:36). Jesus calls his followers to love their enemies and pray for those who persecute them, to judge others leniently, and he offers yet another reason for this command: "You will be children of the Most High; for he is kind to the ungrateful and the wicked" (Luke 6:35) and gives good things to

40. Weights and measures must be calculated by comparisons and ancient descriptions as well as evidence of coinage, and it is not always exact. Marvin A. Powell's conclusions, given above, are still sufficiently reliable ("Weights and Measures," *ABD* 6:897–908, at 907–8). Michael P. Theophilos treats the issues and, notably, shows that the denarius was not simply a laborer's usual "daily wage" but, in many cases, would have been considered generous (*Numismatics and Greek Lexicography*, T&T Clark Biblical Studies [London: T&T Clark, 2020], 92–101).

Act of Love

The connection between love for God and others with forgiveness—God's forgiveness for us and our forgiveness of others—is beautifully recalled in a popular Catholic prayer, the "Act of Love."

> O my God, I love you above all things with my whole heart and soul, because you are all good and worthy of all my love. I love my neighbor as myself for the love of you. I forgive all who have injured me, and ask pardon for all whom I have injured. In this love I resolve to live and die.

those who sin against him (Matt. 5:45). Further, as mercy is an act of love, mercy and forgiveness for others restore God's likeness in us and join us to God in love. God *is* love, and Christ shows the greatest love in his death on the cross, a death he chose out of mercy for sinners (John 15:13; Rom. 5:8; Gal. 2:20; 1 John 4:8, 16). We are called to follow him in forgiveness and love, imitating Christ and the Father (John 13:34–35). And when we are perfected in Christlike love, we will know him and be like him, restored to the love and glory for which humanity was made (1 John 3:1–3; 4:12, 17).

That is the goal of Jesus's mercy toward the fallen: to bring the lost home to live in love and obedience to the Father, to restore us to the likeness of God. This is what our practices of penance and self-denial ultimately aim at. It is what Christ calls for in his earthly ministry. It is what he died for. And, through the power of the Holy Spirit, Jesus's work of mercy and restoration continues after Easter in the apostolic Church.

8

Christ, the Spirit, and the Ministry of Forgiveness

> If you forgive the sins of any, they are forgiven them; if you retain the sins of any, they are retained.
>
> —John 20:23

Jesus came to save. In him the salvation of God is revealed to "all flesh"—Israel and the nations (Luke 3:6). In him Isaiah's prophecies are fulfilled of a coming king who would rule the world in righteousness and of a Servant who would suffer to redeem his people. Ezekiel's promises that God would come to shepherd his people and that the Davidic king would be their shepherd are fulfilled at once in Christ, both Son of God and son of David. He delivers and ransoms his people from the debt of guilt, and he not only commands them to a life of repentance but also models it himself. He is both their "leader" (Heb. 12:2 NABRE) on the way back to the Father and "the way" itself (John 14:6).

Christ's work to renew humanity and reconcile the fallen to God forgives guilt and restores sinners through repentance and love. After his resurrection and ascension into heaven, he continues this saving mission through the Church. He sends forth the Holy Spirit upon the Church to unite believers to himself and to the Father, and he commissions the apostles to preach repentance and to forgive sins by the power of his Spirit in them. Through their ministry, the Spirit forms Christ's followers in faith and love so that Adam's children might be restored "day by day" to the glory of God's "image" (2 Cor. 3:18; 4:16). This work of the Spirit is accomplished through the mediation of the apostles and others preaching, baptizing, and conferring Christ's sanctifying Spirit on others, as well as the ministry of disciplining sinners and pronouncing forgiveness in Jesus's name. As we consider the sacrament of reconciliation in Scripture, we should reflect on the saving work of Christ and its mediation through the Spirit in the Church.

Christ the Mediator and His Mediating Spirit

The problem of sin and its effects is multifaceted. Sin incurs guilt and ruptures the sinner's relationship with God. The fall into sin also leads to death, condemning to decay humans whom God created to receive the gift of immortality. Sin also has effects within. "Original sin," inherited along with human nature, inclines one to prioritize one's own desires and pride in ways that go against the love and righteousness for which humanity was created—distorting the image of God in us. Sinful acts ("actual sin") can reinforce that inclination and create patterns of behavior that do further harm to ourselves and to our relationships with God and others.

Christ's work to redeem is also, therefore, multifaceted, counteracting and surpassing sin and its effects. Christ, as God and man, bridges heaven and earth, divine and human. In joining the divine nature to humanity, Christ also rejoins humanity to the life of God. The incarnate Christ himself "is the image of the invisible God" (Col. 1:15; cf. 2 Cor. 4:4), revealing the glory that he shares with the Father for our salvation (John 1:14, 18). Jesus pays the ransom to free us from the debt of sin by his righteous life and death, bringing about forgiveness for our past. His death becomes our death, as we "die" and are "crucified" with him (Rom. 6:3–6). And by his resurrection to immortal, bodily life, he opens the way for humans to share or "participate" in the reality of his divine immortality (2 Pet. 1:4; cf. Rom. 6:8–11). Joined to Christ, humans are joined again to the fullness of the image they were created to bear. This will be seen supremely at the general resurrection, when all in Christ will be "changed" and will bear the "image" of Christ in incorruptible bodies (1 Cor. 15:49, 51; cf. John 3:31). Before then, too, being joined to Christ brings a gradual renewal not necessarily of our external bodies but in love and righteousness. Those in Christ are joined through him to the Father, and their inward selves—according to Paul, their very humanity (Greek *anthrōpos*)—begin to be renewed. The "old self . . . corrupt and deluded by its lusts" no longer reigns, and "the new self, created according to the likeness of God in true righteousness and holiness," takes root to restore us within (Eph. 4:22, 24; cf. 2 Cor. 4:16; 5:17; Col. 3:9–10).

All of this comes about through Jesus Christ. It is through the incarnate God, who he is and what he has done, that humanity is ransomed from sin and death and restored to life with God. As 1 Timothy 2:5–6 puts it, there is "one mediator between God and the human race, Christ Jesus, himself human, who gave himself as ransom for all" (NABRE). Those who seek the Father come to him through Christ, and those who join themselves to Christ are joined to the Father (John 6:45; 14:6–11). Those who receive Christ's body and blood, who receive Christ's words by faith, and who keep his commandments dwell or "abide" in him, taking part in the reality of who he is, and they are joined to the Father through him (cf. John 3:36; 5:24; 6:34–58; 15:7–10; 17:20–23).

Christ is the only one in whom all of this could come about. Yet, if humans must be united to the divine life through the God-man, Christ, how is our access to Christ mediated? The New Testament ascribes this role first and foremost to the *Holy Spirit*. Indeed, according to John the Baptist, this is one distinctive aspect of Christ's saving work: he is the one who will bring and give God's Holy Spirit (John 1:32–33; cf. Matt. 3:11; Mark 1:8; Luke 3:16). The Spirit is both the Spirit of the Father and the Spirit of the Son (cf. Matt. 10:20; Rom. 8:14; Gal. 4:6), and being filled with the Spirit of God's Son joins one to Christ and to his identity as God's beloved child and heir (Rom. 8:12–17; Gal. 4:4–7). As Jesus himself promised, the Spirit is poured out so that, after his departure, Christ may dwell "in" the hearts of his people on earth and they, in turn, may dwell "in" him (John 14:17). The presence of Christ and his divine image is mediated through the work of the Holy Spirit.[1]

Jeremiah foretold a New Covenant in which God's people would be forgiven their sins under the law of Moses and in which their hearts would be restored to a relationship of intimacy and obedience to God (Jer. 31:31–34). Ezekiel, similarly, prophesied that God would purify the people with water, renew them in obedience, and give them new life by sending his own Spirit into them (Ezek. 36:25–27). Christ, by his great sacrifice, becomes "the mediator of a new covenant" surpassing the covenant of Sinai, bringing forgiveness and restoration to life (Heb. 9:15; cf. Luke 22:20; 2 Cor. 3:6). And he mediates this

---

1. Outright rejection of the Holy Spirit is thus said to block one's forgiveness and salvation (see Mark 3:29–30).

to individuals by sending the Holy Spirit. The Lord who has "life in himself" (John 5:26) shares his life with the fallen through "water and Spirit" (John 3:5). The Spirit works to convict the world of sin and to make the Church preserve the life-giving words of Jesus (John 14:25–26; 15:26; 16:7–15). Christ's one-time death in Jerusalem atones for the sins of the whole world, and individuals in ancient Corinth or modern America are purified through the power of the Spirit that joins them to Christ in baptism (1 Cor. 6:11; 12:13). Further, when one receives the Spirit, the Spirit works within to "pour out" God's love in one's heart and to fuel repentance and renewal in love (Rom. 5:5). Christ's mission of restoration is driven by the power of the Spirit within to "strengthen" believers in their "inner being with power" (Eph. 3:16). Union with Christ, for forgiveness and for inner renewal, is forged by the power of God's Holy Spirit. When that renewal is complete, the Father will raise fallen mortals to share Christ's divine image perfectly in immortality:

> Anyone who does not have the Spirit of Christ does not belong to him. But if Christ is in you, though the body is dead because of sin, the Spirit is life because of righteousness. If the Spirit of him who raised Jesus from the dead dwells in you, he who raised Christ from the dead will give life to your mortal bodies also through his Spirit that dwells in you. (Rom. 8:9–11)

Union with Christ's death and resurrection joins the fallen human to Christ's atoning death and to his life as God's Son. This union is mediated, forged, and continued by the power of Christ's Holy Spirit. And the Spirit works this ministry of mediation further *through the Church.* Christ commissioned his apostles to be his witnesses, by preaching and baptizing and making disciples of all in his name (Matt. 28:18–20). And he promised his presence and divine power would be with them through the Spirit after his departure (Luke 24:49; Acts 1:8). By Christ's authority and power, the apostles will be part of the Spirit's work to mediate Christ to others and will tend the flock of the Good Shepherd under him—by carrying out his ministry of forgiveness and restoration in his name.

Christ's Under-Mediators: The King and His Spiritual Stewards

The Father shares all things with the Son, and the Son receives all things from the Father (John 3:35; 13:3; 17:2). Christ bears this in himself as God's Son,

The Nicene Creed: The Third Article

The ministry of Christ on earth through the sacraments is energized by the power of the Holy Spirit in the Church. This is why the Christian creeds place belief in the Church, baptism, and forgiveness in the third article on the Holy Spirit, as here in the Nicene Creed:

> I believe in the Holy Spirit, the Lord, the giver of life, who proceeds from the Father and the Son, who with the Father and the Son is adored and glorified, who has spoken through the prophets. I believe in one, holy, catholic and apostolic Church. I confess one Baptism for the forgiveness of sins and I look forward to the resurrection of the dead and the life of the world to come.

always working in concert with the Father. The Spirit, Jesus says, will take what is Christ's and declare it to the Church after Easter (John 16:13–15). The Church's ministry is grounded in the power and mission of Christ, shared with them through the Holy Spirit. The Spirit will remind the apostles of Jesus's words and lead them in their understanding of the fullness of truth (John 14:25–26; 16:13). The Spirit will support them and guide them in their mission, moving them to speak faithfully even when they are persecuted (Luke 12:11–12).

The Spirit mediates the risen Christ to the Church on earth and works particularly through the apostles' mission to preach, baptize, and hand on the faith. The Gospels and Acts use different images to describe the Spirit's work. John can describe the Spirit as "the Paraclete," a helper or advocate aiding the Church in its life in God for its mission in the world (e.g., John 14:16, 26). The language of "power" is also used of the Spirit's presence and work in the apostles to convert unbelievers by their preaching (Luke 24:49; Acts 1:8; 6:8). Another image used in Christ's commissioning of the apostles for ministry is that of "authority." Christ, who bears "all authority" in heaven and earth (Matt. 28:18), commissions the disciples for their ministry on the basis of his authority, which they are to exercise in his name and at his command. He gives them authority to share in his work of casting out demons, healing, preaching repentance, and also forgiving and retaining sins by the power of his Spirit in them.

Authority Vested: The Church's Ministry

Christ opposed sin and freed people from it by his own life of righteousness and also by his work to free individuals from demons, to forgive sins, and to call people to repentance (e.g., Matt. 9:35). He shares such authority with his disciples, even sending them out at different points in his ministry. "Then Jesus called the twelve together and gave them power and authority over all demons and to cure diseases, and he sent them out to proclaim the kingdom of God and to heal" (Luke 9:1–2; cf. Matt. 10:1, 6–8). After his departure, too, Christ's enduring, heavenly authority is the basis on which they continue this ministry: "All authority in heaven and on earth has been given to me. Go therefore and make disciples of all nations. . . . And remember, I am with you always, to the end of the age" (Matt. 28:18–20).

The term "authority" (Greek *exousia*) is sometimes also translated "power." When Jesus offers to come to the home of a centurion for a healing, the centurion says that he is unworthy to receive Jesus, but he is confident in Jesus's "authority" to heal from a distance. He knows about authority, being under that of others and exercising it himself: "For I also am a man under authority, with soldiers under me; and I say to one, 'Go,' and he goes, and to another, 'Come,' and he comes, and to my slave, 'Do this,' and the slave does it" (Matt. 8:9). He believes that Jesus has the authority to command and be obeyed, to just "speak the word" and make things happen (Matt. 8:8). Similarly, people are amazed at Jesus's authority when even demons have to obey his word (Mark 1:27). Yet authority does not merely indicate power over others. Ideally, authority also implies that one's use of that power is lawful. When Jesus overturns the tables of the money changers at the temple, the chief priests and elders ask him, "By what authority are you doing these things, and who gave you this authority?" (Matt. 21:23). Their question is not about where he got his strength to overturn tables, but whether he legitimately represents someone who can make decisions about what should be going on in the temple. When Jesus pronounces forgiveness upon the man who was paralyzed, the scribes doubt both that he is able to pronounce such forgiveness and that it is legitimate for him to do so. So he heals the man in order to prove that he has this authority (Mark 2:1–11).

When Christ commissions his disciples with authority over diseases and unclean spirits to preach authoritatively of his kingdom, it is an authority they possess under him and in his name. Christ possesses authority to make commands and to take action not from a human commander or from temple priests but through his own divinity, because of who he *is*. As the eternal Son, he is able to explain not merely a valid interpretation of the law of Moses but the reason God gave certain laws in the first place (Mark 10:4–9). As the Son with whom the Father shares all things, decisions about judgment and life are in his hands (see John 5:19–30). The apostles have authority not because of who they *are* in themselves, but because they are *connected* to the Son. By the Spirit, the Son shares all things with them and grants them power to act in his name. They act as his representatives, by his authorization, through his power, and they do so for the sake of his own kingdom and for his creatures.

The metaphor from the human world that appears often in Jesus's parables is that of a king or landowner granting authority to his *stewards*. The head of the kingdom, or the head of a household, delegates authority to his stewards—over business decisions and finances, over planting decisions, over other servants, and so forth. The servants a steward manages are expected to obey the steward, but they are the master's servants. The money a steward manages is at his disposal to manage, but it is the master's money, and the steward is expected to manage it to the master's benefit (and, of course, their own benefit, since they are part of the master's economic household too). If they misuse that authority, they will be accountable for it. Jesus emphasizes that his stewards must be faithful: if so, they will be rewarded, but if they think that in his delay to return they can be lazy, abuse his subjects, or act in a way that misrepresents him, they will be punished (Matt. 24:45–51; Luke 12:42–48). Nonetheless, their authority as stewards means that they do have power to make decisions and do business with what has been entrusted to them if the Lord's will is to be done, even if this power can be misused. The kingdom of heaven is like a man who went away and "summoned his slaves and entrusted his property to them" (Matt. 25:14). He gives large sums of money ("talents") to each so that they may carry on his business. The ones who put the money to good use are rewarded. But the one who, in fear, intentionally only preserves his talent rather than doing business with it is punished (Matt. 25:14–30).

Christ gives authority to his disciples so that they may share in his mission, doing the kingdom's business, making decisions in his name, and authoritatively serving those under their charge. They represent Christ in his work to preach the kingdom and call people to repentance. They represent him in his work to exorcise demons. They represent him because they are connected to him, and they are made *authoritative mediators* of Christ's presence and

Christ's saving work to others. If none can come to the Father except through the Son, the Son is similarly represented by his Church: "Whoever listens to you listens to me, and whoever rejects you rejects me, and whoever rejects me rejects the one who sent me" (Luke 10:16; cf. John 13:20). Just as Christ was sent by the Father, so in the same way, after Easter, Christ sends out the Church by the Holy Spirit: "'As the Father has sent me, so I send you.' When he had said this, he breathed on them and said to them, 'Receive the Holy Spirit'" (John 20:21–22).

The work of the Church to represent Christ authoritatively for the salvation of souls is grounded on Christ's own authority to share what is his. And he mediates it to the Church through the power of the Holy Spirit. This is why the Christian creeds place belief in the Church within the third article, "I believe in the Holy Spirit." The presence and power of Christ mediated through the Spirit gives the Church authority to speak in his name and discern divine truth. Christ's authoritative mediators are given the ability to *confer* the Spirit on others: on all through baptism (Acts 2:38) and for particular charisms

The Stewardship of Christ's Apostolic Ministers

The role of the apostles' appointed successors as Christ's stewards and representatives was received as an essential mark of the Church early on. Ignatius of Antioch, writing to various churches around AD 110, uses imagery from the household and the symphony.

> For everyone whom the Master of the house sends to manage his own house we must welcome as we would the one who sent him. It is obvious, therefore, that we must regard the bishop as the Lord himself.[a]

> For Jesus Christ, our inseparable life, is the mind of the Father, just as the bishops appointed throughout the world are in the mind of Christ. Thus it is proper for you to run together in harmony with the mind of the bishop, as you are in fact doing. For your council of presbyters . . . is attuned to the bishop as strings to a lyre. Therefore in your unanimity and harmonious love Jesus Christ is sung.[b]

a. Ignatius, *To the Ephesians* 6.1 (trans. Holmes, 187).
b. Ignatius, *To the Ephesians* 3.2–4.1 (trans. Holmes, 185, 187).

and ministries by the laying on of hands (cf. Acts 6:6; 13:3). They are given Christ's Spirit to preach repentance and to be examples of it themselves. By the same power and as part of the same mission of salvation, Christ grants the apostles also the authority to forgive and retain sins.

Authority Vested: Forgiving and Retaining Sins

Christ's work to oppose sin is shared with the Church through the Spirit in word and sacrament. The Spirit energizes the Church's ministry of preaching the *word*. The Spirit guides the Church to understand and hand on Jesus's words (John 14:25–26), leads the Church into all truth, and testifies concerning sin and righteousness (John 16:7–15). The apostles, by the power of the Spirit, call sinners to repentance and life in Christ by this word. Through that word, the Church calls unbelievers to believe and receive grace through *sacrament*. In baptism, which is not a mere bath but "the bath of water with the word" (Eph. 5:26 NABRE), Christ shares his Spirit to purify and give new life to sinners and make them part of his body (cf. 1 Cor. 6:11; Titus 3:5; 1 Pet. 3:21). Indeed, in administering baptism and in calling all to faith, the Church takes part in Christ's work not merely to rebuke sin but to *forgive* it: for baptism into Christ brings "forgiveness" and a "washing away" of former sins (Acts 2:38; 22:16).

The apostles, then, are commissioned with authority to forgive sins by administering the sacrament of baptism. But if the restoration of the divine image in human beings is the goal, continued sin after baptism needs to be dealt with also. Christian sin has consequences and can incur penalty. This is clearly the case in the potential for believers to fall from grace. Paul, speaking to people he says have already received baptism and the gift of the Spirit (Gal. 3:1–5, 26–29), warns that they will "fall from grace" and forfeit their share in God's kingdom if they reject the apostolic gospel or turn to live in grave sin (Gal. 5:2–4, 19–21; 6:8). Even in less extreme cases, however, sin still needs to be addressed and forgiven. Paul also teaches that even those who remain in Christ will be requited and endure fiery "testing" and purification at their judgment (1 Cor. 3:12–15; cf. 2 Cor. 5:10). First John 5:16 likewise calls Christians to intercede for their "brothers"—fellow Christians—when they commit sins not leading to death. Indeed, as our previous chapter noted, Jesus builds this reality into the Lord's Prayer, calling his disciples to pray for forgiveness of their own sins as a necessity on par with daily bread (Matt. 6:12). Sins after baptism and conversion incur guilt and penalty, potentially eternal (not just temporal) penalty if one falls from grace, and they need to be dealt with.

Jesus shares with the disciples his authority to deal with Christian sin by forgiveness and discipline. Jesus has the authority not simply to pronounce forgiveness as a human forgiving those who wrong him personally, but to pronounce sins forgiven in heaven, in the sight of God. The synoptic Gospels show Jesus demonstrating this in his healing of the man who was paralyzed (Matt. 9:1–8; Mark 2:1–11; Luke 5:17–26). When Jesus sees the faith of the man's friends, he tells him, "Son, your sins are forgiven" (Mark 2:5). Quickly, many bystanders understand this as blasphemy, that Jesus is speaking on God's behalf with no authority or power to do so: "Who can forgive sins but God alone?" (Mark 2:7). Jesus, however, identifies his authority to forgive with his ability to heal—both equally sourced in his divinity—and heals the man with his word in order to prove "that the Son of Man has authority on earth to forgive sins" (Mark 2:10). Christ, as the divine Son, has the authority to pronounce forgiveness of sins on earth, a pronouncement made with his human mouth and heard by human ears, but one that is nonetheless valid in heaven.

Jesus is the divine creditor, and he gives his apostles authority to manage the forgiveness of debts owed to their Lord as stewards of "the household of God, which is the church" (1 Tim. 3:15; cf. Luke 16:1–8). This is explicit in two passages from Matthew and one from John. First, and centrally, we see it in Jesus's commissioning of Peter. Jesus gives Simon the name "Peter" (Greek *Petros*), a name derived from one of the Greek terms for "rock" (*petra*): "You are Peter, and on this rock I will build my church, and the gates of Hades will not prevail against it" (Matt. 16:18). You are *Petros*, and on this *petra* I will build my Church.[2] In biblical-theological terms, we can see here Jesus sharing his authority with Peter already in the name: God is the "rock," and Christ is the "rock" on which the foundation of the Church and one's salvation are built (Deut. 32:4; Matt. 7:24–25; 1 Pet. 2:4–8; 1 Cor. 10:4). In John 21:15–19, the Good Shepherd entrusts his flock to Peter for Peter to shepherd. Here, similarly, Peter is made a rock, not separate from Christ, but in him, on which

---

2. This correlation is even clearer in Aramaic, as the name *Kepha'* is identical with the term *kepha'*, "rock." Peter's Aramaic name *Kepha'*, spelled *Kēphas* in Greek ("Cephas" in Latin and English), is visible at several points in the New Testament, most notably John 1:42: "Jesus looked at him and said, 'You are Simon the son of John; you will be called Cephas' (which is translated Peter)" (NABRE). Paul uses this untranslated version of Peter's name frequently (e.g., 1 Cor. 1:12; Gal. 1:18).

the solid "foundation" of Christ's Church will be established in Peter's time and thereafter.[3]

Peter's role as the rock on which Christ's Church will be built is directly connected, likewise, with Jesus's conferral of high authority on Peter's office. "I will give you the keys of the kingdom of heaven, and whatever you bind on earth will be bound in heaven, and whatever you loose on earth will be loosed in heaven" (Matt. 16:19). Peter will be given the "keys" to the kingdom of which Christ, as the Son, is king. The metaphor of "keys" is, again, an image of stewardship, as when Eliakim is made high steward of the Davidic kingdom when he receives "authority" and "the key" to the kingdom (Isa. 22:15–24). In God's kingdom, keys are thus associated with teaching authority, administration, and also with the priesthood (cf. Matt. 23:13; Luke 11:52).[4] The exercise of this authority of the keys is summarized in the promise that Peter will be able, on earth, to perform heavenly "binding and loosing." These terms indicate, again, authoritative teaching and governance of God's people—to "loose" a commandment or its interpretation as nonbinding or to "bind" people to follow a commandment in a particular way (cf. Matt. 5:19)—and thus also judicial activity. In teaching, an authority figure can bind and loose by giving permissions or requirements for behavior. When the same authority is applied in governance and judgment, "'to bind' and 'to loose' correspond to 'to put in fetters' or 'to acquit,'" pronouncing guilt and forgiveness.[5] Peter, as steward of Christ's kingdom, will have the authority to teach and make decisions about guilt and obedience in governing the community.

This authority is given to Peter, here with the "keys" to the kingdom. Later in Matthew, we see that Peter's authority to bind and loose is also shared with others who hold apostolic office with him, though they do not possess the "keys" as Peter does.[6] Jesus speaks to his apostles about dealing with sin in

3. A similar image in Ephesians depicts Christ as the great, all-important "cornerstone" of the Church, with the apostles then being the "foundation" stones fit onto and supported by that cornerstone (Eph. 2:20). This architectural imagery appears also in, e.g., Rev. 21:14 and *Shepherd of Hermas* 13.1 (Vision III.2).

4. See Michael Patrick Barber, "Jesus as the Davidic Temple Builder and Peter's Priestly Role in Matthew 16:16–19," *JBL* 132 (2013): 935–53.

5. Ulrich Luz, *Matthew 8–20*, trans. James E. Crouch, Hermeneia (Minneapolis: Fortress, 2001), 365.

6. Jesus, in designating Peter as the "rock," declares with singular verbs that Peter particularly (singular "you") possesses the keys and bears power to bind and loose (Matt. 16:19). In Matt. 18:18 he ascribes the same authority to all of the apostles (plural "you"). The latter verse is sometimes taken to remove any singularity from the promise to Peter. But, while Matt. 18 shows that this authority is not solely *restricted* to Peter, it does not equate their office with his

the community (Matt. 18:15–20). If a fellow disciple sins against you, Jesus says, he is to be rebuked, first by the one wronged, then by more witnesses, and finally, if he is still unrepentant, by the Church. "If he listens to you, you have gained your brother," Jesus says (Matt. 18:15 ESV). But if the person refuses to repent, even after being rebuked not just by a friend but by the Church, then the Church is to use its authority to "bind" and cast that person out by the power of Christ. "Truly I tell you, whatever you bind on earth will be bound in heaven, and whatever you loose on earth will be loosed in heaven" (Matt. 18:18). Paul, as we will see in the following chapter, exercises this authority by pronouncing judgment against a publicly unrepentant sinner and commands that he be excommunicated (1 Cor. 5:1–5). Paul, though not one of the Twelve, also bears apostolic authority as a "steward" of Christ by the power of the Spirit (cf. 1 Cor. 4:1). Here, he exercises it both in determining the man's unrepentance and in binding him in his sin until he repents, just as later, after the man has repented, Paul uses his authority to "loose" by forgiving the man and calling for his readmission to the community (2 Cor. 2:6–11).

In John's Gospel, the risen Christ confers this authority on the apostles not in terms of "binding" and "loosing" but in terms of "forgiving" and "retaining" sins. After his resurrection, when he appears to the apostles, he commissions them to do so directly: "As the Father has sent me, so I send you" (John 20:21). The Lord sends them out for his same mission (the same "sending"), not independent of him but by his own power as the crucified and risen Son of God. As we have seen, he does this by communicating his Holy Spirit to them: "When he had said this, he breathed on them and said to them, 'Receive the Holy Spirit. If you forgive the sins of any, they are forgiven them; if you retain the sins of any, they are retained'" (John 20:22–23). John's language of Jesus "breathing the Spirit on"—or, perhaps, "into"—them (Greek *enephysēsen*) recalls the creation of humanity in Genesis 2:7: "And God formed the man as dust from the earth and breathed [*enephysēsen*] into his face the breath of

---

in every respect. The other apostles are not promised the "keys" given to the kingdom's head steward, and it is better to assume that the other apostles exercise their authority interdependently ("if two of you agree," Matt. 18:19) and in connection with Peter. As W. D. Davies and Dale C. Allison Jr. argue, Matt. 16:19 seems to speak of a "wider authority," associated as it is with the foundation of the universal Church: "If power to bind and loose was also given to others, that does not entail that those others exercised their power in quite the same way as did Peter, or that they too held the keys of the kingdom" (*The Gospel according to Saint Matthew*, 3 vols., ICC [Edinburgh: T&T Clark, 1988–2004], 2:635).

"The Manifold Mercy of God"

The source and ground of apostolic authority in Christ's role as mediator, and Christ's ongoing power exercised through apostolic ministers to restore sinners by penance and reconciliation, is emphasized well in this letter from Leo the Great:

> The manifold mercy of GOD so assists men when they fall, that not only by the grace of baptism but also by the remedy of penitence is the hope of eternal life revived. . . . For the Mediator between GOD and men, the Man Christ Jesus, has transmitted this power to those that are set over the Church that they should both grant a course of penitence to those who confess, and, when they are cleansed by wholesome correction, admit them through the door of reconciliation. . . . In which work assuredly the Saviour Himself unceasingly takes part and is never absent from those things, the carrying out of which He has committed to His ministers, saying: "Lo, I am with you all the days even to the completion of the age."[a]

a. Leo the Great, *Letter* 108.2 (in *NPNF*[2] 12:80).

life, and the man became a living soul."[7] The mission of Christ to deliver the world from the effects of sin and death is a work of new creation: he casts down Satan and takes away the sins of the world (John 1:29; 12:31), bringing life through repentance and forgiveness. And now, by the power of the Spirit, he commissions the disciples to carry out the same.[8]

The disciples are given the authority and task of forgiving sins, of pronouncing absolution. They do this directly, representing Jesus as Jesus represents the Father: "Whose sins *you* forgive are forgiven them" (John 20:23 NABRE; italics added). As Jesus was sent as representative of the Father—"Whoever has seen me has seen the Father" (John 14:9)—so now he sends them as his representatives. "Whoever receives one whom I send receives me" (John 13:20). Or, in Luke, "Whoever listens to you listens to me" (Luke 10:16). We might rephrase this in the confessional: "Whoever *confesses* to you confesses to me" or "Whoever hears your absolution hears mine." The

7. I have translated from the Greek Septuagint here. Similarly, with the same verb, see Wis. 15:11.
8. See Marianne Meye Thompson, *John: A Commentary*, NTL (Louisville: Westminster John Knox, 2015), 422: "The disciples' mission reflects and extends Jesus' own mission by participating in God's mission to bring life to the world, here expressed in terms of the forgiveness of sins."

power to effect this forgiveness remains, as noted above, that of God, but it becomes theirs *in* God by the power of the Spirit.[9]

In addition to pronouncing forgiveness, the apostles are also tasked with the responsibility to "retain" sins. "This latter aspect may seem harsh, but it flows naturally from the story of Jesus."[10] Jesus meets some who would like to be told they do not need repentance, but he leaves them in their sins (John 9:39–41). Jesus's own words and miracles condemn those who respond to them with apathy or unbelief rather than saving faith (John 12:47–50; 15:22–24; cf. 3:16–18). The Spirit continues the same in the Church, bringing Christ's ministers to hand on his word, convicting the world of sin and righteousness (John 14:25–26; 16:7–11), and, in specific cases, forgiving or retaining sins. Bringing life to human souls means forgiving sins and renewing sinners through repentance. It also means diagnosing those who want forgiveness but are not in fact repentant, like a prodigal asking his father for more money but refusing to live again in his household.

The Ministry of Repentance for the Forgiveness of Sins

The Church, by the power of the Spirit, continues Christ's work to bring life to the world. Christ prepared his apostles for this vocation by sending them out during his earthly ministry to preach, heal, and drive out demons. And Jesus promised that, when the Spirit infused Jesus's apostles, they would be empowered to preach "repentance for the forgiveness of sins . . . to all nations" (Luke 24:47 ESV). In the book of Acts, after Pentecost, we see Christ continue his powerful work to free people from sin in the Church.

Through the Spirit in his apostles, the risen Jesus continues to oppose sin by casting out demons, healing, and purifying. The apostles do many "wonders" and "signs" (Acts 2:43; 5:12), casting out unclean spirits (Acts 8:7; 15:16; 16:16–18) and healing the sick by their word through the name of Jesus (Acts 3:1–8; 9:33–35; 14:8–10; 28:8–9). They also raise the dead by Christ's Spirit of life (Acts 9:36–43; 20:6–12). Many sick and possessed people are delivered just by coming into contact with Peter's shadow (Acts 5:15–16) or by cloths and handkerchiefs that Paul had touched (Acts 19:11–12). Jesus had said that his

9. Urban C. von Wahlde calls this power "sacramental, in the sense that the power is mediated through human action and volition" (*The Gospel and Letters of John*, 3 vols., ECC [Grand Rapids: Eerdmans, 2010], 2:860).

10. Francis J. Moloney, *The Gospel of John*, SP 4 (Collegeville, MN: Liturgical Press, 1998), 533.

followers would do works even "greater" than his by the power of his name (John 14:12–14), and this is precisely what occurs in the Church through the ministry of the Spirit.

The disciples do many miracles and signs of God's power and God's plan of restoration. Perhaps the greatest wonder worked through them, though, is the conversion of sinners. The apostles preach. They preach from the basis of the Scriptures, reading them in light of Christ and by the guidance of the Spirit (cf. Acts 2:22–36; 15:13–21). Paul, particularly, also preaches to pagans from the witness of their culture or from nature (Acts 14:1–18; 17:16–31). But to any audience and by any argumentation, the apostles' message to unbelievers is a call to repent and believe in Jesus for the forgiveness of sins. "Repent therefore, and turn to God so that your sins may be wiped out" (Acts 3:19), Peter proclaims in Jerusalem. Paul summarizes his mission to the pagans as a mission "to open their eyes so that they may turn from darkness to light and from the power of Satan to God, so that they may receive forgiveness of sins" (Acts 26:18). Christ has risen from the dead, and he will return to judge all, so now is the time for all to repent (Acts 17:30–31). "Save yourselves from this corrupt generation" (Acts 2:40). "Repent and be baptized every one of you in the name of Jesus Christ for the forgiveness of your sins, and you will receive the gift of the Holy Spirit" (Acts 2:38 ESV).

The apostles call people to turn from their sins and receive forgiveness and new life with God through faith and baptism. And through their preaching, God works to "open" people's "hearts" so that they are moved to faith and seek baptism (Acts 16:14). Thousands convert, Jews and pagans, impious and pious—even priests and Pharisees (Acts 6:7; 15:5)—such that, by the end of Acts, the gospel has spread from Judea and Syria to Greece and Rome.

The apostles do not exercise the ministry of forgiveness and repentance only in calling people to faith and baptism, however. They continue to exhort Christians in regular self-denial for Christ in prayerfully enduring persecution (cf. Acts 4:23–31; 5:41; 14:22). They continue the discipline of fasting (Acts 13:2–3; 9:9; 14:23). They give alms, selling their possessions to give to the Church's communal life and to aid those who are suffering (Acts 4:34–37; 9:36; 11:29; 24:17; cf. 10:2, 4). In general, the apostles devote themselves to the ministry of prayer and "the word" (Acts 6:4), preaching faith and charity in Christ, while the faithful "devoted themselves to the apostles' teaching and fellowship, to the breaking of bread and the prayers" (Acts 2:42). The apostles lead and guide the faithful in communal life, in repentance, in prayerful worship, and in love for their neighbors.

The apostles also have to use their authority to bind and loose in governing the Church and dealing with disputes and sin. They do so in deciding to appoint deacons under them to manage the affairs of the Church and communal distribution when their tasks become unmanageable (Acts 6:1–6). They do so in their teaching and governance, determining the Church's practice in the case of Gentile (non-Jewish) converts and whether they should be required to undergo circumcision and adopt Mosaic purity customs. They consider God's work to bring "the repentance that leads to life" to Gentiles when they believe (Acts 11:18), confirmed by God's sending the Spirit manifestly upon them and purifying their hearts (Acts 15:9). And they read the books of the prophets afresh in seeking divine guidance (Acts 15:13–21). Having let the Spirit lead them in the truth of God's revelation, the apostles and presbyters use the language of legal decree (woodenly "it seemed good") to communicate their decision: "It is the decision of the holy Spirit and of us" that Gentiles may receive baptism and be admitted to full participation in Christ's Church without being circumcised (Acts 15:28 NABRE).[11] It is their decision and the Spirit's decision, loosed on earth as in heaven.

They exercise their binding and loosing authority also in dealing with unrepentant sin. They do this often in the case of unbelievers who simply reject the gospel, declaring that they are still in their sins and unforgiven unless they repent: they condemn themselves as "unworthy of eternal life" by their unbelief (Acts 13:46); their blood is on their own hands (Acts 18:6).[12] But the apostles also exercise this authority among the *baptized*. Two examples stand out. One is Peter's rebuke of Ananias and his wife, Sapphira (Acts 5:1–11). The first believers in Jerusalem, Acts narrates, were quickly moved to sell properties—if they had them—and give the proceeds for the apostles to use and distribute (Acts 4:32–37). Ananias did the same, but, with his wife's knowledge, he did not give all the proceeds of the sale. Rather, he *acted* as though he had, but in fact he gave only part of the proceeds—presumably

11. See, e.g., Joseph A. Fitzmyer, *The Acts of the Apostles: A New Translation with Introduction and Commentary*, AB 31 (New York: Doubleday, 1998), 566, who offers one of many imperial examples in which "it seemed good" (Greek *edoxen*, as in Acts 15:28) introduces an authoritative decision: "It has been decided by me [Caesar Augustus] and my council under oath . . ." (Josephus, *Jewish Antiquities* 6.163 [trans. Fitzmyer]).

12. The apostles in this way are like prophets, and those who reject them are likened to rebellious Israel and its kings before the exile (Acts 7:51–53; 13:40–41; 28:25–28), joining together with the nations in rejection of God's saving call (Acts 4:23–31).

hoping to benefit twice, monetarily by the sale and also socially in the Church, gaining honor and "glory" for being more generous than he actually was.[13] There seems to have been no requirement that believers sell all to be part of the Church. The sin for which Peter confronts Ananias and Sapphira is not their lack of generosity but their *deception*: "Why has Satan filled your heart to lie to the Holy Spirit and to keep back for yourself part of the proceeds of the land? . . . You have not lied to man but to God" (Acts 5:3–4 ESV). Peter's words result in a "punitive miracle," as when Paul pronounces blindness on a magician trying to obstruct the gospel (Acts 13:9–11).[14] Ananias immediately falls down dead. When Sapphira arrives later, Peter questions her: "Tell me, did you sell the land for this amount?" (Acts 5:8 NABRE). Like God asking Cain about his brother, Peter's question is an invitation to confess. If she had, we might expect him to prescribe some penance to deal with the sin. But she does not. Not yet knowing her husband's fate, Sapphira continues their self-interested lie. Peter then rebukes her, too, for "testing" the Spirit and pronounces death upon her (Acts 5:9), and she dies immediately.

This episode is somewhat dramatic, and it is the only example of an apostle's authoritative rebuke resulting in death. A second example comes in the rebuke of Simon the Magician ("Simon Magus") in Acts 8:4–25. Philip, the deacon (Acts 6:5), had preached and performed signs in Samaria, and a well-known sorcerer there named Simon, though surely initially jealous of Philip's apparent power and acclaim, was moved to faith. "Even Simon himself believed. After being baptized, he stayed constantly with Philip and was amazed when he saw the signs and great miracles that took place" (Acts 8:13). However, Simon's desire for glory through power and magic reemerge at the arrival of the apostles. Philip's evangelization of Samaria had been independent, and, as elsewhere in similar situations, an apostolic delegation from Jerusalem comes to validate the new mission and bless it under the Church's authority (cf. Acts 8:14; 11:19–26).[15] In this case, Peter and John come to pray and lay their hands on the Samaritans to give their blessing and confer the Holy Spirit upon them with great signs of power.[16]

---

13. Fitzmyer, *Acts*, 316. Similarly, Craig S. Keener, *Acts: An Exegetical Commentary*, 4 vols. (Grand Rapids: Baker Academic, 2012–15), 2:1186; Luke Timothy Johnson, *The Acts of the Apostles*, SP 5 (Collegeville, MN: Liturgical Press, 1992), 92.

14. Fitzmyer, *Acts*, 317.

15. The episode, in that sense, says something of "apostolic jurisdiction" (Carl R. Holladay, *Acts: A Commentary*, NTL [Louisville: Westminster John Knox, 2016], 184–85).

16. The reception of the Spirit is consistently related in Acts and elsewhere with conversion and baptism (Acts 2:38; cf. 1 Cor. 12:13). This correlation is assumed to such a degree that,

But Simon, the old wonder-worker, becomes covetous of the apostles' power to give the Spirit by laying on hands, and he tries to buy it: "He offered them money, saying, 'Give me also this power so that anyone on whom I lay my hands may receive the Holy Spirit'" (Acts 8:18–19). The apostles *did* in fact lay their hands on people to appoint them to various ministries. But Simon does not, it seems, desire to receive the Spirit's gift for the sake of actual ministering. "Magic seeks a craft that can rationally control the divine powers," and this magician covets this exclusive authority in spiritual things.[17] Peter rebukes him for his evil intention and pronounces a curse on him as deserving death for this sin. Yet, more directly than with Sapphira, he calls him to repentance: "Repent therefore of this wickedness of yours, and pray to the Lord that, if possible, the intent of your heart may be forgiven you" (Acts 8:22). Peter employs his authority, "binding" Simon in his sin until he repents. And, apparently, Simon does. He begs for Peter to intercede for him, to pray that he not, in fact, die for this sin. What happens after that? The narrative simply ends with Simon's plea and moves on. According to some second-century sources, Simon would become a false teacher and opponent of the Church, suggesting either that he did not repent or that his repentance was impermanent. However, within Acts, though his forgiveness is not explicitly narrated, Peter's rebuke in this moment seems effective.[18] This is suggested particularly in the contrast between Simon and Ananias and Sapphira: in

---

when the Spirit descends on uncircumcised Gentiles before they are baptized, Peter infers that God is manifesting his will that Gentiles *should* henceforth be baptized and admitted to the Church without circumcision (not without baptism), since God has already given them the gift usually conferred in baptism (Acts 10:44–48; 11:15–17). When Paul meets some who have not received the Spirit, it is because they received only John's baptism and need to be baptized into Christ (Acts 19:1–7). In Samaria here, they apparently do not need rebaptism, but we are told that "they had only been baptized in the name of the Lord Jesus" and that "the Spirit had not come upon any of them" (Acts 8:16). It is unclear whether there was a particular insufficiency in Philip, or whether here Acts only means to say that the Spirit did not "come upon them" with powerful manifestations (such that they did not need rebaptism but did need the apostles' laying on of hands), and explanations abound (see Keener, *Acts*, 2:1522–27). The narrative does, at least, indicate divine approval of the Samaritan community through the Jerusalem apostles by the Spirit's powerful signs, which occasion Simon's sin.

17. Johnson, *Acts*, 149.

18. One manuscript tradition appears to accentuate Simon's repentance, adding that, in pleading for Peter's intercession in Acts 8:24, "he did not stop weeping greatly." But it is an outlier. Tertullian notes Simon's repentance in Acts but says that it was "vain" (*Treatise on the Soul* 34). Other Church Fathers point to Acts for Simon's evil beginnings but do not treat its apparent depiction of his contrition (e.g., Irenaeus, *Against Heresies* 1.23.1). Depictions of Simon as a false, heretical Christian compared to Marcion (ca. 140) can be found in Justin Martyr (*First Apology* 26; *Dialogue with Trypho* 120) and, more imaginatively, in the Pseudo-Clementine *Homilies* 2 and 3 and the *Acts of Peter*.

both cases Peter diagnoses their sins and pronounces them worthy of death, but, while Ananias receives no recourse to repentance and Sapphira does not confess when given the opportunity, Simon displays at least imperfect contrition and begs forgiveness. And Simon, unlike Ananias and Sapphira, does not drop down dead. If we are to understand that he lived where others died because of this repentance, we might infer that Peter "loosed" what he had "bound" in this case, even if Simon later turned away from his repentance.[19]

The Pattern of Penance in the Apostolic Church

The authority Christ grants to Peter and the other apostles by the Spirit is ordered "to save people from the consequences of their sins" by bringing all to repentance and life.[20] This is their participation in Christ's mission, and it is one that they hand on as the Church grows and spreads internationally, conferring the Spirit onto others for this ministry by the laying on of hands (cf. Acts 13:3; 14:23; 1 Tim. 4:14; 5:22; 2 Tim. 1:6). The Spirit works in all believers, uniting them to Christ and empowering them to live in self-denial and love for God and neighbor through various "ministries" (Greek *diakonia*, 1 Cor. 12:5) and "gifts" apportioned to different individuals (1 Cor. 12:4–13, 27–30). The apostles and their successors are hardly the only people in whom the Spirit's power is at work. But the Spirit is at work in apostolic ministers for a unique purpose. They are made shepherds over God's "flock" under the Good Shepherd and with Peter, whom Jesus commissioned to feed his sheep, to lead them by exhortation and by rebuke (John 21:15–19; Acts 20:28; Eph. 4:11; 1 Pet. 5:2). Their authority is managerial and representative, representing Christ in the Church and, by their words in his name, making decisions for the sake of the whole body of believers—in Acts at an international level with their pronouncement about Gentile circumcision. This authority over bodies of people, as well as the responsibility of publicly binding and loosing for discipline and forgiveness within the Church, is necessarily one that can be exercised by some but not all, whether in the international Church or in a particular congregation. Not all agreed with the apostles and presbyters in Jerusalem about admitting Gentiles without circumcision. As we will see in

19. See Johnson, *Acts*, 152–53; similarly, Fitzmyer, *Acts*, 407; Holladay, *Acts*, 186.
20. Robert W. Wall, "The Acts of the Apostles: Introduction, Commentary, and Reflections," *NIB* 10:1–368, at 140 (commenting on Peter's authority over Simon Magus in connection with Matt. 16:19).

Paul's excommunication of the immoral brother in Corinth, as well, many in that congregation approved of that man's immorality. But if this authority is not held by all, it is to be held by some for the *benefit and salvation* of all, as part of Christ's continued mission on earth to rebuke sinners so that they will know how far they have fallen, to forgive and readmit the penitent, and to guide all the faithful in the path of life.

Christ has died and made atonement for the sins of the world, a perfect and eternally effective offering that is like but surpasses the sacrifices prescribed for particular sins in the Levitical system (Heb. 10:11–14). By the Spirit's work to unite believers to Christ and conform them to his glorious image, the effects of Christ's sacrifice bring a new and superabundant glory in the New Covenant (2 Cor. 3:4–18). And the *pattern of penance* is, likewise, elevated in greater glory through the grace of the Spirit in the Church. Like Moses, yet as a minister of a more perfect covenant, the apostles mediate and intercede before God. Like the prophets, the apostles call unbelievers to turn from sin to God if they desire forgiveness and life, yet they are entrusted not merely with preaching and intercession but with directly forgiving sin and conferring God's transformative Spirit. Like prophets and faithful kings, the apostles call God's people—faithful yet still beset by weakness and temptation—to humble themselves and grow in obedience and love. And by uniting people to the Son through word and sacrament, the apostles not only tell people what faithfulness demands but take part in God's restoration of fallen humanity by joining souls to the immortal glory and image of God. This is the mission in which they take part as they preach "repentance for the forgiveness of sins" (Luke 24:47 ESV), as they baptize, and as they use their authority to rebuke and forgive sin among believers before the final judgment. This chapter allowed us to consider the apostolic ministry exercised in the book of Acts. Our final chapters will allow us to see this ministry exercised in teaching and administration in the rest of the New Testament.

9

Be Reconciled to God!

Sin and Restoration in the Pauline Letters

> So we are ambassadors for Christ, since God is making his appeal
> through us; we entreat you on behalf of Christ, be reconciled to
> God.
>
> —2 Corinthians 5:20

Through the work of the Holy Spirit, sinners are joined to the death and resurrection of Christ and are made new in him. They are joined to him in his
lowliness and crucifixion and called to imitate his self-giving love for others
and his self-offering to God. They are also joined to him in his resurrection
and identified with the glorious Son of God and restored in the glory and likeness of God by his life-giving Spirit, through the Spirit's work in the Church's
ministry of word and sacrament.

The Pauline Letters are especially instructive as we consider the restoration
of sinners to friendship with God—God's work of reconciliation. Writing to
particular churches, Paul says much about salvation in Christ, from its beginning in conversion to its end. He calls people to heed the leading of God's
Spirit to conform them to the love and righteousness of God in Christ. His
teaching and example also show us ways in which this apostle, a "steward" of
the mysteries of Christ (1 Cor. 4:1), exercised his ministry to call the faithful

to repentance and to use his authority to "bind" and "loose" in the name of Jesus. In this chapter we will consider the thirteen letters that bear Paul's name in the New Testament, looking especially at how they speak of the life of the baptized and how the apostle deals with the problem of Christian sin. We will also draw on the Letter to the Hebrews, which does not claim to be by Paul but has often been considered Pauline and stands alongside the Pauline corpus in the biblical canon.[1] It too has much to say about repentance.

Justified and Reconciled: The Gift of Life in the New Adam

Paul proclaims the good news that, in the death and resurrection of Christ, God has brought about the solution to the problem of sin and death. The coming of Christ and his life, death, and resurrection are to the human race an act of divine love and gift. "God proves his love for us in that while we still were sinners Christ died for us" (Rom. 5:8). All, he says, "have sinned and fall short of the glory of God," and sinners "are now justified by his grace as a gift, through the redemption that is in Christ Jesus" (Rom. 3:23–24). Paul can describe this multifaceted reality in many ways. He can conceive of Christ's death as a definitive sin offering (Rom. 3:25; 8:3), as the new Passover (1 Cor. 5:7), as "freeing" transgressors from sin's power (Rom. 6:12–23), as renewing the fallen to "glory" (Rom. 5:2; 2 Cor. 3:18), and much more besides.

One fairly comprehensive way in which Paul can sum up the saving significance of Christ is to speak of him as the New Adam (see Rom. 5:12–21; 1 Cor. 15:45–49). Adam's sin brought the reality of sin into the world, along with the tendency to sin and heed the passions of the flesh over God's command to love. With sin came guilt and condemnation and, ultimately, death for Adam's heirs. But, with the advent of Christ, Adam proved to be only a "type" of the one to come (Rom. 5:14). For Christ, the Son of God, came as the New Adam, and he brings about the *reversal* of the consequences of Adam's sin for humanity.

1. The biblical canon lists the thirteen letters that bear Paul's name in order of descending length by addressee: letters to churches (Romans being the longest, 2 Thessalonians the shortest) followed by letters addressed to individuals (1 Timothy being the longest, Philemon the shortest). Hebrews, a long letter not addressed to an individual, is placed outside this collection after Philemon, yet alongside it as a letter often thought to be by Paul or by someone connected to Paul's apostolate. Jerome rehearses a few ancient disagreements and states that it is "of no interest" (*nihil interesse*) whose letter it is precisely, "since it is of a churchman and is daily celebrated in the lection of the churches," and so it is received among the "canonical and ecclesiastical" writings (*Epistle* 129.4; my translation).

For the judgment following one trespass brought condemnation, but the free gift following many trespasses brings justification. If, because of the one man's trespass, death exercised dominion through that one, much more surely will those who receive the abundance of grace and the free gift of righteousness exercise dominion in life through the one man, Jesus Christ. Therefore just as one man's trespass led to condemnation for all, so one man's act of righteousness leads to justification and life for all. For just as by the one man's disobedience the many were made sinners, so by the one man's obedience the many will be made righteous. (Rom. 5:16–19)

Paul highlights in this passage the contrast of *condemnation and death* in the first Adam and *justification and life* in the New Adam. Adam's one sin brought about guilt and condemnation for Adam's heirs. Sin brings death as its worthy wage (cf. Rom. 1:32; 6:23), and so Adam's sin brought death into the world. But if Adam's condemnation came in answer to his one fault, Christ's self-gift paid the redemption price for all sins and all sinners for *forgiveness*. In Christ "we have redemption, the forgiveness of sins" (Col. 1:14; cf. Rom. 3:25; 4:6–7; Eph. 1:7). Those joined to Christ by the Spirit share in his inheritance, not a condemnation that leads to death but a *justification* that leads to life (Rom. 8:10–11; Gal. 3:21; Phil. 3:9–11).[2]

Christ also deals with the effects of sin in human relations with God and within the human person. Adam's sin brought not only guilt and condemnation but also a ruptured relationship with God. Living in sin, apart from grace, is not only to be guilty but to stand as an "enemy" against God (Rom. 5:10; cf. James 4:4). The New Adam's work of justification thus brings with it the gift of *reconciliation*, restoring humans to friendship and love with God. Whereas sinners had rebelled and stood against God, those in Christ now have "peace with God through our Lord Jesus Christ," for "while we were enemies, we were reconciled to God through the death of his Son" (Rom. 5:1, 10). Those joined to Christ are adopted and made partakers of the Son, prodigals restored to the life of the family in love and obedience under the Father (Rom. 8:12–17).

The New Adam brings newness and restoration in atoning for sin's guilt and bringing justification and reconciliation to sinners. Further, as the divine

2. "Justification," as the opposite of condemnation here, trades on a legal image of divine judgment, yet the image is not separate from images of friendship and reconciliation or renewal to new life. See James B. Prothro, *A Pauline Theology of Justification: Forgiveness, Friendship, and Life with God*, Lectio Sacra (Eugene, OR: Cascade Books, 2023).

gift counteracts Adam's trespass and its effects, this restoration to love and righteousness also involves *liberation* from sin. Paul speaks of sin as a kind of power that makes its "headquarters" in the flesh, drumming up sinful passions and desires within, prodding and inclining humans away from love and toward self-gratification and disobedience (Rom. 7:5, 8, 17).[3] Without grace and the influence of God's Spirit, life under sin is like life under a slave master because of the weakness of the flesh (Rom. 6:16). But those baptized into Christ have, in Christ, been *freed* from sin and come under the dominion of their new Lord. "But thanks be to God that you, having once been slaves of sin, have become obedient from the heart to the form of teaching to which you were entrusted, and that you, having been set free from sin, have become slaves of righteousness" (Rom. 6:17–18). God sends his Spirit into human hearts to renew them in righteousness and strengthen them in love: "The love of God has been poured out into our hearts through the holy Spirit that has been given to us" (Rom. 5:5 NABRE). Through the Spirit of Christ, the redeemed are brought to imitate Christ's self-giving and charity, not earning the lethal wages of sin but sowing seeds from which they will reap eternal life (cf. Gal. 6:8; Phil. 2:5–11; Col. 3:12–17). This is their sanctification, whose end or goal (Greek *telos*) is eternal life (Rom. 6:22).

This is the New Adam's work: to restore what was lost in humanity's fall. It is the same work that was prophesied in God's promise of the New Covenant: forgiveness and restoration to obedience and life through God's Spirit (Jer. 31:31–34; Ezek. 36:25–27).[4] Christ's death atones for the guilt of sin and brings about forgiveness for former trespasses, restoring communion and intimate friendship between the sinner and God. And through the gift of the Spirit, God works to "conform" sinners more and more to the image of Christ (Rom. 8:29), who is himself the image of God (2 Cor. 4:4; Col. 3:10; Eph. 4:23–24). They are conformed to Christ's image now in Christlike behavior, joined to his cross (Rom. 6:6; Gal. 2:19–20), and they will be conformed to his image in glory at the resurrection, "the redemption of our bodies" (Rom.

---

3. James D. G. Dunn, *The Theology of Paul the Apostle* (Grand Rapids: Eerdmans, 1998), 67. The personification of "sin" as a kind of power or slave master is sometimes taken to be the polar opposite of the idea of "sin" as transgressions and guilt. But slavery to sin, in Paul's depiction, is slavery to sinning (Rom. 6:16), and he identifies forgiveness of trespasses as well as liberation from sin's power as elements of salvation. For a treatment of Paul's complex discussion of sin, see Matthew Croasmun, *The Emergence of Sin: The Cosmic Tyrant in Romans* (New York: Oxford University Press, 2017).

4. See Brant Pitre, Michael P. Barber, and John A. Kincaid, *Paul, a New Covenant Jew: Rethinking Pauline Theology* (Grand Rapids: Eerdmans, 2019).

8:23), when the Spirit through whom the Father raised the Son will bring all God's adopted children to the glory and life that Adam forfeited (cf. Rom. 8:11, 17; 1 Cor. 15:43; Phil. 3:21; Heb. 2:10).[5]

Receiving the Gift: Baptism and Faith

This wonderful reversal is a gift of love to the world from the triune God. It is a gift given for "all" (cf. Rom. 1:16; 3:23–24; 1 Cor. 15:22). Yet not all receive it. Indeed, though Paul says it brings him sorrow, it is simply true that many reject the gift of reconciliation and live still as "enemies" of the Crucified One (Phil. 3:18). Christ's death makes atonement for all sin, but not every sinner receives the benefit of the New Adam's work (cf. 2 Cor. 4:3; Eph. 5:6; 2 Thess. 2:10).

If not all Adam's heirs receive the saving gift, how is it received? The Pauline Letters lead us to two summary answers: faith and baptism. As we saw in the Gospels and Acts, the sacramental means by which this gift is received is *baptism*. Compare the following passages, with italics added to some key elements:

> For in the one *Spirit* we were all baptized into one *body*—Jews or Greeks, slaves or free—and we were all made to drink of one Spirit. (1 Cor. 12:13)

> Do you not know that all of us who have been baptized into Christ Jesus were baptized *into his death*? Therefore we have been buried with him by baptism into death, so that, just as Christ was raised from the dead by the glory of the Father, so we too might walk in *newness of life*. (Rom. 6:3–4)

> In him also you were circumcised with a spiritual *circumcision*, by putting off the body of the flesh in the circumcision of Christ; when you were buried with him in baptism, you were also raised with him through faith in the power of God, who raised him from the dead. And when you were dead in trespasses and the uncircumcision of your flesh, God *made you alive* together with him, when he *forgave* us all our trespasses. (Col. 2:11–13)

> He saved us through the bath of *rebirth*
> and *renewal* by the holy *Spirit*,

5. See especially Michael J. Gorman, *Cruciformity: Paul's Narrative Spirituality of the Cross* (Grand Rapids: Eerdmans, 2001).

> whom he richly poured out on us
>   through Jesus Christ our savior,
> so that we might be *justified* by his grace
>   and become *heirs* in hope of eternal life. (Titus 3:5–7 NABRE)

Through baptism, the sinner is joined to Christ by the Holy Spirit. Those who were unrighteous are in baptism washed clean of former sins, justified, and consecrated to God in Christ and by the power of God's Spirit (cf. 1 Cor. 6:11). The sacrament confers the Spirit and joins one to Christ, to his death and to the power of his life. The sacrament also joins all to the Church, Christ's body, as circumcision joined male infants to the covenant family of Israel—and now in an even more perfect and spiritual communion. The rite of circumcision for Israelite boys now fulfilled by baptism is for all, men and women, who are adopted into God's family and made spiritual heirs of Abraham in Christ (Gal. 3:26–29). The rite in which a bit of physical flesh was removed is fulfilled in baptism, through which one is joined to Christ and disjoined from sin's power and manipulation of one's fleshly desires.

Yet the one-time event of baptism is not the end of the process of one's salvation, but rather its sacramental beginning. Forgiven former sins, one is joined to Christ for an ongoing life of renewal and friendship with Christ. In Paul, then, the "objective side" of the saving union in baptism is necessarily complemented by the "subjective side of the same event"—namely, *faith*.[6] Colossians 2:12 joins the two together, stating that we are buried with Christ "in baptism" and now continue to live in him "through faith." Faith matches baptism in Paul's thought as a mode of participation in Christ, a means by which one receives the Spirit: we "receive the promise of the Spirit through faith" (Gal. 3:14; cf. 3:1–5). Through the Spirit, Christ dwells in the believer to empower new life and virtue within, and this is mediated through the ongoing relationship of faith. Note the prayer in Ephesians 3:16–17, "that you may be strengthened in your inner being with power through his Spirit, and that Christ may dwell in your hearts through faith." As Paul says of himself and indeed of all who are joined to Christ, Christ now lives in him and he now lives in Christ "by faith" (Gal. 2:20).

Faith is, thus, at the center of one's justification in the New Adam: "We have come to believe in Christ Jesus, so that we might be justified" (Gal. 2:16). It

---

6. Christian Stettler, "Die Taufe im Neuen Testament—und heute," *TBei* 46 (2015): 24–41, at 32 (my translation).

Augustine: Salvation through Ongoing, Living Faith

While Augustine quoted Paul to argue against some who taught that salvation could be attained by works without divine grace, he was also at pains to emphasize that, for Paul, faith that is salvific is embodied in works of love.

> But people who did not understand the words of the apostle, *We hold that a human being is made righteous through faith without works of the law* (Rom. 3:28), thought that he said that faith was enough for a man, even if he lives a bad life and does not have good works. Heaven forbid that the vessel of election should have thought that. For, after he had said in a certain passage, *For in Christ neither circumcision nor the lack of circumcision is worth anything,* he immediately added, *but faith which works through love* (Gal. 5:6). This is the faith which separates the faithful of God from the unclean demons. For they too, as the apostle James says, *believe and tremble* (James 2:19), but they do not do good works. They, therefore, do not have this faith from which the righteous live, that is, *the faith which works through love,* so that God gives them eternal life in accord with their works.[a]

a. Augustine, *Grace and Free Choice* 7.18 (in *Answer to the Pelagians IV,* trans. Teske, 82).

is an ongoing mode of participation in Christ.[7] It is part of receiving the gift at one's conversion and part of maintaining one's relation to Christ, a kind of channel through which one receives the continued "supply" of the Spirit and the renewing effects of grace (Gal. 3:5; Phil. 1:19). This means that faith, faith by which one lives in this saving union, must also be *dynamic.* Faith, in Paul, is not merely notional, nor does it refer only to the initial moment of conversion, as though one's entire salvation ("by faith") could be settled only in that one moment. Paul can speak of one first coming to faith, turning to the Lord, and entrusting oneself to him (Rom. 13:11). But faith can become "weak" and slacken, and one can even fail to endure such that one's faith

7. See Jeanette Hagen Pifer, *Faith as Participation: An Exegetical Study of Some Key Pauline Texts,* WUNT 2/486 (Tübingen: Mohr Siebeck, 2019). Hebrews 11:1, though often translated in terms of personal "assurance" (NRSV) or "evidence" (NABRE), states that faith is the "substance" (DRV) of what is hoped for, which some understand also to indicate its participatory value, as faith grasps and receives the reality of its object. See the discussion in Benedict XVI, *Spe salvi,* §§7–9.

and conversion prove to have been "in vain" (cf. Rom. 12:11; 14:1; 1 Cor. 15:2; Gal. 6:9; 1 Thess. 3:5). Paul's ministry, therefore, aims to nurture faith so that believers may be "strengthened" and "grow" in *faithfulness*, not only in believing more truths about God but in believing them more strongly in the Lord so that one trusts him, obeys him, and stands firm in him against temptation and the weakness of the flesh (cf. Col. 1:10–11; 1 Thess. 3:11–13). Paul's work to evangelize the pagans is aimed both to bring them to convert from idolatry to God (1 Thess. 1:9–10) and, as he summarizes it, "to bring about the obedience of faith" in the enduring faithfulness of the converted (Rom. 1:5; 16:26). Through endurance and growth in faith, by the power of the Spirit, one is continually conformed to Christ, by "faith working through love" (Gal. 5:6).

The Battle of Faith: The Danger of Sin and the Guidance of the Spirit

Faith is at the center of one's justification and reconciliation to God, from the first moment of conversion and throughout one's life of growth and repentance in the Spirit. But the life of faith is a struggle. Paul uses images of athletic contest and of battle, calling all to fight against sin, to train themselves in endurance, and to arm themselves with spiritual weapons (cf. Rom. 6:12–13; 1 Cor. 9:24–27; 2 Cor. 6:7; 10:3; Eph. 6:10–20; Phil. 1:30). This battle is waged within each believer, and it reflects a greater cosmic battle between the Spirit of God and the influence of sin and malevolent, demonic powers in the world (cf. 1 Cor. 7:5; Gal. 5:17; Eph. 6:12). Those in Christ have been delivered from sin's dominion, living now under grace and no longer as sin's slaves. Yet they can still submit to sin's "dominion" again by their own choices (Rom. 6:12, 16). Paul and the author of Hebrews both use Israel's wandering as a figure for the experience of the Church on earth: delivered from death by Christ in the new Passover (1 Cor. 5:7), Christians are led to salvation through water in baptism (like the Red Sea) and nourished by spiritual food in the Eucharist (like the manna) on their journey to the promised land. But they should, for that reason, be warned against laxity, for many rebelled and were destroyed in the wilderness, not reaching the goal for which they were redeemed, and the same can happen to those in Christ (see 1 Cor. 10:1–12; Heb. 3:1–4:11). "Take care, brothers, that none of you may have an evil and unfaithful heart, so as to forsake the living God . . . , so that none of you may grow hardened by the deceit of sin. We have become partners of Christ if only we hold the beginning of the reality firm until the end" (Heb. 3:12–14 NABRE).

The ongoing life of faith is a struggle, and one with high stakes. Just as many Israelites in the wilderness tried to reverse their redemption by returning to Egypt, a Christian can "turn back" to become a willing "slave" of the idolatry and evil from which God freed him or her (Gal. 4:8–9). The Pauline Letters describe this as "falling" from grace (Gal. 5:4), "turning" away to follow Satan (1 Tim. 5:15), and "sowing" seed from which one will reap destruction (Gal. 6:8). One who does so has received grace but received it "in vain" (2 Cor. 6:1). Paul warns of this happening both in the case of apostasy—rejection of the apostolic gospel—and in practices of willful, grave sin. He warns against both in Galatians, speaking to people he says were baptized and had genuinely received God's Spirit (Gal. 3:1–5, 27). If they turn away to follow "a different gospel" and reject that of the apostolic Church, Paul warns, they will fall from grace and forfeit the saving benefits of Christ (Gal. 1:6; 5:2–4). He speaks likewise of the "works of the flesh," particular grave acts by which, if pursued willfully in rejection of God, one can forfeit the inheritance for which one was adopted: "fornication, impurity, licentiousness, idolatry, sorcery, enmities, strife, jealousy, anger, quarrels, dissensions, factions, envy, drunkenness, carousing, and things like these. I am warning you, as I warned you before: those who do such things will not inherit the kingdom of God" (Gal. 5:19–21).

The phrase "and things like these" in Paul's list of vices indicates that he is not giving an exhaustive catalog. It is also clear that, like Jesus, Paul does not envision every single act of strife or jealousy or other things in his list to have an immediately mortal effect in one's soul. Paul spends much of his letters and ministry correcting Christian misbehavior or telling believers to forgive one another because Christians can misbehave and fail and still be Christians, still living "under grace" (Rom. 6:14). Jesus also taught his disciples to ask for forgiveness from God regularly, assuming that they would sin regularly in their lives as disciples. Indeed, even when writing to the Galatians, Paul expresses confidence that God will keep them or draw them back to the faith (Gal. 5:10). God is faithful, Paul insists, and will not simply discard his children who turn to him in penitence, even after serious sin (Phil. 1:6; 1 Thess. 5:23–24). "If we are faithless, he remains faithful—for he cannot deny himself" (2 Tim. 2:13). Nonetheless, he has not promised to save all, but those who, though struggling with faithfulness, remain with him: "If we deny him, he will also deny us" (2 Tim. 2:12).

The Letter to the Hebrews warns quite strongly against willful sin and particularly of the danger of apostasy. The author addresses Christians who have been "enlightened," fully initiated into the mysteries of Christ, and who have suffered public persecution and endured in faith (Heb. 10:32–36). He calls them not to go backward or become lax, not to neglect their faith, but to endure to the end, so that they are prepared for martyrdom if need be (cf. Heb. 2:1–4; 4:14–16; 10:19–31; 12:1–17). And he adds a warning: none should presume that they will be restored and take falling away lightly. The purifying death of Christ—the perfect fulfillment of Israel's annual sin offering—is not repeatable. So too one's "foundation" in "repentance from dead works" and the plenary remission of guilt and punishment in baptism are unrepeatable (Heb. 6:1–3; 10:18, 26). Indeed, if one has been fully initiated into the Christian mysteries and truly known the saving power of grace, and then willfully makes the choice to apostatize, restoration to such repentance is "impossible" (Heb. 6:4–6).[8] The argument turns on the theme of liturgical singularity. Hebrews focuses its view of salvation in a typology of Israel's yearly sin offering at Yom Kippur: Christ's death effects a complete purification, and it need not and cannot be repeated as were the Levitical offerings (Heb. 10:1–18; cf. Rom. 6:9).[9] If one returns to willful, grave sin, one does not have the option of simply resacrificing Christ or being rebaptized (Heb. 10:26). The claim that it is "impossible" to restore an apostate can, of course, be overread. So too can the argument by liturgical singularity, as though Hebrews is denying that God can save anyone who sins intentionally after baptism.[10] Paul, at least, states that "God has the power" to restore apostates "again" if they "do not persist in unbelief" (Rom. 11:23). Indeed, to deny the possibility of restoration would also contradict non-Levitical means of repentance in the Old Testament, on which the typology in Hebrews is based. David's willful sins of adultery and murder disallowed his use of the Levitical system, which did

8. The sin from which repentance is "impossible" in Heb. 6:4–6 is clearly envisioned as apostasy, willful rejection of the gifts of salvation by which one makes a public mockery of God. Compare William L. Lane, *Hebrews*, 2 vols., WBC 47A–B (Nashville: Nelson, 1991), 1:142; Harold W. Attridge, *The Epistle to the Hebrews*, Hermeneia (Philadelphia: Fortress, 1989), 168–69.

9. See David M. Moffitt, *Rethinking the Atonement: New Perspectives on Jesus's Death, Resurrection, and Ascension* (Grand Rapids: Baker Academic, 2022), 87–99.

10. The traditional explanation is simply that rebaptism is impossible. Alternately, some interpret the claim more subjectively or psychologically: that one who goes so far as to apostatize after knowing the saving power of grace has, in doing so, hardened himself severely and cannot be restored in that state. Compare Alan C. Mitchell, *Hebrews*, SP 13 (Collegeville, MN: Liturgical Press, 2007), 128–30.

not provide sacrificial atonement for grave, intentional sins done in rejection of God (Num. 15:30–31; cf. Heb. 10:26–31). David, as we saw, was restored, but only through contrition and penance, and not without temporal punishment. One can fall and repent. But after the complete washing in the water of baptism, as many patristic authors put it, the only way of restoration that remains is through the water of *tears*, the path of contrition and repentance for particular sins.[11]

Hebrews warns sternly of the danger of apostasy and calls believers not to grow slack but to press on in faith and endurance, training themselves and soldiering on in the struggle. The author of Hebrews shares this concern with Paul, who calls all to follow his example as one who has hope but rejects presumption, not assuming that he has reached perfection in righteousness, but always "straining forward" and disciplining his body that he might not be disqualified from salvation but receive the promised reward (cf. 1 Cor. 9:24–27; Phil. 3:12–16). This is Paul's goal for believers, that they would not only *not* fall away but that they would grow and endure in obedience and so receive a reward. Indeed, Paul emphasizes that all sin—grave or light—will be requited at the judgment, even for those who have not fallen away: "For all of us must appear before the judgment seat of Christ, so that each may receive recompense for what has been done in the body, whether good or evil" (2 Cor. 5:10).[12] Paul uses an image of a fire through which all must pass that will "test" and purify their works. Those who stand on the foundation of Christ will be saved, but sins and impurities in one's Christian life, after they have laid the one-time "foundation" of conversion and baptism, must be burned away. Their salvation will be achieved through a final purification. "The fire will test what sort of work each one has done. If the work that anyone has built on the foundation survives, he will receive a reward. If anyone's work is burned up, he will suffer loss, though he himself will be saved, but only as through fire" (1 Cor. 3:13–15 ESV).[13]

<hr>

11. Cf. Origen, *Homilies on Leviticus* 2.4; Gregory of Nazianzus, *Oration* 39.17; John Damascene, *Exposition of the Orthodox Faith* 4.9; Ambrose, *Letter* 41.21; Pseudo-Ambrose, *Concerning Repentance* 2.2.10; John Chrysostom, *Homilies on Hebrews* 9.4. Later, compare Thomas Aquinas, *Commentary on Hebrews*, chapter 6, lecture 1, §291.

12. For the place of the final judgment in Paul's theology and moral exhortations, see recently Brendan Byrne, *Paul and the Economy of Salvation: Reading from the Perspective of the Last Judgment* (Grand Rapids: Baker Academic, 2021).

13. On salvation through fire as involving purification here, see Daniel Frayer-Griggs, "Neither Proof Text nor Proverb: The Instrumental Sense of διά and the Soteriological Function of Fire in 1 Corinthians 3.15," *NTS* 59 (2013): 517–34.

God's gifts of faith and baptism aim to bring people to convert and to remain in Christ, not only to avoid condemnation but to grow in virtue and receive God's "reward" (cf. 1 Cor. 3:14; 4:5; 9:25; 2 Tim. 4:8). In baptism and through the continued channel of faith, God supplies the Spirit to his people to prompt and lead and empower them in obedience and faithfulness. The battle of faith is *not one that the believer fights alone* but is one in which the Spirit of God himself is engaged to lead Christians against the influence of sin and carnal passions.

> For what the flesh desires is opposed to the Spirit, and what the Spirit desires is opposed to the flesh; for these are opposed to each other, to prevent you from doing what you want. (Gal. 5:17)

> For those who live according to the flesh have their outlook shaped by the things of the flesh, but those who live according to the Spirit have their outlook shaped by the things of the Spirit. For the outlook of the flesh is death, but the outlook of the Spirit is life and peace, because the outlook of the flesh is hostile to God, for it does not submit to the law of God, nor is it able to do so. Those who are in the flesh cannot please God. You, however, are not in the flesh but in the Spirit, if indeed the Spirit of God lives in you. (Rom. 8:5–9 NET)

The Spirit intervenes in our hearts and lives to lead us away from sin and toward obedience. This can mean that one does not do what one wants (as in Gal. 5:17, above), if we think of what we "want" in terms of our carnal, short-sighted desires for pleasure and self-preservation. From a different perspective, inasmuch as we let the Spirit renew us in the truth of Christ, the Spirit's intervention in fact brings us to do what we truly *do* want to do. God calls, pulls, prompts, and renews believers so that their mind or "outlook"— their worldview and values—and their behavior are transformed and shaped by God's truth, by God's commands and promises (cf. Rom. 12:1–2; Eph. 4:23).[14] God works in believers not only to bring them to be able to do his will but also to want it, not just directing their actions but renewing them

---

14. Most translations of Rom. 8:5–7 render Paul's Greek in terms of "mindset" or "concern." The NET, above, uses "outlook," adding an explanatory note that the language indicates not simply what one's mind is preoccupied with. The verb *phroneō* and the noun *phronēma* here are related to mindset, but they point especially to the shape of one's values, interests, and worldview. Indeed, to "have the mindset/outlook of" someone is a phrase often used to indicate allegiance in contexts of war or conflict: in a war between Greece and Persia, for instance, one who "takes the side of" the Greeks "has the mindset/outlook of the Greeks," meaning that they

in their desires and values and habits according to the "mind of Christ" (cf. 1 Cor. 2:16; Phil. 2:5, 13; Eph. 4:23).

With the power of God's grace at work through the Spirit, Paul calls all to arm themselves with divine virtue and wisdom in the fight against sin. For the day of judgment—the general judgment and, naturally also, every believer's particular judgment—is drawing nearer.

> Therefore, sin must not reign over your mortal bodies so that you obey their desires. And do not present the parts of your bodies to sin as weapons for wickedness, but present yourselves to God as raised from the dead to life and the parts of your bodies to God as weapons for righteousness. (Rom. 6:12–13 NABRE)

> For salvation is nearer to us now than when we became believers; the night is far gone, the day is near. Let us then lay aside the works of darkness and put on the armor of light; let us live honorably as in the day, not in reveling and drunkenness, not in debauchery and licentiousness, not in quarreling and jealousy. Instead, put on the Lord Jesus Christ, and make no provision for the flesh, to gratify its desires. (Rom. 13:11–14)

Those who have been joined to Christ have been joined to his crucifixion, freed in him from the dominion of sin and death and led to imitate his self-giving for others. Paul calls them to let the work of God's Spirit have full sway, to put to death—to *mortify*, in traditional language—their sinful deeds in continued repentance, and to let God lead them in ever greater conformity to Christ toward eternal life. For, he promises, "if you live according to the flesh, you will die; but if by the Spirit you put to death the deeds of the body, you will live" (Rom. 8:13).

Fallen and Restored: Christian Sin and Repentance in Corinth

The work of God's Spirit through the Church is to free humans from sin and join them to Christ. Accordingly, the apostle preaches, baptizes, and exhorts people to grow in faith, hope, and self-giving love. Because sin still threatens believers, Paul also calls his people to repent, to turn from sin and live in a manner that befits their calling in Christ (e.g., Col. 3:1–17). And he calls them

---

are allied with and support the cause of the Greeks and hope for their victory. Compare, e.g., 1 Macc. 10:20; Josephus, *Jewish Antiquities* 7.286; *Jewish War* 4.209.

to encourage and rebuke each other in the local congregation and restore those who are faltering from transgression (cf. 1 Cor. 5:11; Gal. 6:1–2; Phil. 4:2–3; 2 Thess. 3:14–15).

We also see Paul use his representative authority as Christ's "steward" who represents and "works together" with God (1 Cor. 3:9; 4:1; 2 Cor. 6:1) to deal directly with grave, unrepentant sin. The most lucid example comes in 1 Corinthians, where Paul uses his authority to "bind" by commanding that a man be ousted from the communion of the Church—ex-*commun*icated, in other words. Paul, writing from Ephesus (1 Cor. 16:8), says that the Corinthian believers have gained a wide reputation for tolerating sexual immorality, of a kind that even pagans find offensive: a man is "having"—engaging in sexual congress with—his father's wife (1 Cor. 5:1).[15] And the congregation, at least in large part, has responded to this not with fraternal rebuke but with pride and boasting (1 Cor. 5:2). Paul shames them for their attitude and calls for the man to be cast out from the Church. The action he calls for here is communal, to be carried out by those in Corinth. But their action stems from his authority: they are to do so in Corinth because he, though currently in Ephesus, has already pronounced judgment as an apostle.

> For though absent in body, I am present in spirit; and as if present I have already pronounced judgment in the name of the Lord Jesus on the man who has done such a thing. When you are assembled, and my spirit is present with the power of our Lord Jesus, you are to hand this man over to Satan for the destruction of the flesh, so that his spirit may be saved in the day of the Lord. (1 Cor. 5:3–5)

Paul here uses his authority to bind the man in his sins. He has pronounced his judgment in Jesus's name, and the Corinthian leaders are to follow through with this by the power and presence of Paul's "spirit" that is with them. The man is to be "handed over to Satan"—that is, to be put outside the community of salvation, the Church (cf. 1 Tim. 1:20).

What is the purpose of this excommunication? Clearly, on the one hand, it is a judgment delivered on a grave and apparently habitual sin. But there are, it seems, other instances of grave sin in Corinth that Paul does not deal

15. "Having" renders the Greek verb (*echō*) directly here. The translation "living with" (e.g., NABRE, NRSV) is euphemistic. Paul uses the same language of "having" here that he uses of sexual intercourse between spouses in 1 Cor. 7:2. The phrase can be used of marriage broadly, but Paul's comments about the egregious scandal and unheard-of character of this union with his father's "wife" suggest we are not dealing with a young widow later marrying her adult stepson.

with in a public excommunication like this (though he does call people to examine themselves in repentance before they approach the Eucharist: 1 Cor. 11:27–28). However, the Pauline Letters, and 1 Corinthians in particular, stress the *communal* significance of sin. The Church is Christ's body, with many members (1 Cor. 12:12–26). Sinning against a brother or sister is, then, to "sin against Christ" (1 Cor. 8:12). Likewise, as a body, what happens to the individual parts affect the whole. When one member of the body suffers, all the other members suffer "with" it (1 Cor. 12:26). Likewise with the influence of sin in the body, as he comments here: "A little yeast leavens the whole batch of dough" (1 Cor. 5:6). The Church of Christ is to be pure, and, as in the celebration of Passover, the community that will partake of Christ's paschal sacrifice should remove the "yeast," here referring to moral evil and impurity, from its midst (1 Cor. 5:7–8). There are secret sins, of course, ones that will not be made public until the final judgment (Rom. 2:15–16; 1 Cor. 4:5). But even small sins—grudges, small but consistent patterns of selfishness, excessive laxity or rigorism—can spread and affect the community. All the more, in this case, with grave public sins. Not only can Christian sin affect the Church's witness to outsiders, but it can cause other believers to stumble (cf. 1 Cor. 8:8–13; 10:27–28; 1 Tim. 3:7). Paul addresses the Church with a warning: "Do you not know that you are God's temple and that God's Spirit dwells in you? If anyone destroys God's temple, God will destroy that person. For God's temple is holy, and you are that temple" (1 Cor. 3:16–17).

The public and unrepentant nature of this man's apparently habitual sin has harmful consequences in the body of Christ. If apostles are like undershepherds serving the Good Shepherd's flock, the wrongdoer here may be likened to a sheep that has become rabid and is harming the rest of the flock. The apostle's goal is to remove the sin, but when the sinner only boasts and rejects instruction, the good of the flock may require removing the sinner. However, the excommunication is also meant to serve the health of the ousted sinner as well. The judgment Paul pronounces is not final but is meant to have a *remedial* effect. Paul says that the man is to be cast outside the community, with the hope that he will *learn* through this discipline and ultimately be *saved* (1 Cor. 5:5; 1 Tim. 1:20). The immediate effect is punishment for the wrong and the protection of the community, but the ultimate goal is for the good of both the Church *and* the transgressor, as a rebuke through which this sheep might be returned to the fold. If the witness of apostolic teaching was ineffective, and the man continued to be unrepentant despite smaller rebukes and warnings while he still held the esteem of his fellows, he may finally see the seriousness of what his sin has wrought when he is removed from the community of Christ on earth—an anticipation of the divine judgment, when the unrepentant will be sent away from the heavenly communion of Christ. Some in Israel repented at the prophets' words, but for the nation overall the final rebuke that brought repentance was exile. In a similar way, for some it is exile from the Church—excommunication—that finally cracks hardened hearts and brings them to repentance.

The example of this excommunication is particularly instructive not only because it shows us the purposes of this penalty but also because the excommunication appears to have *worked*. First Corinthians gives us a snapshot of Paul using his "binding" authority to protect Christ's body from sin and discipline the sinner. But we have more than one letter from Paul to Corinth. Reading across the letters, we can reconstruct what transpired in the wake of Paul's rebuke. Indeed, we can see Paul "loose" what he bound and reconcile the sinner back to the fellowship of the Church.

After Paul wrote 1 Corinthians and called for that unnamed man to be ousted from the Church's fellowship, his relationship with the Corinthians proved to be fraught, and sexual immorality remained a problem in Corinth (2 Cor. 12:21). He returned for another visit that proved somehow painful to him, at which time he rebuked some for immorality and licentiousness and then left (2 Cor. 13:2). After the visit, however, Paul wrote them a letter "with many tears" (2 Cor. 2:4), apparently with threats and rebukes about a particular wrongdoer and about the congregation's lack of appropriate response to the man. He wrote, he says, in the hopes that they would respond by proving their obedience to Paul (2 Cor. 2:9). The result of the letter was, happily, positive: Paul's words caused the Corinthians grief, but a "godly grief" that galvanized them not to despair but to *repentance* (2 Cor. 7:9). The letter rebuked them, and they responded with indignation at sin and contrition for having enabled it (2 Cor. 7:11). What they did in response—or at least "the majority" of them—was to carry out "punishment" on the offender (2 Cor. 2:6; 7:11). This response showed their obedience, brought on by Paul's rebuke and their contrition, restoring them to obedience and reconciling them with the apostle whose commands they had neglected (cf. 2 Cor. 2:3, 9; 7:10–11, 15).

Paul does not name the man or his specific offense, but it is quite likely that this is the same man Paul had excommunicated for sexual immorality. Sexual immorality was an ongoing problem in Corinth, true, and it is possible

this wrongdoer is different from the one who was to be excommunicated
for relations with his father's wife. Yet for the same reason it is simplest to
assume we are dealing with the same man: there *was* an ongoing problem
with sexual immorality in Corinth, discussed in 1 Corinthians, yet only one
person was to be excommunicated for an egregious instance of immorality, for
which Paul had to correct the congregation and command them not to glory
in his sin but instead to cast him out (1 Cor. 5:1–13). Paul's words describing
the tearful letter indicate that he had told them to oust the man, at least at
some point, otherwise their response of shunning him would not have proved
their obedience to Paul. And nothing prohibits this from being not a new
issue but a long-standing issue that reached its boiling point in Paul's painful visit and the tearful letter.[16] Indeed, reconstructing the narrative requires
little imagination: the man had not repented after the congregation received
1 Corinthians, and his fellow believers had not sufficiently enforced Paul's
excommunication—perhaps because of the man's clout, their reluctance, a
lack of a united leadership among the notoriously factious Corinthians (cf.
1 Cor. 1:10–12), or some other reason. This became visible and caused conflict
on Paul's subsequent visit, leading Paul to write the tearful letter, after which
the "majority" finally enforced the excommunication.

However, what is most instructive for us in this event is not that Paul's
rebuke brought the Corinthian church to obedience but that the Church's
rebuke—authoritatively bound by Paul and joined in by the community—
brought the *wrongdoer* to repentance. Paul not only writes of the effect of his
tearful letter on them but hints also at the effect the excommunication had on
the sinner. "This punishment by the majority is enough," and the Corinthians
now should "forgive and console him, so that he may not be overwhelmed by
excessive sorrow" (2 Cor. 2:6, 7). Paul has "forgiven" the man, he says, "for
your sake in the presence of Christ"—apparently emphasizing the ecclesial

16. Paul's description of the tearful letter in 2 Cor. 2 and 7 does not name the wrongdoer's
sin per se, and he protests that he is not forgiving an injury to himself (2 Cor. 2:5, 10); to some,
this suggests that this wrongdoer is not the man excommunicated in 1 Corinthians. But if the
congregation knows of the sin, and if Paul is calling for forgiveness and reconciliation, he may
have thought naming the sin again to be unnecessary or counterproductive. Paul's protests, likewise, may be his way of clarifying that his calls to excommunicate and to readmit are not results
of his personal vendettas but are ecclesial matters—any forgiveness from Paul is enacted "for
your sake in the presence of Christ" (2 Cor. 2:10). Naturally, questions of the letter's composition and historical background are also relevant here. For an overview of the issues, see James B.
Prothro, *The Apostle Paul and His Letters: An Introduction*, Verbum Domini (Washington, DC:
Catholic University of America Press, 2021), 119–31.

character of this forgiveness—and they should be united with their apostle in this forgiveness (2 Cor. 2:10).[17] They should now not shun him but, Paul says, "reaffirm your love for him" (2 Cor. 2:8). We do not have all the details about what change took place in the man. But Paul's warning that the man's grief will consume him if they continue to shun him suggests that he, too, came to the "godly grief" of contrition. And his longing to be readmitted to the community suggests at least a willingness to submit to the Church and amend his life. This means that the excommunication did its job, not as a final and irreversible penalty but as a rebuke and a kind of *penance*. Now, by Paul's authority in Christ, the Corinthians are to welcome the man back into the life of Christ's body to share with them the divine gifts of unity (particularly in the Eucharist, given Paul's words in 1 Cor. 10:16–17) and the mutual edification and love that the Spirit supplies (cf. 1 Cor. 12:4–13; 12:27–14:1).

Excommunication and communal shunning are a weighty form of ecclesiastical discipline that Paul does not often use. They are diagnoses not simply of grave or willful sin but of ardent unrepentance in a grave matter even after being rebuked, in rejection of God and God's Church (see Matt. 18:14–20). As Paul describes and uses it, though, it is hoped to be a remedial measure, so that those who refuse to repent at smaller rebukes from friends or in their consciences, or even at stern warnings from Christ's stewards, will finally see what their sin has wrought and long to be readmitted through contrition and penance. Moved to repentance, they receive that forgiveness and readmission to the Church's fellowship and are restored by grace to rejoin the battle against sin. For the penitent, as Cyprian writes,

> God grants both the weapons by which he who was once overcome is rearmed, and restores and strengthens his powers by which faith reestablished can be energized. The soldier will rejoin his battle, he will repeat his assault, and he will challenge the enemy, having been made stronger for the battle through his remorse.[18]

Further, the man's restoration is good for the community, not only in the restoration of their numbers but in their own endurance in the battle against

---

17. The Greek in 2 Cor. 2:10 states that Paul has forgiven "in the face of Christ" (*en prosōpō Christou*). Most take this as a Semitism locating the action *before* the face (and so in the "presence") of Christ, although the Septuagint usually renders such Semitic idioms by other prepositions (e.g., Gen. 30:33; Exod. 32:34). Interpreting "face" to indicate the "person" or representative role *in* which Paul forgives (the term "face" was used to indicate an actor's role, for instance), the Vulgate notably translates it as *in persona Christi*—"in the person of Christ" (DRV).

18. Cyprian, *The Fallen* 36 (trans. Brent, 142–43).

sin. They, too, grow in virtue and in learning love through the practice of reconciling with and welcoming the sinner. If they should refuse, they would be like the prodigal son's elder brother, or like those who refused fellowship with sinners that Jesus absolved and welcomed. Indeed, Paul says, if the congregation should refuse to forgive the man, "Satan" may gain a foothold in *them* through their unforgiveness (2 Cor. 2:11). Sin causes rupture in one's relationship with God and with others, and the Church must deal with sin for the good of the whole body of Christ—both in rebuking sin and in forgiving the penitent.

Put Off the Old Self and Put On the Image of Christ

Restoration through penance is possible for one who has fallen. That should be a great comfort to those who have fallen and to those who care for them and seek to call such prodigals home. God forgives. Yet, as the Letter to the Hebrews warns, we should not presume that we will seek that forgiveness if we fall away. Believers are not called to presume on an easy return, but to persevere and grow in their life of faith, to "lay aside every weight and the sin that clings so closely, and let us run with perseverance the race that is set before us" (Heb. 12:1). "Repentance" and "turning" from sin are necessary for Christians as well as for unbelievers (Rom. 2:4; 2 Cor. 3:16; 7:9–10; 12:21; 1 Thess. 1:9–10). Righteousness and wickedness are opposites: one living in wickedness must turn from it to God, and one walking in righteousness must avoid sin and strive to remain with God (see 2 Cor. 6:14–18). God has promised the inheritance of eternal life to the faithful in Christ. Therefore, "since we have these promises, beloved, let us cleanse ourselves from every defilement of flesh and spirit, making holiness perfect in the fear of God" (2 Cor. 7:1 NABRE).

Paul's theology of repentance is a part of his theology of salvation, particularly his descriptions of baptism and union with Christ. The chief language used in the Pauline Letters to refer to baptism is that of *death and life* and of *putting off and putting on*. Those baptized into Christ have been put to death—"crucified" even—and buried with Christ (cf. Rom. 6:3; Gal. 2:19; Col. 2:12). They have been joined to his death and are now freed from the dominion of sin, and they share now in his life and hope in its perfection when they, with Christ, are raised from the dead (cf. Rom. 6:4; Gal. 2:20; Col. 2:12–13). This theology of sharing in Christ's fate—his death and life—is complemented also by a clothing metaphor. Those who are baptized have "put on" Christ as clothing, letting Christ's identity and character envelop them and supersede their identities outside Christ (Gal. 3:27 ESV).

This is our salvation, being united to Christ. Yet it is "in hope" that we were "saved" (Rom. 8:24), and the final realization of our salvation grows nearer every day for those in Christ (Rom. 13:11). In the present life, salvation is a *hope*, one into which we have been baptized but whose completion has not yet been reached. Our task, in the meantime, is to live more deeply into the graces of our baptism. We have been put to death with Christ and died to sin, freed from the dominion of sin in our flesh, so we are called now to "put to death the deeds of the body" (Rom. 8:13) and our lingering inclinations and habits of malice and immorality and selfishness (Col. 3:5). We have put on the Lord Jesus in baptism, and we must clothe ourselves with his virtues by ridding ourselves of our old rags: "Let us cast off the works of darkness, and put on the armor of light. Let us walk properly as in the daytime, not in orgies and drunkenness, not in sexual immorality and sensuality, not in quarreling and jealousy" (Rom. 13:12–13 ESV; cf. Col. 3:8–10). We are already clothed with Christ, and now we must not let Christ remain merely as clothing outside of us but allow him to permeate our being, shaping us in his love and self-denial for others. Paul calls us to "put on the Lord Jesus Christ, and make no provision for the flesh, to gratify its desires" (Rom. 13:14).

The Pauline Letters show a good deal of ways in which one can live into one's baptism, becoming further detached from sin and growing in faith. These include traditional mainstays of penance. Paul calls for prayer, whether in contemplation, or in work, or for the gospel and the salvation of sinners (cf. Rom. 10:1; Eph. 6:18; 1 Thess. 5:17, 25). Paul fasts and mortifies his flesh (1 Cor. 9:27; 2 Cor. 6:5; 11:27).[19] He endorses almsgiving according to one's ability as a participation in God's grace, as an act of love and self-gift, and as an offering to God that will be repaid (cf. 2 Cor. 8:1–7; Eph. 4:28; Phil. 4:18–19). He also calls for sincere self-examination and self-discipline before approaching the Eucharist: "Whoever, therefore, eats the bread or drinks the cup of the Lord in an unworthy manner will be guilty concerning the body

---

19. Most English translations (with the exception of the NABRE) translate "fasting" language in Paul (Greek *nēsteia*) merely to indicate involuntary hunger. But Paul distinguishes this "fasting" from mere "hunger and thirst" in 2 Cor. 11:27, and the catalog of sufferings in which he lists it includes not only things imposed upon him involuntarily by circumstance (like shipwrecks or mere hunger) but also voluntary acts that are part of his apostolate and piety (like his "anxiety for all the churches," 2 Cor. 11:28).

and blood of the Lord. Let a person examine himself, then, and so eat of the bread and drink of the cup" (1 Cor. 11:27–28 ESV). Indeed, Paul here states that some are sick and even dying as a "judgment" from God because of their sins at the Lord's Supper (1 Cor. 11:29–30). The proper response to such "disciplines" is repentant self-judgment, and he seems to suggest that such self-judgment can obviate further divine punishment of one's sin. "But if we judged ourselves, we would not be judged. But when we are judged by the Lord, we are disciplined so that we may not be condemned along with the world" (1 Cor. 11:31–32).

But putting our sins to death by the grace of the Spirit encompasses so much more besides. Hospitality, willingly associating with the lowly, putting away pride and vengeance for humble patience, forgiving others, ceding one's interests for the good of others, defending the truth and rebuking evil, growing in knowledge and praise of God—and so many other acts of self-denial and charity—are ways of dying to sin, participating in Christ's death, and being made new by his Spirit of life (cf. Rom. 12:9–21; Phil. 2:1–11; Col. 3:1–17; Eph. 4:1–5:21). Indeed, every self-denial, every "putting off" of the sinful inclinations that cling to us, is a means by which we "put on" Christ and his love, and every act of love in imitation of Christ calls us necessarily beyond ourselves toward the praise of God and the good of our neighbor. Every suffering willingly born for others not only draws us deeper into the mystery of Christ's redemptive death (cf. Phil. 3:9–11; Col. 1:24) but also "produces" the glorification that we will receive finally in the resurrection (2 Cor. 4:17 NABRE; cf. Rom. 8:17). It is a means by which we grow to be like Christ, conformed "to Christ's *character* in the present" so that we may be conformed "to Christ's *body* in the future."[20] It is the mode by which the children of Adam put on the New Adam, being renewed in the "image" of God (Col. 3:10).

As we saw in the Gospels, the call of the gospel is ultimately a call to love. Love is patient, kind, not proud or envious, forgiving, and looks out always in hope (1 Cor. 13:4–7). Love corrects wrongs with gentleness while pursuing what is good and right (Gal. 6:1–2). Love fulfills the law of God because love "does no wrong to a neighbor" (Rom. 13:10). Toward God, love is the means by which true faith is expressed, a living "faith working through love" (Gal. 5:6). By faith in Christ, and in hope, we love God and render to him the

---

20. Michael J. Gorman, *Romans: A Theological and Pastoral Commentary* (Grand Rapids: Eerdmans, 2022), 208.

Living the Life of Our Baptism

Being clothed with Christ in baptism calls us to know the identity forged for us not only as we look to our conversion and baptism in the past but also as we seek to be ever more faithful to that identity in the present.

> We cannot stay still. We must keep going ahead toward the goal Saint Paul marks out: "It is not I who live, it is Christ that lives in me" [Gal. 2:20]. This is a high and very noble ambition, this identification with Christ, this holiness. But there is no other way if we are to be consistent with the divine life God has sown in our souls in Baptism. To advance we must progress in holiness. Shying away from holiness implies refusing our Christian life its natural growth. . . . Conversion is the task of a moment; sanctification is the work of a lifetime. The divine seed of charity, which God has sown in our souls, wants to grow, to express itself in action, to yield results which continually coincide with what God wants. Therefore, we must be ready to begin again, to find again—in new situations—the light and the stimulus of our first conversion.[a]

a. Josemaría Escrivá, *Christ Is Passing By* (New York: Scepter, 1974), §58.

honor and thanksgiving and obedience that he is owed, giving our very selves as offerings to God (Rom. 12:1). It is how those dead in Christ continue to die to sin, and how those who have put on Christ continue to clothe themselves with his virtues and life. In the same way, it is how those who were made God's friends, who have been "reconciled to God through the death of his Son" (Rom. 5:10), may now live and grow in that relationship. When God's children are faltering, the call to repentance and love is a call to be renewed and to reengage that friendship, as the apostle appeals on behalf of Christ: "Be reconciled to God" (2 Cor. 5:20).

10

Growing in Christ, Confessing in Hope

The Catholic Epistles and Revelation

The Lord does not delay his promise, as some regard "delay," but he is patient with you, not wishing that any should perish but that all should come to repentance.

—2 Peter 3:9 (NABRE)

We come finally to the Catholic Epistles—letters ascribed to James, Peter, John, and Jude—and the book of Revelation. We saw in the Gospels and Pauline Letters that the call to faith and repentance was often framed against the horizon of the coming kingdom and divine judgment. After Christ's resurrection and ascension, his promise to return and judge the living and the dead brings an urgency to this call: idolaters and unbelievers must *turn* to the Lord in conversion before the final day, and believers, too, must grow in faith and, if they fall, *return* to the Lord through confession and repentance. That the Lord will return is promised and sure, but we cannot predict precisely when. None should presume that they will have the opportunity to repent tomorrow. The time is now.

The Catholic Epistles and Revelation underscore this well, and their call makes a fitting conclusion to a book about confession and repentance. "Behold, I am coming soon, bringing my recompense with me, to repay each one for what he has done," promises Jesus (Rev. 22:12 ESV). The faithful are to wait for the Lord in hope and fortify themselves in faith and love so that, at the Lord's coming, they will receive his approval (James 5:7–11; 2 Pet. 3:11–13; Jude 20–21). "You also must be patient. Strengthen your hearts, for the coming of the Lord is near" (James 5:8). "Be on your guard, so that you do not lose what we have worked for, but may receive a full reward" (2 John 8). These texts call believers to grow, not regress, in the gifts received in baptism and conversion. Pertinent to our study of the sacrament of reconciliation, they also give particular instructions about the need to deal with Christian sin through confession, repentance, and intercession before the final day.

Nothing Unclean: The Hope of Life and the Call to Repentance

The message of Christ proclaims the greatest news and promises the greatest hope. The good and loving creator of all is reclaiming his world from Satan and sin and the enemies that have filled it with chaos and hatred. In the dead and resurrected flesh of Christ, God has "condemned" sin itself (Rom. 8:3). Christ has loosed the stranglehold of death and of the devil on God's creatures (John 12:31; 16:11; Col. 2:15; Heb. 2:14–15). And through the Spirit, Christ is "making all things new" (Rev. 21:5). Seated at the right hand of the Father in glory, the Son reigns over the universe now and is at work to put all things under his feet (cf. 1 Cor. 15:20–28; Eph. 1:20–23; 1 Tim. 6:14–15; Heb. 2:18; Rev. 11:15). When he returns, he will end all evil finally and completely. Satan will be crushed and cast out forever, and the "last enemy"—death itself—will be destroyed when Christ raises all the dead for judgment (cf. Rom. 16:20; 1 Cor. 15:26; Rev. 20:10, 13–14).[1] The world that God made for justice and life will be purified with fire and remade: a "new heavens and a new earth in which righteousness dwells" (2 Pet. 3:13 ESV; cf. Rev. 21:1) and in which there is "nothing unclean" (Rev. 21:27).

All that sin has disordered will finally be reversed. This is cosmically good news. And it is good news for individual humans fallen in sin, because the righteous Victor gives us the grace to share in his victory. Believers have been

1. Early Christian belief in the judgment of all, living and dead, is sufficiently clear. There seems to have been different views as to whether all the dead would be *raised* for judgment, or whether (after the judgment?) only the righteous would be raised. The Pauline material is debated, and the very early *Didache* 16.6–7 has only the righteous being raised. Texts like John 5:25–29 and Rev. 20:13 seem to affirm a general resurrection before judgment, with only the righteous then living eternally with God in glory.

made heirs of God in Christ, and at Christ's return they will participate in his judgment of evil and enjoy life with him in the new creation. God will crush Satan "under your feet" (Rom. 16:20). Children of Adam, created to be little lords and representatives of God on earth, will, restored in the New Adam, *reign* alongside Christ and even judge angels (Rom. 5:17; 1 Cor. 6:2–3; Rev. 3:21; 22:5). When Christ raises his people to glory in the resurrection, death will be defeated in the bodies of every one of the redeemed. They will be restored to the glory Adam forfeited and eat from the tree of life (Rev. 2:7). The harmony that sin disturbed will be renewed, and the redeemed will live in a new paradise in eternal intimacy with God—with no sin to separate them and no corruption or loss to cause grief. Revelation presents us with a startling vision of intimate communion between God and the whole Church: heaven comes down to earth, uniting the Church militant and the Church triumphant together as one spotless *bride* to celebrate her perfect union with God (Rev. 21:9–10). God "will dwell with them, and they will be his people, and God himself will be with them as their God. He will wipe away every tear from their eyes, and death shall be no more, neither shall there be mourning, nor crying, nor pain anymore, for the former things have passed away" (Rev. 21:3–4 ESV).

This is the inheritance to which all in Christ have been reborn, "an inheritance that is imperishable, undefiled, and unfading, kept in heaven for you" (1 Pet. 1:4). But for those on earth, until that day, it lies still in the future. The promise of this future, then, becomes a *call* and command in the present. For, though many are reborn to the hope of this inheritance, it will be finally received only by those children who are found faithful at the end. "The victor will inherit these gifts, and I shall be his God, and he will be my son" (Rev. 21:7 NABRE). Endurance to the end is here depicted as a "victory" or "conquest" in a kind of battle, a battle one must win to receive the final inheritance. Demonic forces like the devil, and political forces that serve his ends, oppose and make "war" against the Church and pressure believers to deny the Lord (cf. 1 Pet. 5:8; Rev. 2:10; 12:17; 13:7; 17:6). There are threats also from within. False teachers and hypocrites cause scandal and division within the community, "denying" the Lord by their behavior and influencing others to do the same (cf. 2 Pet. 2:1, 18–20; 3:17; 1 John 4:1–6; 2 John 7–10; 3 John 9–10; Jude 4–19). Within each believer, too, sinful inclinations and habits threaten to seduce God's children away from the truth (James 1:14–15; 4:1; 1 Pet. 2:11; 1 John 2:16–17).

Christians hope for the return of Christ and for the day when evil is finally condemned and the cosmos is restored. We "look forward" to the resurrection and the life of the world to come, as we confess in the Nicene Creed. But if we hope for inheritance in a world purified of sin, *we must also prepare ourselves for that day* by repenting and purifying ourselves. In the words of 1 Peter 1:17–18, "If you call on him as Father who judges impartially according to each one's deeds, conduct yourselves with fear throughout the time of your exile, knowing that you were ransomed from the futile ways inherited from your forefathers" (ESV). Those called and chosen by God should now endeavor to validate and confirm their election by growing in virtue (2 Pet. 1:10). Those who have been purified through the blood of Christ and the waters of baptism must now purify themselves, hastening to be "without spot or blemish" before God (2 Pet. 3:14). We *avoid sin* that would stain the soul that Christ died to cleanse (cf. James 1:27; Jude 23; Rev. 3:4). We grow in purity by faith and continued *hope*, by which we are joined to Christ (1 John 3:3; cf. Heb. 10:22–23). We purify ourselves through *repentance*: "Cleanse your hands, you sinners, and purify your hearts" (James 4:8). We do so also through *obedience and love*, practicing our religion in a way that is undefiled by caring for the needy and loving our brethren in obedience to God (James 1:27; 1 Pet. 1:22). By such means, we prepare ourselves for our share in the new world, which nothing unclean can enter.

The present time is a time of grace and promise, a time of hope. For that reason, it is also a time of repentance. The Lord desires "that all should come to repentance" (2 Pet. 3:9 NABRE). He waits and works to bring about his final union with his bride, the Church, who is to be adorned in splendor with a pure garment that consists of "the righteous deeds of the saints" (Rev. 19:8). The Good Shepherd wants the wanderers home, and he wants none to abandon the fold. At the beginning of the visions in Revelation, Jesus addresses seven congregations in Asia Minor. Some he praises for their endurance. Others he rebukes for their faithlessness or weakness. But he calls *all* to stoke the fire of their faith, lest they be found unfaithful when he returns to judge. "I am coming soon; hold fast to what you have, so that no one may seize your crown" (Rev. 3:11). "Remember then from what you have fallen; repent, and do the works you did at first" (Rev. 2:5). "Remember then what you received and heard; obey it, and repent. If you do not wake up, I will come like a thief, and you will not know at what hour I will come to you" (Rev. 3:3). Jesus's warnings, and his rebukes even for those who are enduring, may sound harsh. As we have seen throughout Scripture, however, God's rebukes are motivated by love and a desire for our good. He calls us to repentance because he wants us to receive, and not to lose, the grace he has given and the inheritance he has won for us. "Those whom I love," he says, "I reprove and discipline, so be zealous and repent" (Rev. 3:19 ESV).

Maturing in Faith: Knowledge, Memory, and Love

The call to repentance is strongly motivated by Christ's future return to judge and restore all things. As we saw above, the threat of punishment is part of that motivation. In its most perfect form, though, repentance is motivated by *love* for our gracious Father.[2] According to 1 John 4:18, "perfect love" dispels fear of punishment. One who loves perfectly will sorrow over sin because sin offends the beloved. One who loves God perfectly will pursue what God wants, love what God commands, and imitate God's own love for others. But perfect love is not mere emotion or passion. It is active and habitual, involving both heart and action. For, as John says in the same letter, the love of God truly reaches "perfection" only in one who "obeys" God's word and commandments (1 John 2:3–6). This love is developed over time, and it is threatened by temptation, sinful desires, and doubt.

Christians, thus, are called not only to maintain the purity and graces given in baptism but also to increase in them as they grow in love. One image that recurs frequently is that of *rebirth* and, following that rebirth, growth and development. Those born as heirs of Adam, subject to death and sin, are granted a new "birth" in Christ through baptism—forgiven former guilt and restored through the Spirit as children of God (James 1:18; 1 John 3:1, 9; cf. John 3:5; Philem. 10; Titus 3:5). God "has given us a new birth into a living hope through the resurrection of Jesus Christ" (1 Pet. 1:3). Corruptible, mortal humans have been "born anew" to incorruptibility through the "imperishable seed" that is God's "living and enduring word" (1 Pet. 1:23). The divine word is like a seed planted in us, capable of saving our souls (James 1:21) and granting us new life in God as "participants of the divine nature" (2 Pet. 1:4).

If our incorporation into Christ is a rebirth, the Christian life after that rebirth is one of *growth and maturity*. The image is, in some ways, parallel

2. For a distinction between "servile fear" of punishment and "filial fear," which is part of love, see Thomas Aquinas, *Summa Theologiae* III, q. 85, art. 5. According to Augustine, such fear can be a means to perfection in love, inasmuch as it brings us to correct ourselves and grow (*Homilies on the First Epistle of John* 9.5).

to one we have seen elsewhere of a plant bearing fruit. Believers are to "grow" in grace that leads to salvation (1 Pet. 2:2; 2 Pet. 3:18). But the image of human rebirth accents the psychological and behavioral dimension of this growth. The newborn, like a plant, is nourished and supplied with life from its source—God's grace through the "milk" of the Spirit (1 Pet. 2:2). But the child's growth is not automatic or merely passive. It involves the development of the mind and will by which God's children cultivate habits of Godliness and virtue. Those who have been reborn by the word of God must continue to receive or "welcome" that word and "put away all filth and evil excess" that may stunt its effects (James 1:21 NABRE). Those in Christ are like "newborn infants" (1 Pet. 2:2), and these newborns must grow to become "obedient children" (1 Pet. 1:14). Children reborn through God's love are to resemble God, reflecting the spiritual DNA encoded in their new birth by walking in love, truth, and righteousness (1 John 3:9–10). This is how one maintains one's place as God's beloved child, growing in faith and keeping the commandments (1 John 2:24; 3:17–18; 4:8; 5:1–2; 2 John 4–6).

The opening exhortations of 2 Peter assure us that God has granted believers "all things that pertain to life and godliness, through the knowledge of him who called us to his own glory and excellence" (2 Pet. 1:3 ESV). Because God has done so, the letter continues, we must supplement our faith with virtue, knowledge, self-control, endurance, piety, and love (1:5–7). These traits can, if their growth is cultivated, "keep you from being ineffective and unfruitful in the knowledge of our Lord Jesus Christ. For anyone who lacks these things is short-sighted and blind, and is forgetful of the cleansing of past sins" (1:8–9).

Supplementing faith with deeper knowledge and virtue is important in one's life of repentance, as it fortifies us to endure in times of trial and in our pursuit of love and self-denial. It is through *knowledge* of who God is and what God has done and has promised that one can grow in faith and hope.

> Therefore prepare your minds for action; discipline yourselves; set all your hope on the grace that Jesus Christ will bring you when he is revealed. Like obedient children, do not be conformed to the desires that you formerly had in ignorance. Instead, as he who called you is holy, be holy yourselves in all your conduct. (1 Pet. 1:13–15)

It is through such knowledge that the immature child can grow in virtue, knowing the goodness of God that we have received and that we are called to imitate. "The way we came to know love was that he laid down his life for us; so we ought to lay down our lives for our brothers" (1 John 3:16 NABRE; cf. 4:16).

Knowledge of God's character and promises also fortifies us for *endurance* through times of suffering and temptation. Deuteronomy called the Israelites to fortify themselves for obedience by "remembering" the Lord—specifically, God's great power, sternness, and mercy toward Israel in the exodus and the wilderness (Deut. 8:1–20). Similarly, Jude and 2 Peter call Christians to remember God's judgments of old on those who rebelled against him, pointing to examples from the time of the flood and Israel's wandering in the wilderness (2 Pet. 2:1–22; Jude 5–16). This knowledge offers comfort to those who suffer under the influence of false teachers and hypocrites, and it warns any who are tempted to join them: "The Lord knows how to rescue the godly from trial, and to keep the unrighteous under punishment until the day of judgment" (2 Pet. 2:9). Such remembrance and knowledge is part of "building" oneself up in faith, gained through the testimony of the Scriptures and the teaching of the apostles (Jude 20).

More than just remembering the Lord's grace and justice in Israel's past, however, Christians are called to fortify themselves with the knowledge of God's grace and justice manifested in Christ Jesus. First Peter calls Christians to endure in suffering by remembering *Christ's suffering* for all (cf. 1 Pet. 2:21–25; 3:13–18; 4:12–16; 5:9). Christ himself suffered innocently, and those who are in Christ should expect no better treatment—whether they suffer for their faith specifically or simply at the hands of cruel people. They are, rather, called to "arm" themselves with the same mindset, ready to endure sufferings at the hands of others (1 Pet. 4:1). Suffering for the sake of righteousness and out of obedience to God is a participation in Christ's sufferings, part of one's continued dying to sin in union with Christ (1 Pet. 4:1–2, 8), which produces heavenly "credit" for them in God's sight (1 Pet. 2:19–20).

Knowledge of God and, particularly, the revelation of God's love and mercy in Christ should also lead believers to cultivate habits of *self-denial and love*. Knowledge of God must engender love in God's children: "Whoever does not love does not know God, for God is love" (1 John 4:8). First John calls us to know and recall the love of God manifested in the cross in order to imitate it by the power of God's grace in the Spirit (1 John 4:7–21). The Petrine Epistles call us also to remember the fact that we have been forgiven and purified, ransomed with the precious blood of Christ and forgiven our sins (1 Pet. 1:14–19; 2 Pet. 1:9). If we do not keep this in mind, we may forget the life from which we were redeemed and fall into it once again—like the Israelites desiring to return to Egypt. Indeed, maintaining our purity and striving in obedience is a part of our life of self-denial and self-giving, our life of love in Christ. Note the connection in 1 Peter 1:22: "Having purified your souls by your obedience to the truth for a sincere brotherly love, love one another earnestly from a pure heart" (1 Pet. 1:22 ESV). Believers must turn with tears from their own sources of pride and strife, putting away their temptations and evil desires for wealth or glory, that they may live at peace with God and others (James 4:1–6; 5:1–6; Rev. 3:15–18). They must be submissive to leaders and others who instruct or rebuke them in the Church (1 Pet. 5:3–6; 3 John 5–8). And they must show humility in service, hospitality, and love for others (cf. James 3:14–16; 1 Pet. 3:8; 4:7–11). Believers must direct their efforts to self-control in their speech, behavior, and attitudes, denying their pride for the sake of love and obedience (James 1:26–27; 2:1; 4:16). They must remember their own lowliness and be merciful rather than judgmental toward others, knowing that they too will be judged (James 2:12–13; 4:11–12; Jude 22–23). Indeed, James calls all to hasten to self-denial and repentance in view of the judgment and God's promised reward:

> Submit yourselves therefore to God. Resist the devil, and he will flee from you. Draw near to God, and he will draw near to you. Cleanse your hands, you sinners, and purify your hearts, you double-minded. Lament and mourn and weep. Let your laughter be turned into mourning and your joy into dejection. Humble yourselves before the Lord, and he will exalt you. (James 4:7–10)

The call to supplement our faith with repentance can be difficult. There are "growing pains," so to speak, for Christ's newborns. But growth in self-denial and repentance is part of our progress in the perfection of Christlike love. If we refuse such growth, we not only fail in love, but we forget the grace of our rebirth and disregard the precious blood by which we were redeemed. It would, James says, be like a person who gets a good look at who he is in the mirror and then, turning to leave the house, forgets who he is and acts like someone he is not (James 1:22–25). God calls us to know who he is and to know who he has redeemed us to be, as well as to live and grow in that identity. Moreover, this knowledge and growth bear the promise of a reward and exaltation that far exceed any discomfort. Repentance and self-denial now prepare us for our inheritance in the future.

Dealing with Sin: Confession, Intercession, and Intervention

The call of the Christian life is to be more deeply rooted in knowledge of God, as well as of one's salvation and calling, and to grow in virtue and love. To this call, as we saw above, are added rebuke and warning, a call for all to repent and endure in view of the coming judgment.

As we continue our investigation of the final books in the New Testament, with a particular view to considering the realities involved in the sacrament of reconciliation, we can turn now to ask how we see Christian sin being dealt with in these books. What is to be done when a Christian falters or fails? What about when a newborn heir of God decides to play the prodigal and forsake his Father and his family, the Church? The Catholic Epistles highlight three elements of dealing with Christian sin: *confession* and *repentance* on the part of the sinner, and *intercession* and *intervention* on the part of the sinner's fellow believers and presbyters.

Confession and Repentance

Growing in knowledge of God brings one to know the depth of God's love and God's holiness. This, in turn, should lead also to greater self-knowledge. Christians are called to imitate God's holiness (1 Pet. 1:15–16) and God's love in Christ (1 John 4:16), and if our minds are enlightened by the light of God, we will know that we fall far below that standard. First John underscores this strongly: "If we say that we have no sin, we deceive ourselves, and the truth is not in us" (1 John 1:8). The light of truth that is God shines on our imperfections to call us out of darkness (1 John 1:5–6). Our need to be saved from sin is revealed in Christ, certainly through his teaching, but also in the very fact of his crucifixion. In John 3:14 Jesus compares his being "lifted up" on the cross to the lifting up of the bronze serpent in Israel's wilderness period (see Num. 21:4–9). The people grumbled, and God sent fiery serpents to bite them as a punishment and discipline. When Moses interceded for them, God told Moses to fashion a serpent of bronze and mount it up on a pole, promising that anyone who was bitten had only to look at the bronze serpent to be delivered. The image is striking: they were forced to look upon an exalted representation of the consequence of their own sin and, by doing so, were saved from the full penalty themselves. Looking with faith upon the Crucified One, likewise, delivers Christians from the full penalty of sin. Yet in contemplating the cross, we too are gazing on an image of our sins' consequences. To insist that one has no such sin is to deny that one needs this salvation and, in effect, to falsify this aspect of what the cross reveals. "If we say that we have not sinned, we make him a liar, and his word is not in us" (1 John 1:10).

First John calls quite adamantly for obedience, stating strongly that those born of God will walk in love and righteousness and not pursue sin (1 John 2:1; 3:6–10; 5:18). Yet the reality of Christian sin is acknowledged, and so too is the danger that our own hearts and consciences may condemn or accuse us (cf. 1 John 3:19–20; 5:16).[3] Awareness of one's sins, of how far one ha "fallen," is important to repentance (Rev. 2:5). Self-examination is a part of developing self-control, diagnosing ourselves so that we can see more clearly how to repent and grow in virtue or what graces to pray for. Such self-diagnosis is also part of submitting ourselves for healing, so that we can know and name our sins before the God who forgives: "If we confess our sins, he who is faithful and just will forgive us our sins and cleanse us from all unrighteousness" (1 John 1:9).

Christ has paid the redemption price for all sins, not only our former sins, and Christ presents his sacrifice in heaven on our behalf. "My children, I am writing this to you so that you may not commit sin. But if anyone does sin, we have an Advocate with the Father, Jesus Christ the righteous one. He is expiation for our sins, and not for our sins only but for those of the whole world" (1 John 2:1–2 NABRE). First John 1:9 assures us that God will *forgive* our sins if we submit them to him in *confession*. God desires our salvation, and he will not spurn one who turns to him with contrition. And his word of forgiveness is stronger than even the sharpest condemnation of our consciences (1 John 3:20).

John's promise of forgiveness for one who confesses, however, also builds in the need for reconciliation and *repentance*. One who is forgiven must turn from sin to live in renewed friendship and love for God. According to 1 John, we abide in God and have "confidence" in view of the final judgment not merely by virtue of being forgiven but by being transformed to walk in his perfect love and keep his commandments (see 1 John 2:5; 3:21; 4:16–17). To know God and to enjoy the continued benefits of Christ's cleansing sacrifice is to live a *life* of perseverance in faith and love: "If we walk in the light as he himself is in the light, we have fellowship with one another, and the blood

3. For a discussion of sin and Christian perfection in 1 John, see Urban C. von Wahlde, *The Gospel and Letters of John*, 3 vols., ECC (Grand Rapids: Eerdmans, 2010), 3:48–50.

198 The Bible and Reconciliation

of Jesus his Son cleanses us from all sin" (1 John 1:7). "Whoever does not love abides in death" (1 John 3:14). Christian sin is to be dealt with through confession and repentance, as one receives forgiveness and is renewed to live in love with God and neighbor.

Confession and Priestly Intercession

First John promises that God, in his faithfulness and justice, will forgive sins confessed, and the same letter enjoins the forgiven to return to a life of obedience and love. In 1 John 1:9 the promise of forgiveness for Christian sin is conditioned simply on confession. But the Johannine writings affirm the authority of apostolic presbyters to forgive and retain sins in Christ's name (John 20:23) and to rebuke the disobedient and command the community to shun them (2 John 7–11; 3 John 9–10). Likewise, 1 John later makes a distinction between sins that lead to death and sins that do not (1 John 5:16–17), and the author insists that believers will not go on sinning (1 John 3:6; 5:18). Is the promise of forgiveness "if we confess" in 1 John 1:9 imagined as a secret prayer to God or as a confession to God in the hearing of others? Is this promise perhaps limited only to inadvertent or nondeadly sins? Many interpreters take 1 John 1:9 to envision communal confession of some kind, though the verse is unspecific about the work of the Church in dealing with sin in its members.[4]

We find the role of the Church in dealing with sin especially in the call to *intercession*. James 5:16 and 1 John 5:16 in particular promise that, when a believer sins, God will grant forgiveness in response to the prayers of other believers on the sinner's behalf.

> Is anyone among you sick? Let him call for the elders of the church, and let them pray over him, anointing him with oil in the name of the Lord. And the prayer of faith will save the one who is sick, and the Lord will raise him up. And if he has committed sins, he will be forgiven. Therefore, confess your sins to one another and pray for one another, that you may be healed. The prayer of a righteous person has great power as it is working. (James 5:14–16 ESV)

> If anyone sees his brother sinning, if the sin is not deadly, he should pray to God and he will give him life. This is only for those whose sin is not deadly.

4. See further Raymond E. Brown, *The Epistles of John*, AB 30 (New York: Doubleday, 1982), 208; Georg Strecker, *The Johannine Letters: A Commentary on 1, 2, and 3 John*, Hermeneia (Minneapolis: Fortress, 1996), 32.

There is such a thing as deadly sin, about which I do not say that you should pray. (1 John 5:16 NABRE)

The Letter of James calls believers to let the word of God, implanted in them, grow unto salvation (James 1:18) by pursuing wisdom and righteous behavior (cf. James 1:21–27; 2:18–26) and cleansing themselves through repentance so that they may endure and receive the crown of life at the last day (James 1:12).[5] Against the horizon of judgment, amid his call for believers to wait prayerfully for the Lord's return, James calls believers to confess their sins and to intercede for one another's forgiveness. First he calls for prayer related to (presumably significant) illness. One who is sick should summon the presbyters or "elders" (Greek *presbyteroi*) of the Church, an office of leadership apparently understood to be shared by the apostles with their successors through the laying on of hands (cf. Acts 14:23; 15:2; 20:17; 1 Tim. 4:14; 5:17; Titus 1:5; 1 Pet. 5:1, 5; 2 John 1; 3 John 1). They will pray over him and anoint him with oil, and through their "prayer of faith" the sick man will be saved and, if he had committed sins, he will be forgiven. James moves then to a more general instruction, but one logically connected ("Therefore," 5:16) to what he has just said of the power of such prayer to bring healing and forgiveness. They are to confess and pray for one another so that they might be healed. Not all illness is caused by a particular sin, even in the case of the one anointed (note "*if* he has committed sins" in 5:15), and not all who have sins to confess are physically ill. The promise of "healing" for those who confess seems, then, to be one of "spiritual" healing "from sin" through forgiveness.[6] Different from 1 John 1:9, however, the promise of forgiveness is not merely tied to the confession. Rather, forgiveness is connected to the work of advocacy, in which one who has heard the confession *intercedes as a mediator* for the sinner before God. The prayer of a "righteous" person, James says, is powerful. And he reminds his audience of the example of Elijah, a mere man like others, at whose prayer God both began and later ended a drought (James 5:17–18).

5. James has often been read as a kind of pastiche of instruction and exhortation. For a unified reading of James against the horizon of divine judgment, see now Daniel K. Eng, *Eschatological Approval: The Structure and Unifying Motif of James*, NTM 45 (Sheffield: Sheffield Phoenix, 2022).

6. See Eng, *Eschatological Approval*, 181–82. With a similar but more communal focus, compare Luke Timothy Johnson, *The Letter of James: A New Translation with Introduction and Commentary*, AB 37A (New Haven: Yale University Press, 2008), 342.

First John 5:16 makes a similar promise. If one sees a fellow Christian (a "brother") sinning, one should pray to God, and God will give "life" to the sinner in response to the intercessor's prayer. Here again intercessory prayer is offered as a way of dealing with Christian sin; however, in this verse the promise is not conditioned on hearing the sinner's confession. If one *sees* another sinning, he should pray to God, and God will grant mercy and restoration to the sinner, at least in the case of sin that is not "deadly"—that is, that does not lead to spiritual death.[7] John does not necessarily prohibit praying for a person who has committed mortal sin. To refuse to seek the salvation of one who is in sin and heading for death would seem to contradict the divine love that sent Christ to save the "world" and "us"—when we too were dead—precisely the act of love that we must imitate (John 3:16–17; 1 John 4:9–11). But John does say that his promise of life for intercession does not apply to cases of deadly sin. To translate more woodenly: "I am not saying that one should pray about *that sin*."[8] If this leaves open the possibility of praying for a *person* who has committed deadly sin, it emphasizes that the kind of intercession John promises will bring "life" to the sinner applies only in cases of nondeadly sin. One who has strayed from the way of life must be converted to be saved, as we will see below. Merely asking God to renew life in one who has, through deadly sin, cut himself off from the source of life is insufficient. But in the case of nondeadly sin, John's promise is simple and striking. One who sees a Christian sin—without even needing to hear their confession or assess their contrition—should intercede for them, and God will hear that prayer and forgive them.

7. We are not told explicitly in this text what distinguishes deadly from nondeadly sin other than its effect (leading to death). For a detailed list of options, see Brown, *Epistles of John*, 612–19. A theological synthesis about what conditions are required to commit "mortal" sin, as the NRSV translates 1 John 5:16 (grave matter, committed deliberately, knowingly, and freely), must be a synthesis of this and many other texts that explicitly or implicitly distinguish grades or kinds of sinning within moral theology and anthropology. Limiting themselves to the Johannine writings, many authors take the deadly sin here to be that of secession or apostasy (cf. 1 John 2:19). Notably, in John's Gospel, Jesus speaks of sin and condemnation remaining on persons when they persist in opposition to Christ out of culpable ignorance (John 9:40–41; 15:22–24; cf. 3:18–19).

8. The negated Greek phrase *ou peri ekeinēs*, "not about that," is clearer in its reference than some English translations betray. The pronoun "that" (*ekeinēs*) is feminine, and its antecedent is the feminine noun *hamartia*, "sin," earlier in the verse. Note also that the negated verb is "I say," not "pray"—that is, John is saying that his words do not pertain to such a case of sin (not that he is telling them that they must not pray about it). See von Wahlde, *Gospel and Letters of John*, 3:203–4.

We can learn several things from these texts, at least three pertaining to sin and the need for confession. First, and fundamentally, we can see that *Christian sin still needs to be dealt with and forgiven.* The person sinning in these texts is a Christian, envisioned as a "brother" and one who is a regular part of the community, not an apostate or one excommunicated. He is washed in Christ's healing waters, but he still needs forgiveness and a renewal of life when he sins. If John and James viewed sins after baptism to be immaterial to one's life with God, they would presumably not have gone out of their way to make such commands or promises in God's name. Indeed, elsewhere in the Catholic Epistles, 1 Peter 3:7 warns that mistreatment of one's wife can "hinder" one's prayers. Whether this envisions a divine penalty—similar to Jesus's warning that God will not forgive one who persists in unforgiveness—or a kind of relational breakdown due to one's sin, it affirms that Christian sin has consequences in one's relationship with God, here one that is potentially "dangerous . . . in view of the eschatological urgency that demanded prayer" (see 1 Pet. 4:7).[9] Second, the need to deal with Christian sin pertains not simply to sinfulness or fallenness in general but to *particular, actual sins.* This seems implied from the occasion for intercession in the two passages: James calls for mutual intercession in the context of confession, where particular sins are divulged, and John calls believers to intercede for others when they see them committing a sin. Third, Christian sin has *communal effects*, so it is properly dealt with in and through the community of the faithful. James's call to confess to "one another" indicates the communal and interpersonal nature of confession, though it is unclear whether he envisions that one (or many) will confess in front of the whole assembly or only to select persons.[10]

To whom are people told to confess? Or, we might ask, whose intercession is promised to have such power? A note in the Challoner Douay-Rheims (DRV), followed by many Catholic readers, insists that James 5:16 is a call to confess only to presbyters (priests), since "to confess to persons who had no power to forgive sins would be useless." However, the context of the verse focuses on the power of intercessory *prayer*, not the apostolic authority to pronounce forgiveness or retain sins directly in Christ's name. James's communal call does not rule out, and rather seems to include, the intercession

9. Craig S. Keener, *1 Peter: A Commentary* (Grand Rapids: Baker Academic, 2021), 251.
10. See the discussions in Peter H. Davids, *The Epistle of James: A Commentary on the Greek Text*, NIGTC (Grand Rapids: Eerdmans, 1982), 196; Dale C. Allison Jr., *A Critical and Exegetical Commentary on the Epistle of James*, ICC (London: Bloomsbury, 2013), 768–71.

of particularly faithful and "righteous" persons, regardless of whether they hold ministerial office. And 1 John 5:16 calls "anyone" who sees a sister or brother sinning to pray for them so that God will give the sinner life. This is a great promise and a great task laid upon the whole community of faith. It is a *priestly* task, though it is not limited to those who hold priestly office. All who are in Christ—whether ordained or lay—participate in his priestly office and, together, constitute a "royal priesthood" within the world (1 Pet. 2:5, 9; Rev. 1:6; 5:10).[11] They offer their very being and their possessions as pleasing sacrifices to God through Christ (cf. Rom. 12:1; Phil. 4:18). They mediate Christ's love to the world by word and example. And they imitate Christ, the great High Priest, not only by offering prayers in general but also by praying for those who sin against them (cf. Matt. 5:44; Luke 23:34; Acts 7:60). They too are called to intercede for others when others sin. God desires the life and purification of all, and God, through these inspired texts, promises to hear believers when they intercede for the forgiveness of others. Their intercession is hardly "useless."

Believers today should hear such calls and turn to this duty of intercession on behalf of others, no matter their vocation. At the same time, it would be a mistake to read these promises as somehow making the role of clergy unnecessary for the forgiveness of sin in the Church. All who are in Christ participate in Christ's royal priesthood, just as the nation of Israel was made a priestly nation when God redeemed them from Egypt (Exod. 19:6). But, as we saw in God's judgment of Korah in Numbers 16, God ordained a place for ministerial priests *within* the priestly kingdom to represent them to God and represent God authoritatively to them. In the New Testament, Jude condemns Christians who flout authority and follow in the way of Korah (Jude 11, cf. 8). First Peter and Revelation, which describe the whole Church as a priestly kingdom, simultaneously assume the distinct ministerial office of apostles and presbyters (1 Pet. 5:1–5; Rev. 4:4; 14:3; 21:14). All in Christ are called to intercede and represent others before God, and they represent Christ to others in their various vocations. In Pauline terms, all in Christ have received the same Spirit, and all have been given different gifts for the edification of Christ's body. But not all the gifts have the same purpose, and not all believers are apostles or preachers (1 Cor. 12:4–11, 27–31). Not all have been given the authority of stewards who manage the Master's household and other servants

11. See Vatican Council II, *Lumen gentium*, §10.

(Matt. 24:45–46). Not all have been appointed to bind, to loose, and to manage debts owed to the Lord and pronounce forgiveness authoritatively in his name (Matt. 16:19; 18:18; John 20:23). To note that James 5:16 is not limited to confession before a priest and to infer from this "the clear non-need of a priest" is a biblical-theological non sequitur.[12]

Indeed, our particular texts in James and 1 John seem to hint at, or at least make space for, a need for Christ's authoritative representatives in dealing with Christian sin, particularly in the limitations they imply to the efficacy of intercession. The promise in 1 John 5:16 that God will "give life" to a sinner when the intercessor asks, without the sinner necessarily confessing and doing penance, is limited to sins that are not deadly. James's promises related to intercession are conditioned not on the gravity of the sinner's sin but on the status of the intercessor. James points especially to the efficacy of prayer by the "righteous" in the community. And he seems to assume that presbyters are not only included among such powerful intercessors, but also that they are to be sought especially in serious cases. James's call to communal confession and his promise that a righteous person's intercession is powerful follows logically ("Therefore," James 5:16) from his instructions for the sick: the sick should call not simply for any righteous person but specifically for the *presbyters of the Church*, because *their* prayer will bring healing and forgiveness (James 5:14–15). There is no reason to think that James envisions serious sins, any more than serious illness, being dealt with apart from the governance and authority of the presbyters. Peter H. Davids notes that the presbyters clearly hear confessions when anointing (James 5:15) and infers also that they "guide the process" of communal confession and intercession.[13] But, if they are intercessors to be sought out in serious cases of illness in James 5:14–15, and if powerful intercession is what needs to be sought for forgiveness of sin in 5:16, we may infer that the presbyters are not merely organizers for others' prayer but are themselves authoritative and powerful intercessors—whether for all sins confessed in the assembly or for particular ones brought to them.

It would be a mistake to read these texts and 1 John 1:9 as promising forgiveness only through sacramental confession with an ordained minister, but it would also be a mistake to read these texts as obviating the need for sacramental confession, especially in cases of deadly sin. Biblical Christianity

12. The quotation is from Scot McKnight, *The Letter of James*, NICNT (Grand Rapids: Eerdmans, 2011), 446.
13. Davids, *James*, 196.

should aim to say yes to all the biblical data and give coherent expression to it in its forms of faith and practice. For Catholics, these verses should recall the opening of the divine liturgy, wherein we make a general confession and ask intercession from the whole Church and our fellow congregants ("and you, my brothers and sisters"), to which the priest responds with his own prayer of intercession. We should be assured of God's promises to hear such prayer and galvanized to intercede for others in our private prayer lives. But we should also be reminded of the good of bringing particular sins—especially grave ones—to the priest in the context of the sacrament, where he has the opportunity to hear, to counsel, and to pronounce forgiveness directly as an authoritative conduit for Christ's restorative grace. This gift of sacramental confession, too, is divinely established as a mode of dealing with sins after baptism and bears God's clear promise of forgiveness in Scripture. And it, too, is far from useless.

Merciful Intervention

James and 1 John, as we have seen, prescribe explicit confession and intercession as ways of dealing with Christian sin. However, the promise in 1 John 5:16 is limited to nondeadly sin, at least for a person's restoration through intercession without confession. And the promises of forgiveness through confession and intercession in 1 John 1:9 and James 5:16 assume someone who is already repentant and seeking forgiveness. What about a believer who departs from the path of life? How is such Christian sin to be dealt with?

We saw in Hebrews 6:4–6 a stark warning against apostasy, one which—though open to varying interpretations—warned of the impossibility of restoration from apostasy. The example of the Corinthian sinner punished and then forgiven and restored through Paul's ministry showed an example of restoration through the path of repentance. In the Catholic Epistles, we find hope for those who have strayed from the faith and life of the Church, as well as a call to all Christians to go and restore them. Indeed, we find it highlighted in the letters of the brothers James and Jude, which frame the Catholic Epistles collection and its themes of love and faithful endurance amid trials and crises.[14] The final words of the first Catholic Epistle and the final exhortation of the last call the Church to mercy.

---

14. See Darian R. Lockett, *Letters from the Pillar Apostles: The Formation of the Catholic Epistles as a Canonical Collection* (Eugene, OR: Pickwick, 2017), 188–96; David R. Nienhuis

My brothers, if anyone among you should stray from the truth and someone bring him back, he should know that whoever brings back a sinner from the error of his way will save his soul from death and will cover a multitude of sins. (James 5:19–20 NABRE)

And have mercy on those who doubt; save others by snatching them out of the fire; to others show mercy with fear, hating even the garment stained by the flesh. (Jude 22–23 ESV)[15]

James and Jude here give instructions regarding believers who have strayed from the truth to the extent that, to be saved, they must be returned. This is not a person who is willingly bringing her or his sins to the community or presbyters for confession, at least not yet. This is the case of one wandering away from God and the Church—one who, in Jude's terms, is heading for the "fire" of condemnation. This person is not irrevocably lost: this is a sin from which one *can* be restored. But this is not a sin that mere intercession is sufficient to cover (1 John 5:16). Nor is this a sin that the faithful can decide makes the person no longer worth trying to save. Rather, "the saints are called to an ongoing rescue operation that seeks the merciful restoration of all who walk in error."[16] In the case of one who has strayed so far, Christians are called to *intervention*.

Such intervention is something that those in apostolic office do as part of their calling (2 Tim. 4:2; Titus 2:15). It is also, as in these texts, something that all Christians are invited to do as part of their life of love in Christ: to call their prodigal brothers and sisters home. It is an act of love that involves rebuke as well as invitation, and it must be done not merely with zeal but also with gentleness and a genuine desire for the person's good (Gal. 6:1; 2 Thess. 3:15). It can also involve temptation and requires believers to fortify themselves lest they, too, fall into error (Gal. 6:1; Jude 23). But, through the word of God's mercy and rebuke delivered through a believer, God's Spirit prompts and pulls the sinner to contrition and repentance. Through the intervention of

and Robert W. Wall, *Reading the Epistles of James, Peter, John, and Jude as Scripture: The Shaping and Shape of a Canonical Collection* (Grand Rapids: Eerdmans, 2013), 47–48.

15. The text of Jude 22–23 is notoriously disputed, and its transmission history is complex. Though it often goes unnoted in Bible translations, many commentators opt for a shorter reading found in our earliest Greek witness to Jude and in some early versions and Church Fathers: "Snatch some out of the fire; and on those who dispute have mercy with fear, hating even the garment stained by the flesh."

16. Nienhuis and Wall, *Reading the Epistles of James, Peter, John, and Jude*, 237.

the Church, and God's Spirit working in the Church, the prodigal is returned from his wanderings and reconciled to his Father's household. He is saved from the death and condemnation toward which his sins lead and is restored to life with God.

Further, when a prodigal is restored, it enriches the whole household and brings healing to the body of Christ. Polycarp of Smyrna, in the early second century, encourages the Philippians to think in this way about a presbyter who has fallen away through love of money: "Do not regard such people as enemies, but, as sick and straying members, restore them, in order that you may save your body in its entirety."[17] Such loving intervention is an act of righteousness that adorns the beauty of Christ's body. And it is, for the one who undertakes it, a way of building on the foundation of one's baptism with precious stones, one that will garner a "reward" (1 Cor. 3:12–15). Indeed, in this way, to work for the conversion of sinners can itself be considered a form of penance, an act of love and mercy that covers one's own trespasses and that will be met with mercy at one's own judgment. Many early Christians speak of converting or restoring sinners as a way of "covering" or "paying" for sins alongside penances such as alms, fasting, or steadfast prayer.[18] It is a spiritual work of mercy, an act of love by means of which God's grace is operative to purify his Church for the last day. It is an act by which one abides in the love of God for the world, a life-giving love that covers a multitude of sins (cf. 1 Pet. 4:8). It is one of the "righteous deeds" by which believers adorn Christ's bride for the wedding feast at the last day (Rev. 19:8).

Waiting in Repentance and Hope

Dealing with Christian sin before the judgment is necessary, and all believers are called to work against sin or work for its removal in different ways in their own vocations. One who sees nondeadly sin in others should intercede. One who sees others straying into death should intervene. One who is conscious of sin should confess in hope to God and call others—especially presbyters

17. Polycarp, *To the Philippians* 11.4 (trans. Holmes, 293, 295).
18. Cf. *2 Clement* 16.4; *Barnabas* 19.10; Clement of Alexandria, *Salvation of the Rich* 38; Tertullian, *Antidote for the Scorpion's Sting* 6; Origen, *Homilies on Leviticus* 2.4. Indeed, though most recent commentators read the "multitude of sins" covered in James 5:20 to be the sins of the one restored, the verse has often been read as a promise that the *restorer's* sins will be covered by this act of charity.

Repentance and Intervention in *2 Clement*

The parable of the lost sheep (Luke 15:1–7) emphasizes God's desire that none be lost from the fold. Apostles such as Paul, James, and Jude called believers to share in this concern for God's flock both by keeping themselves in the faith and by evangelizing those who go astray. Their successors emphasized the same, as we see in this exhortation by a second-century presbyter that was attributed to Clement.

> Let us repent, therefore, with our whole heart, lest any of us should perish needlessly. For if we have orders that we should make it our business to tear men away from idols and to instruct them, how much more wrong is it that a soul that already knows God should perish? Therefore let us help one another to restore those who are weak with respect to goodness, so that we may all be saved, and let us admonish and turn back one another. And let us think about paying attention and believing not only now, while we are being admonished by the elders; but let us also remember the Lord's commands when we have returned home and not allow ourselves to be dragged off the other way by worldly desires. Let us come here more frequently and strive to advance in the commandments of the Lord, in order that all of us, being of one mind, may be gathered together into life.[a]

a. *2 Clement* 17.1–3 (trans. Holmes, 161).

in a case of grave sin—to hear that confession, and should show forth his or her repentance in renewed acts of faithfulness and love toward God and others. And all are called to supplement their faith with self-control, knowledge, and love. All must endeavor to turn ever more from sin and to grow in love, in gratitude for our past deliverance and in view of the future for which we were redeemed. All are called, in a word, to a life of *repentance*.

The Catholic Epistles, like the Pauline literature, invite Christians to see themselves in the figure of Israel in the wilderness, redeemed and still pressing forward to follow God toward our final inheritance. In 1 Peter, we are also invited to see ourselves in Israel's "new" wilderness, the exile: "If you invoke as Father the one who judges all people impartially according to their deeds, live in reverent fear during the time of your exile" (1 Pet. 1:17). As we saw,

Israel's exile brought a purification of the nation's past infidelities. Living in exile was a time of suffering, repentance, and waiting in which the nation was to turn again to God and await God's salvation, when God would judge the nations that held them captive and deliver them. Christians, too, forgiven former sins through faith and baptism, are also waiting for the final day of judgment and deliverance. But this time of waiting is a time of trial, a time for active repentance as believers prepare themselves for the day when all are judged.[19] As 1 Peter 4:17 has it, "The time has come for judgment to begin with the household of God; if it begins with us, what will be the end for those who do not obey the gospel of God?" Indeed, according to 2 Peter, this is one reason that God himself is "waiting," so to speak, to bring that final day: "The Lord does not delay his promise, as some regard 'delay,' but he is patient with you, not wishing that any should perish but that all should come to repentance" (2 Pet. 3:9 NABRE). The delay of the final judgment aims to leave opportunity for all to repent, not merely for unbelievers to convert for the first time but also for "you," for Christ's newborns already in the Church, to continue to repent and "grow into salvation" (1 Pet. 2:2).

We should therefore count every day that passes before Christ's return as an opportunity for repentance, not as a delay of our salvation but as an opportunity to progress toward it (2 Pet. 3:15). Our call, every day, is to endure in hope, to say no to our sinful inclinations and say yes to the gospel through which God grows new life within us (James 1:21). Through his promise and grace God grants us new birth so that we, fallen children of Adam, can "become partakers of the divine nature," having escaped the "corruption that is in the world because of sinful desire" and participating in Christ's divine righteousness and immortality (2 Pet. 1:4 ESV). Our call, in our various vocations and the opportunities put in front of us, is to mature in knowledge and virtue so that we newborns grow in obedience. God is faithful and just. He will not neglect the prayer of those who turn to him in confession. And he gives the greatest grace—divine love and strength and enlightenment poured out in our hearts—so that we newborns might grow in knowledge and virtue, redeemed by the Son so that we might become obedient children, prodigals restored to life in our Father's household, heirs of the new creation.

---

19. For a detailed study, see Andrew M. Mbuvi, *Temple, Exile and Identity in 1 Peter*, LNTS 345 (London: T&T Clark, 2007).

11

The Manifold Mercy of God

His divine power has given us everything needed for life and godliness.

—2 Peter 1:3

We began this book with the image of the prodigal son. Jesus's parable depicts the movements of fall, repentance, and restoration. The son takes what he can of his inheritance and leaves home, following his desires for life away from his father and his father's household. When he realizes how far he has fallen, reduced from an honored son to a ragged beggar, he makes the long journey home and confesses his sin. And when he does so, he encounters the mercy and love of his father, who embraces him, restores him to his dignity and honor, and welcomes him back into the life of his household. It is an image of *repentance*. It is an image of *restoration*. And it is an image of *reconciliation* between the son and his father and with the family he spurned.

God wants all of his children to return, to live fully as members of the household, and to receive their full and eternal inheritance in him. And God grants the grace for them to return. Having begun with the prodigal, it is fitting that we close with 2 Peter 1:3–4, which gives a different kind of commentary on the same reality.

His divine power has given us everything needed for life and godliness, through the knowledge of him who called us by his own glory and goodness. Thus he has given us, through these things, his precious and very great promises, so that through them you may escape from the corruption that is in the world because of lust, and may become participants of the divine nature. (2 Pet. 1:3–4)

The heirs of Adam, made in God's image and likeness, have fallen into "corruption" through disordered "lusts" and desires to enjoy the benefits of God's creation apart from God. They must be restored by God's power and grace. And God *gives* that grace. Through Christ Jesus, the Son of God, fallen humans are brought out from corruption to share in the "divine nature," restored to the perfection of God's image in love and holiness. In Christ, sinners are forgiven, and those who opposed God in sin are reconciled to God and restored through Christ's body, the Church. God calls the fallen to be restored through the proclamation of the gospel and the witness of believers, and he grants forgiveness and grace by the gift of the Holy Spirit received by faith and baptism. The Spirit works in believers to renew them in knowledge and love and godliness, to lead Adam's heirs to oppose sin and escape the "lusts" and corruption of the world through self-denial, and to form them again in the image of the New Adam in his self-giving love, so that they may receive the full inheritance of eternal, divine life in Christ.

The grace given in the sacrament of reconciliation is part of this work of salvation through restoration. For one who has been restored to God through conversion and baptism, *sin is still a problem*. When Christians choose to pursue sin after baptism, it affects the whole body of Christ, and it has effects on individual Christians and their relationship with God. Most extremely, there is the danger of losing what one has gained in Christ (Gal. 5:2; 2 John 8), of failing to bear fruit and cutting oneself off from Christ the Vine (John 15:2, 6, 10; cf. Luke 8:13; Gal. 6:8). But even for one who remains in Christ, sin has consequences and needs to be dealt with. It needs to be confessed and its guilt forgiven, a need for which Jesus invites disciples to pray regularly (Matt. 6:12). Sin can be penalized with divine rebukes and can even hinder one's prayers (1 Cor. 11:27–32; 1 Pet. 3:7). And if sin is not dealt with now, it will be dealt with at one's judgment when all deeds are requited and all that is not conformed to Christ in a believer must be purified (1 Cor. 3:10–15; 2 Cor. 5:10). If we do not humble ourselves, we will be humbled; if we judge ourselves now in self-examination, we will not be judged (Luke 18:9–14; 1 Cor. 11:27–32).

Sin is to be dealt with by *repentance and growth*. Joined to Christ's death and resurrection in baptism, believers live into and draw strength from that grace as they practice self-denial and self-giving in Christlike love. The two are poles of the same reality. In Christ, glory comes through crucifixion. And self-giving love, for one inclined to sin, requires self-denial. A life of repentance in Christ imitates the love of Christ, who bore his cross in love for others and in faith and humility before God. One sacrifices resources (alms) and bodily wants (fasting) with trust in God's provision and in love for God and others. One submits one's pride (and one's time) to glorify God in prayer and humbly submits one's mind to God's instruction in study and contemplation. One forgives others, denying one's pride and desires for vengeance and honor. These and other acts of repentance are ways in which one lives out one's union with Christ's cross and resurrection. When one has failed to avoid sin but instead has fallen into it, the same self-denial and love for God must take the shape of confession, humbly presenting one's sin to God so that it can be forgiven.

God shows great mercy in his provision of ways to deal with Christian sin so that all can be reconciled and restored. He promises forgiveness to those who deny themselves in confession, in self-discipline, and in corporal and spiritual works of mercy toward others (cf. Matt. 6:4, 6, 18; 25:31–46; Mark 11:25; Luke 12:33; 1 John 1:9; James 5:16). And God shows great mercy in working to prompt and encourage repentance in the Church, as the Holy Spirit moves believers to intercede for their brothers and sisters and to rebuke, encourage, and restore those who have gone astray (Luke 17:3; James 5:16, 19–20; 1 John 5:16). The Spirit works through believers to build up the Church in holiness through various gifts, from prophetic speech to charity to teaching to administration (cf. Rom. 12:6–8; 1 Cor. 12:4–11). And the same Spirit is given to work another gift in the *apostolic authority to rebuke and forgive sin in Christ's name* (Matt. 16:19; 18:18; John 20:22–23). This is a gift and part of the saving mission of the risen Christ to oppose sin and forgive sinners, on earth as in heaven. By the Spirit, Christ confers on apostolic ministers the authority to retain or bind people in their sin if they refuse to repent, a rebuke that will hopefully move them to return and be reconciled (1 Cor. 5:5). This is a gift of God for the good of each member of Christ's body and for the health and growth of the body as a whole. Indeed, the authority to bind and loose conferred on Peter and others with him is part of Christ's promise to preserve the Church from being overcome by the onslaught of evil (Matt. 16:18–19; cf. 2 Cor. 2:10–11), a promise that hardly ends with the apostolic age.

According to 2 Peter 1:3, God has in Christ provided manifold gifts—"everything" that is needed—to bring prodigals to salvation through forgiveness, repentance, and restoration. Sacramental forgiveness is one of these gifts. I hope that what has been treated in this book has shown the biblical convictions on which the sacrament of reconciliation is grounded and from which the Church's penitential practice and theology have developed. I also hope that what has been highlighted here can have a rejuvenating effect for those who avail themselves of the sacrament and, especially, for those who administer it and who teach others about it.

One of the benefits of this biblical survey has been to contextualize sacramental penance and reconciliation amid the broader task of repentance as part of one's ongoing conformation to Christ. If the sacrament is isolated in our minds as the only way in which sin is dealt with, we can run the risk of acting as though our life outside the confessional is one of only (hopefully not grave) failings or as if the sacrament is the only place in which we engage our life of repentance for sins. In a different way, if we isolate the sacrament from our life of growth in conformity to Christ, we might think of confessing particular sins or of performing our assigned penances as things we merely have to do to satisfy a requirement, but not really as part of our Christian life and salvation otherwise.[1] But a broader view of salvation as a process of being conformed to Christ reframes the importance of repentance in general and the sacrament within it. Self-denial, for those inclined to sin, is a means to grow in self-giving love. Self-humbling in confession and penance is a part of the Spirit's goal to lead us out of sin and into righteous living that God promises to remember and reward. Considered in the familial image of the prodigal son, self-giving love in imitation of God is the family business or, perhaps better, a family trait of this household. This is the family in which we seek to take part when we confess, and it is the family within which we receive our divine inheritance. The invitation to sacramental confession, with its call to penance, is an invitation to come home to the Father and be renewed for life in this family.

Another benefit of this biblical survey has been the variety of images and metaphorical frameworks within which one can imagine one's life of repentance and holiness. One is that of debt forgiven through absolution and credit

---

1. The effects of dissociating sacramental penance from other practices of penance in the United States are highlighted in Maria C. Morrow, *Sin in the Sixties: Catholics and Confession, 1955–1975* (Washington, DC: Catholic University of America Press, 2016).

gained against future debts through acts of repentance, piety, and love. Another is that of being made clean in baptism and, through confession and repentance, purifying ourselves when we become stained with sin. Another is dying and rising, of living into the reality of our baptism by dying to sin and imitating the risen Christ, who lives in us. Another is the image of bodily health as it pertains both to the whole body of Christ, which Christian sin affects, and also to our own souls being strengthened by grace and wounded by our sins, which we present to Christ in confession and for which we are given a prognosis and prescription. Another is the image of organic growth, clearing away rocks and thorns by repentance so that the seed of God's word in us can bear good fruit that will be reaped at the harvest. Another is an image of warfare, a battle against sin that we fight under our Commander, in which we are often wounded and need renewed grace so that we can reenter the fray with the weapons of righteousness. And of course there is also the image of family and relationship, in which, after running away from home or hurting the family from within, we return with apologies and are reconciled to the God who loves us.

These biblical images and frameworks are helpful as we think of what it is that we are doing when we go to the sacrament or, for priests, when they administer it. Scripture furnishes us also with stories that can function as paradigms as we consider our life under God's mercy from different angles. We can think of our penances—assigned or self-chosen—as expressions of love for our forgiving Lord, washing his feet with our tears. We can think of our sins in terms of Israel's rebellions, calling ourselves to see willful sin not just as breaking a rule but, in larger or smaller ways, as turning away from what we were redeemed for. We can praise God for the joy of forgiveness with the psalmist. We can meditate on the Good Shepherd's heart to restore all of his sheep—thinking of God's loving mercy both for ourselves and for those whom we, in our pride, are inclined to judge. If we are afraid that our own sin is too great and would rather hide from God than confess, we can think of God's patient invitations to Adam and Cain or of the restoration of David and Peter. If we are afraid that our repentance is too little and too late, we can think of Jesus's mercy to the criminal crucified with him, and his promise of the same paradise to those who are "crucified with Christ" through the grace of baptism and repentance.

These and so many more examples from Scripture furnish us with ways in which to frame the Christian life of repentance and the various facets of it,

Suggested Resources

Anderson, Gary A. *Charity: The Place of the Poor in the Biblical Tradition*. New Haven: Yale University Press, 2013.

Bennett, Jana M., and David Cloutier. *Naming Our Sins: How Recognizing the Seven Deadly Vices Can Renew the Sacrament of Reconciliation*. Washington, DC: Catholic University of America Press, 2019.

Chrysostom, John. *On Repentance and Almsgiving*. Translated by Gus George Christo. FC 96. Washington, DC: Catholic University of America Press, 1998.

Fastiggi, Robert L. *The Sacrament of Reconciliation: An Anthropological and Scriptural Understanding*. Chicago: Hillenbrand, 2017.

Feingold, Lawrence. *Touched by Christ: The Sacramental Economy*. Steubenville, OH: Emmaus Academic, 2021.

John Paul II (Pope). *Dives in misericordia* (encyclical letter). November 30, 1980. https://www.vatican.va/content/john-paul-ii/en/encyclicals/documents/hf_jp-ii_enc_30111980_dives-in-misericordia.html.

Poschmann, Bernhard. *Penance and the Anointing of the Sick*. Translated and revised by Francis Courtney. Herder History of Dogma. New York: Herder & Herder, 1964.

Selected Bibliography

Alexander, T. Desmond. *From Paradise to the Promised Land: An Introduction to the Pentateuch*. 4th ed. Grand Rapids: Baker Academic, 2022.

Allison, Dale C., Jr. *A Critical and Exegetical Commentary on the Epistle of James*. ICC. London: Bloomsbury, 2013.

Anatolios, Khaled. *Deification through the Cross: An Eastern Christian Theology of Salvation*. Grand Rapids: Eerdmans, 2020.

Anderson, Gary A. *Charity: The Place of the Poor in the Biblical Tradition*. New Haven: Yale University Press, 2013.

———. *The Genesis of Perfection: Adam and Eve in Jewish and Christian Imagination*. Louisville: Westminster John Knox, 2001.

———. *Sin: A History*. New Haven: Yale University Press, 2009.

Attridge, Harold W. *The Epistle to the Hebrews*. Hermeneia. Philadelphia: Fortress, 1989.

Augustine of Hippo. *Answer to the Pelagians IV*. Translated by Roland J. Teske. Edited by John E. Rotelle. WSA I/26. Hyde Park, NY: New City, 1999.

———. *Expositions of the Psalms 33–50*. Translated by Maria Boulding. Edited by John E. Rotelle. WSA III/16. Hyde Park, NY: New City, 2000.

———. *Homilies on the First Epistle of John*. Translated by Boniface Ramsey. Edited by Daniel D. Doyle and Thomas Martin. WSA III/14. Hyde Park, NY: New City, 2008.

———. *On Christian Belief*. Translated by Edmund Hill et al. Edited by Boniface Ramsey. WSA I/8. Hyde Park, NY: New City, 2005.

Balzer, Klaus. *The Covenant Formulary*. Philadelphia: Fortress, 1971.

Barber, Michael Patrick. "Jesus as the Davidic Temple Builder and Peter's Priestly Role in Matthew 16:16–19." *JBL* 132 (2013): 935–53.

Bautch, Richard J. *Glory and Power, Ritual and Relationship: The Sinai Covenant in the Postexilic Period*. LHBOTS 471. London: T&T Clark, 2009.

Bea, Augustin Cardinal. "Progress in the Interpretation of Sacred Scripture." *Theology Digest* 1 (1953): 67–71.

Benedict XVI (Pope). *Jesus of Nazareth: From the Baptism in the Jordan to the Transfiguration*. Translated by Adrian J. Walker. New York: Doubleday, 2007.

———. *Spe salvi* (encyclical letter). November 30, 2007. https://www.vatican.va /content/benedict-xvi/en/encyclicals/documents/hf_ben-xvi_enc_20071130_spe -salvi.html.

———. *Verbum Domini* (post-synodal apostolic exhortation). September 30, 2010. https://www.vatican.va/content/benedict-xvi/en/apost_exhortations/documents /hf_ben-xvi_exh_20100930_verbum-domini.html.

Bennett, Jana M., and David Cloutier. *Naming Our Sins: How Recognizing the Seven Deadly Vices Can Renew the Sacrament of Reconciliation*. Washington, DC: Catholic University of America Press, 2019.

Bonhoeffer, Dietrich. *The Cost of Discipleship*. London: SCM, 1948.

Bovati, Pietro. *Re-establishing Justice: Legal Terms, Concepts and Procedures in the Hebrew Bible*. Translated by Michael J. Smith. LHBOTS 105. Sheffield: JSOT Press, 1994.

Bovon, François. *Luke 3: A Commentary on the Gospel of Luke 19:28–24:53*. Edited by Helmut Koester. Translated by James E. Crouch. Hermeneia. Minneapolis: Fortress, 2012.

Brown, Raymond E. *The Epistles of John*. AB 30. New York: Doubleday, 1982.

Brueggemann, Walter. *The Message of the Psalms: A Theological Commentary*. Minneapolis: Augsburg, 1984.

———. *Theology of the Old Testament: Testimony, Dispute, Advocacy*. Minneapolis: Fortress, 1997.

Bruno, Chris, Jared Compton, and Kevin McFadden. *Biblical Theology according to the Apostles: How the Earliest Christians Told the Story of Israel*. NSBT 52. Downers Grove, IL: IVP Academic, 2020.

Byrne, Brendan. *Paul and the Economy of Salvation: Reading from the Perspective of the Last Judgment*. Grand Rapids: Baker Academic, 2021.

Childs, Brevard S. *Biblical Theology in Crisis*. Philadelphia: Westminster, 1970.

———. *The Book of Exodus: A Critical, Theological Commentary*. OTL. Philadelphia: Westminster, 1974.

Chrysostom, John. *On Repentance and Almsgiving*. Translated by Gus George Christo. FC 96. Washington, DC: Catholic University of America Press, 1998.

Crenshaw, James L. *Old Testament Wisdom: An Introduction*. 3rd ed. Louisville: Westminster John Knox, 2010.

Croasmun, Matthew. *The Emergence of Sin: The Cosmic Tyrant in Romans*. New York: Oxford University Press, 2017.

Cyprian of Carthage. *On the Church: Select Treatises*. Translated by Allen Brent. SVSPPS 32. Crestwood, NY: St. Vladimir's Seminary Press, 2006.

Dauphinais, Michael, and Matthew Levering. *Holy People, Holy Land: A Theological Introduction to the Bible*. Grand Rapids: Brazos, 2005.

Davids, Peter H. *The Epistle of James: A Commentary on the Greek Text*. NIGTC. Grand Rapids: Eerdmans, 1982.

Davies, W. D., and Dale C. Allison Jr. *The Gospel according to Saint Matthew*. 3 vols. ICC. Edinburgh: T&T Clark, 1988–2004.

Dempster, Stephen G. *Dominion and Dynasty: A Theology of the Hebrew Bible*. NSBT 15. Downers Grove, IL: InterVarsity, 2003.

Downs, David J. *Alms: Charity, Reward, and Atonement in Early Christianity*. Waco: Baylor University Press, 2016.

Dunn, James D. G. *The Theology of Paul the Apostle*. Grand Rapids: Eerdmans, 1998.

Eng, Daniel K. *Eschatological Approval: The Structure and Unifying Motif of James*. NTM 45. Sheffield: Sheffield Phoenix, 2022.

Escrivá, Josemaría. *Christ Is Passing By*. New York: Scepter, 1974.

Eubank, Nathan. *Wages of Cross-Bearing and Debt of Sin: The Economy of Heaven in Matthew's Gospel*. BZNW. Berlin: de Gruyter, 2013.

Fagerberg, David W. "The Sacramental Life." In *The Oxford Handbook of Catholic Theology*, edited by Lewis Ayres and Medi Ann Volpe, 249–62. New York: Oxford University Press, 2019.

Farkasfalvy, Denis. *A Theology of the Christian Bible: Revelation, Inspiration, Canon*. Washington, DC: Catholic University of America Press, 2018.

Fastiggi, Robert L. *The Sacrament of Reconciliation: An Anthropological and Scriptural Understanding*. Chicago: Hillenbrand, 2017.

Feingold, Lawrence. *Touched by Christ: The Sacramental Economy*. Steubenville, OH: Emmaus Academic, 2021.

Feldmeier, Reinhard, and Hermann Spieckermann. *God of the Living: A Biblical Theology*. Translated by Mark E. Biddle. Waco: Baylor University Press, 2011.

Fitzgerald, Allan D. "Penance." In *The Oxford Handbook of Early Christian Studies*, edited by Susan Ashbrook Harvey and David G. Hunter, 786–807. New York: Oxford University Press, 2008.

Fitzmyer, Joseph A. *The Acts of the Apostles: A New Translation with Introduction and Commentary*. AB 31. New York: Doubleday, 1998.

———. *The Gospel according to Luke (X–XXIV)*. AB 28A. New York: Doubleday, 1985.

France, R. T. *The Gospel of Matthew*. NICNT. Grand Rapids: Eerdmans, 2007.

Francis (Pope). *Evangelii gaudium* (apostolic exhortation). November 24, 2013. https://www.vatican.va/content/francesco/en/apost_exhortations/documents/papa -francesco_esortazione-ap_20131124_evangelii-gaudium.html.

———. *Lumen fidei* (encyclical letter). June 29, 2013. https://www.vatican.va/content /francesco/en/encyclicals/documents/papa-francesco_20130629_enciclica-lumen -fidei.html.

———. *The Name of God Is Mercy: A Conversation with Andrea Tornielli*. Translated by Oonagh Stransky. New York: Random House, 2016.

Frayer-Griggs, Daniel. "Neither Proof Text nor Proverb: The Instrumental Sense of διά and the Soteriological Function of Fire in 1 Corinthians 3.15." *NTS* 59 (2013): 517–34.

Giambrone, Anthony. *Sacramental Charity, Creditor Christology, and the Economy of Salvation in Luke's Gospel*. WUNT 2/439. Tübingen: Mohr Siebeck, 2017.

Gibbs, Jeffrey A. *Matthew 11:2–20:34*. ConcC. St. Louis: Concordia, 2010.

Goldingay, John. *Old Testament Theology*. Vol. 1, *Israel's Gospel*. Downers Grove, IL: InterVarsity, 2003.

Gorman, Michael J. *Cruciformity: Paul's Narrative Spirituality of the Cross*. Grand Rapids: Eerdmans, 2001.

———. *Romans: A Theological and Pastoral Commentary*. Grand Rapids: Eerdmans, 2022.

Gregory the Great. *Forty Gospel Homilies*. Translated by Dom David Hurst. Cistercian Studies Series 123. Kalamazoo, MI: Cistercian Publications, 1990.

Hamilton, Victor P. *The Book of Genesis: Chapters 1–17*. NICOT. Grand Rapids: Eerdmans, 1990.

Holladay, Carl R. *Acts: A Commentary*. NTL. Louisville: Westminster John Knox, 2016.

Holmes, Michael W. *The Apostolic Fathers: Greek Texts and English Translations*. 3rd ed. Grand Rapids: Baker Academic, 2007.

Horn, Hieronymus. *Anfänge, die Geschichte Schrieben: Das Buch Genesis (1–11) neu kommentiert*. Stuttgart: Katholisches Bibelwerk, 2013.

Huizenga, Leroy A. *The New Isaac: Tradition and Intertextuality in the Gospel of Matthew*. NovTSup 131. Leiden: Brill, 2009.

Jenson, Phillip Peter. *Graded Holiness: A Key to the Priestly Conception of the World*. JSOTSup 106. Sheffield: JSOT Press, 1992.

John XXIII (Pope). *Paenitentiam agere* (encyclical letter). July 1, 1962. https://www.vatican.va/content/john-xxiii/en/encyclicals/documents/hf_j-xxiii_enc_01071962_paenitentiam.html.

John of the Cross. *The Collected Works of St. John of the Cross*. Translated by Kieran Kavanaugh and Otilio Rodriguez. Rev. ed. Washington, DC: ICS Publications, 1991.

John Paul II (Pope). *Dives in misericordia* (encyclical letter). November 30, 1980. https://www.vatican.va/content/john-paul-ii/en/encyclicals/documents/hf_jp-ii_enc_30111980_dives-in-misericordia.html.

———. *Reconciliatio et paenitentia* (post-synodal apostolic exhortation). December 2, 1984. https://www.vatican.va/content/john-paul-ii/en/apost_exhortations/documents/hf_jp-ii_exh_02121984_reconciliatio-et-paenitentia.html.

Johnson, Luke Timothy. *The Acts of the Apostles*. SP 5. Collegeville, MN: Liturgical Press, 1992.

———. *The Letter of James: A New Translation with Introduction and Commentary*. AB 37A. New Haven: Yale University Press, 2008.

Kass, Leon R. *The Beginning of Wisdom: Reading Genesis*. Chicago: University of Chicago Press, 2006.

Keener, Craig S. *Acts: An Exegetical Commentary*. 4 vols. Grand Rapids: Baker Academic, 2012–15.

————. *1 Peter: A Commentary*. Grand Rapids: Baker Academic, 2021.

Klein, Christoph. *Wenn Rache der Vergebung Weicht: Theologische Grundlagen einer Kultur der Versöhnung*. Forschungen zur systematischen und ökumenischen Theologie 93. Göttingen: Vandenhoeck & Ruprecht, 1999.

Kwakkel, Gert. *"According to My Righteousness": Upright Behaviour as Grounds for Deliverance in Psalms 7, 17, 18, 26 and 44*. OtSt 46. Leiden: Brill, 2002.

Kwon, JiSeong James. "Meaning and Context in Job and Tobit." *JSOT* 43 (2019): 627–43.

Lam, Joseph. *Patterns of Sin in the Hebrew Bible: Metaphor, Culture, and the Making of a Religious Concept*. Oxford: Oxford University Press, 2016.

Lane, William L. *Hebrews*. 2 vols. WBC 47A–B. Nashville: Nelson, 1991.

Leo XIII (Pope). *Providentissimus Deus* (encyclical letter). November 18, 1893. https://www.vatican.va/content/leo-xiii/it/encyclicals/documents/hf_l-xiii_enc_18111893_providentissimus-deus.html.

Léon-Dufour, Xavier. *Dictionary of Biblical Theology*. Translated by P. Joseph Cahill. Rev. ed. by E. M. Stewart. New York: Seabury, 1973.

Levenson, Jon D. *Inheriting Abraham: The Legacy of the Patriarch in Judaism, Christianity and Islam*. Library of Jewish Ideas. Princeton: Princeton University Press, 2012.

Lockett, Darian R. *Letters from the Pillar Apostles: The Formation of the Catholic Epistles as a Canonical Collection*. Eugene, OR: Pickwick, 2017.

Luther, Martin. "Ninety Five Theses." In *Career of the Reformer I*, edited by Harold J. Grimm, translated by C. M. Jacobs and Harold J. Grimm, 17–33. Luther's Works 31. Philadelphia: Fortress, 1957.

Luz, Ulrich. *Matthew 8–20*. Translated by James E. Crouch. Hermeneia. Minneapolis: Fortress, 2001.

Mbuvi, Andrew M. *Temple, Exile and Identity in 1 Peter*. LNTS 345. London: T&T Clark, 2007.

McGrew, Israel. "'What Is Enosh?' The Anthropological Contributions of Job 7:17–18 through Allusion and Intertextuality." *CBQ* 84 (2022): 404–23.

McKnight, Scot. *The Letter of James*. NICNT. Grand Rapids: Eerdmans, 2011.

Meyers, Carol. *Exodus*. New Cambridge Bible Commentary. Cambridge: Cambridge University Press, 2005.

Miller, Robert D. *Covenant and Grace in the Old Testament: Assyrian Propaganda and Israelite Faith*. PHSC 16. Piscataway, NJ: Gorgias, 2012.

Mitchell, Alan C. *Hebrews*. SP 13. Collegeville, MN: Liturgical Press, 2007.

Moffitt, David M. *Rethinking the Atonement: New Perspectives on Jesus's Death, Resurrection, and Ascension*. Grand Rapids: Baker Academic, 2022.

Moloney, Francis J. *The Gospel of John*. SP 4. Collegeville, MN: Liturgical Press, 1998.

Moorman, Mary C. *Indulgences: Luther, Catholicism, and the Imputation of Merit.* Steubenville, OH: Emmaus Academic, 2017.

Morales, Isaac Augustine. *The Bible and Baptism: The Fountain of Salvation.* CBTS. Grand Rapids: Baker Academic, 2022.

Morrow, Maria C. *Sin in the Sixties: Catholics and Confession, 1955–1975.* Washington, DC: Catholic University of America Press, 2016.

Mowinckel, Sigmund. *The Psalms in Israel's Worship.* Translated by D. R. Ap-Thomas. 2 vols. Oxford: Blackwell, 1962.

Muddiman, John. "Fast, Fasting." *ABD* 2:773–76.

Newsom, Carol A. *The Spirit within Me: Self and Agency in Ancient Israel and Second Temple Judaism.* New Haven: Yale University Press, 2021.

Nielsen, Kirsten. *Yahweh as Prosecutor and Judge: An Investigation of the Prophetic Lawsuit (Ríb-Pattern).* Translated by Frederick Cryer. JSOTSup 9. Sheffield: JSOT Press, 1978.

Nienhuis, David R., and Robert W. Wall. *Reading the Epistles of James, Peter, John, and Jude as Scripture: The Shaping and Shape of a Canonical Collection.* Grand Rapids: Eerdmans, 2013.

Nolland, John. *Luke 9:21–18:34.* WBC 35B. Dallas: Word, 1993.

Nutt, Roger W. *General Principles of Sacramental Theology.* Washington, DC: Catholic University of America Press, 2017.

Paul VI (Pope). *Paenitemini* (apostolic constitution). February 17, 1966. https://www .vatican.va/content/paul-vi/en/apost_constitutions/documents/hf_p-vi_apc_196 60217_paenitemini.html.

Pifer, Jeanette Hagen. *Faith as Participation: An Exegetical Study of Some Key Pauline Texts.* WUNT 2/486. Tübingen: Mohr Siebeck, 2019.

Pitre, Brant, Michael P. Barber, and John A. Kincaid. *Paul, a New Covenant Jew: Rethinking Pauline Theology.* Grand Rapids: Eerdmans, 2019.

Pius XII (Pope). *Mystici corporis Christi* (encyclical letter). June 29, 1943. https://www .vatican.va/content/pius-xii/en/encyclicals/documents/hf_p-xii_enc_29061943 _mystici-corporis-christi.html.

Poschmann, Bernhard. *Penance and the Anointing of the Sick.* Translated and revised by Francis Courtney. Herder History of Dogma. New York: Herder & Herder, 1964.

Powell, Marvin A. "Weights and Measures." *ABD* 6:897–908.

Prothro, James B. *The Apostle Paul and His Letters: An Introduction.* Verbum Domini. Washington, DC: Catholic University of America Press, 2021.

———. "Patterns of Penance and the Sin of Cain: Approaching a Sacramental Biblical Theology." *Nova et Vetera* 21 (2023): 1371–89.

———. *A Pauline Theology of Justification: Forgiveness, Friendship, and Life with God.* Lectio Sacra. Eugene, OR: Cascade Books, 2023.

———. "Theories of Inspiration and Catholic Exegesis: Scripture and Criticism in Dialogue with Denis Farkasfalvy." *CBQ* 83 (2021): 294–314.

Rahner, Karl. *Penance in the Early Church*. Translated by Lionel Swain. Theological Investigations 15. New York: Crossroad, 1982.

Ramage, Matthew J. *Dark Passages of the Bible: Engaging Scripture with Benedict XVI and Thomas Aquinas*. Washington, DC: Catholic University of America Press, 2013.

Reiterer, Frederick Vinzenz. *Gerechtigkeit als Heil:* צדק *bei Deuterojesaiah; Aussage und Vergleich mit der alttestamentlichen Tradition*. Graz: Akademische Druck- und Verlagsanstalt, 1976.

Revel, Jean-Philippe. *La réconciliation*. Traité des sacrements 5. Paris: Cerf, 2015.

Sarna, Nahum M. *Understanding Genesis*. Heritage of Biblical Israel 1. New York: Jewish Theological Seminary of America, 1966.

Scott, James M., ed. *Exile: A Conversation with N. T. Wright*. Downers Grove, IL: IVP Academic, 2017.

Sheerin, John B. *The Sacrament of Freedom: A Book on Confession*. Milwaukee: Bruce Publishing, 1961.

Sklar, Jay. *Sin, Impurity, Sacrifice, Atonement: The Priestly Conceptions*. Sheffield: Sheffield Phoenix, 2005.

Stettler, Christian. "Die Taufe im Neuen Testament—und heute." *TBei* 46 (2015): 24–41.

Strecker, Georg. *The Johannine Letters: A Commentary on 1, 2, and 3 John*. Translated by Linda M. Maloney. Hermeneia. Minneapolis: Fortress, 1996.

Tanner, Norman P., ed. *Decrees of the Ecumenical Councils*. 2 vols. London: Sheed & Ward, 1990.

Tate, Marvin E. *Psalms 51–100*. WBC 20. Waco: Word, 1990.

Teresa of Ávila. *The Collected Works of Saint Teresa of Avila*. Vol. 2. Translated by Kieran Kavanaugh and Otilio Rodriguez. Washington, DC: ICS Publications, 2017.

Terrien, Samuel. *The Psalms: Strophic Structure and Theological Commentary*. 2 vols. ECC. Grand Rapids: Eerdmans, 2003.

Theophilos, Michael P. *Numismatics and Greek Lexicography*. T&T Clark Biblical Studies. London: T&T Clark, 2020.

Thiessen, Matthew. *Jesus and the Forces of Death: The Gospels' Portrayal of Ritual Impurity within First-Century Judaism*. Grand Rapids: Baker Academic, 2020.

Thompson, Marianne Meye. *John: A Commentary*. NTL. Louisville: Westminster John Knox, 2015.

Tosato, Angelo. *The Catholic Statute of Biblical Interpretation*. Edited by Monica Lugato. Rome: Gregorian & Biblical Press, 2021.

Vall, Gregory. *Ecclesial Exegesis: A Synthesis of Ancient and Modern Approaches to Scripture*. Verbum Domini. Washington, DC: Catholic University of America Press, 2022.

Vis, Joshua M. "The Purgation of Persons through the Purification Offering." In *Sacrifice, Cult, and Atonement in Early Judaism and Christianity: Constituents and Critique*, edited by Henrietta L. Wiley and Christian A. Eberhart, 33–57. RBS 85. Atlanta: SBL Press, 2017.

von Rad, Gerhard. *Genesis*. Rev. ed. OTL. Philadelphia: Westminster, 1973.

von Speyr, Adrienne. *Confession: The Encounter with Christ in Penance*. Translated by A. G. Littledale. New York: Herder & Herder, 1964.

von Wahlde, Urban C. *The Gospel and Letters of John*. 3 vols. ECC. Grand Rapids: Eerdmans, 2010.

Vos, Geerhardus. *Biblical Theology: Old and New Testaments*. Grand Rapids: Eerdmans, 1948.

Wall, Robert W. "The Acts of the Apostles: Introduction, Commentary, and Reflections." *NIB* 10:1–368.

Waltke, Bruce K., and James M. Houston, with Erika Moore. *The Psalms as Christian Worship: A Historical Commentary*. Grand Rapids: Eerdmans, 2010.

Walton, John H. *Ancient Near Eastern Thought and the Old Testament*. 2nd ed. Grand Rapids: Baker Academic, 2018.

Wenham, Gordon J. *Genesis 1–15*. WBC 1. Nashville: Nelson, 1987.

Wesley, John. *The Works of John Wesley*. 3rd ed. 14 vols. Grand Rapids: Baker, 1986.

Wilckens, Ulrich. "ὑποκρίνομαι, κτλ." *TDNT* 8:559–71.

Williamson, H. G. M. *Ezra, Nehemiah*. WBC 16. Nashville: Nelson, 1985.

Winninge, Mikael. *Sinners and the Righteous: A Comparative Study of the Psalms of Solomon and Paul's Letters*. ConBNT 26. Stockholm: Almqvist & Wiksell, 1995.

Wolter, Michael. *The Gospel according to Luke*. Translated by Wayne Coppins and Christoph Heilig. 2 vols. BMSEC. Waco: Baylor University Press, 2016–17.

Wright, Archie T. *Satan and the Problem of Evil: From the Bible to the Early Church Fathers*. Minneapolis: Fortress, 2022.

Wright, N. T. *The Climax of the Covenant: Christ and the Law in Pauline Theology*. London: T&T Clark, 1991.

———. *The New Testament and the People of God*. Minneapolis: Fortress, 1992.

Subject Index

224

Scripture and Other Ancient Sources Index